Teaching and Researching Computer-assisted Language Learning

APPLIED LINGUISTICS IN ACTION

General Editors:

Christopher N. Candlin and David R. Hall

Books published in this series include:

Teaching and Researching Computer-assisted Language Learning

Ken Beatty

An imprint of **Pearson Education**

London · New York · Toronto · Sydney · Tokyo · Singapore · Hong Kong · Cape Town
Madrid · Paris · Amsterdam · Munich · Milan

Pearson Education Limited
Edinburgh Gate
Harlow
Essex CM20 2JE
England

and Associated Companies throughout the world

Visit us on the World Wide Web at:
www.pearsoned.co.uk

First published in Great Britain in 2003

© Pearson Education Limited 2003

The right of Ken Beatty to be identified as Author
of this Work has been asserted by him in accordance
with the Copyright, Designs and Patents Act 1988.

ISBN 0 582 32900 0

British Library Cataloguing in Publication Data
A CIP catalogue record for this book can be obtained from the British Library

Library of Congress Cataloging in Publication Data
A CIP catalog record for this book can be obtained from the Library of Congress

10   9   8   7   6   5   4
08   07   06   05   04

Typeset in 10.5/12pt Jansan by Graphicraft Limited, Hong Kong
Printed and bound in Malaysia, LSP

The Publishers' policy is to use paper manufactured from sustainable forests.

Contents

General Editors' Preface

Applied Linguistics in Action, as its name suggests, is a Series which focuses on the issues and challenges to practitioners and researchers in a range of fields in Applied Linguistics and provides readers and users with the tools they need to carry out their own practice-related research.

The books in the Series provide readers with clear, up-to-date, accessible and authoritative accounts of their chosen field within Applied Linguistics. Using the metaphor of a map of the landscape of the field, each book provides information on its main ideas and concepts, its scope, its competing issues, solved and unsolved questions. Armed with this authoritative but critical account, readers can explore for themselves a range of exemplary practical applications of research into these issues and questions, before taking up the challenge of undertaking their own research, guided by the detailed and explicit research guides provided. Finally, each book has a section which is concurrently on the Series website *www.booksites.net/alia* and which provides a rich array of chosen resources, information sources, further reading and commentary, as well as a key to the principal concepts of the field.

Questions that the books in this innovative Series ask are those familiar to all practitioners and researchers, whether very experienced, or new to the fields of Applied Linguistics.

- What does research tell us, what doesn't it tell us and what should it tell us about the field? What is its geography? How is the field mapped and landscaped?

- How has research been carried out and applied and what interesting research possibilities does practice raise? What are the issues we need to explore and explain?

- What are the key researchable topics that practitioners can undertake? How can the research be turned into practical action?

- Where are the important resources that practitioners and researchers need? Who has the information? How can it be accessed?

Each book in the Series has been carefully designed to be as accessible as possible, with built-in features to enable readers to find what they want quickly and to home in on the key issues and themes that concern them. The structure is to move from practice to theory and research, and back to practice, in a cycle of development of understanding of the field in question. Books in the Series will be usable for the individual reader but also can serve as a basis for course design, or seminar discussion.

Each of the authors of books in the Series is an acknowledged authority, able to bring broad knowledge and experience to engage practitioners and researchers in following up their own ideas, working with them to build further on their own experience.

Applied Linguistics in Action is an **in action** Series. Its website will keep you updated and regularly re-informed about the topics, fields and themes in which you are involved.

We hope that you will like and find useful the design, the content and, above all, the support the books will give to your own practice and research!

Christopher N. Candlin & David R. Hall
General Editors

Acknowledgements

Great thanks to Chris Candlin and David Hall who shepherded my oft-straggling thoughts into a recognizable book. In particular, Chris's intellectual companionship, good food and fine wines inspired better writing on more interesting tangents.

I also thank my PhD advisors David Nunan and Amy Tsui whose thoughtful and dedicated work on my thesis has in turn ornamented these pages.

For support and patience, I thank my wife Ann. For lost play, I beg forgiveness of my young sons, Nathan and Spencer.

And an apology to the uninvited guest. The ideas of hundreds of researchers are quoted in this book. But as many more have been left out not because their contributions to the field lack merit, but simply because there was not room or, like everyone else, I have not read enough. I welcome correspondence for future editions.

Ken Beatty
Hong Kong

The publishers are grateful to the following for permission to reproduce copyright material:

Example 3.1 © 2001 Adobe Systems Incorporated. Used with express permission. All rights reserved. Adobe, and Atmosphere is/are either [a] registered trademark[s] of Adobe Systems Incorporated in the United States and/or other countries; Example 4.4 reprinted by permission of Dave Sperling; Example 4.5 from Expressions website, http://expressions. heinle.com, copyright 2002 © Heinle, a division of Thomson Learning, Inc; Example 5.2 reprinted by permission of Inspiration Software, Inc, this diagram was created using Inspiration®, published by Inspiration Software, Inc; Figure 6.1 after figure in *Implementing Computer Supported Cooperative Learning*, Kogan Page (McConnell, D. 1994); Figure 7.3 from *Young Learners and the Microcomputer*, Open University Press on behalf of D. Chandler (Chandler, D. 1984); Example 8.2 reprinted by permission of Macromedia, Inc; Example 9.2 reprinted by permission of WebCT, Inc; Figure 9.3 after figure in *The Practicing Administrator's Leadership Series: Roadmaps to Success* by J. McLean, copyright © 1995. Reprinted by permission of Corwin Press, Inc; Screenshot on page 226 reproduced with the kind permission of Questionmark (http://www.questionmark.com).

In some instances we have been unable to trace the owners of copyright material, and we would appreciate any information that would enable us to do so.

Introduction

A century or so ago a child opening an atlas of the world would gaze over large portions invitingly labelled *terra incognita*. The idea of so much of the world being in the realm of the unknown was a compelling invitation to exploration. For others, the excitement was in the refining of the edges of the map, more clearly understanding and defining known details and charting the inevitable changes that occur over time.

These ideas are very much alive today in a new landscape, that of computer-assisted language learning (CALL). CALL is filled with areas that are unknown and in need of exploration. Even where much is known, details have not been made clear or need to be made clearer as other factors and conditions change, such as the introduction of new technologies and broader adoption of existing technologies. The field of CALL is also constantly undergoing change because of technological innovation that creates opportunities to revisit old findings, to conduct new research and to challenge established beliefs about the ways in which teaching and learning can be carried out both with and without a human teacher. At the same time, advances in parallel fields inform CALL and help direct the research agenda.

The metaphor of the *map*, used in this book and throughout this series, *Applied Linguistics in Action*, serves to fulfil the needs of a range of readers. A map shows territory we know and that which we do not know, except in outline. This is particularly important for the researcher who hopes to avoid taking up the study of topic which was thought unknown, but which turns out to have been clearly explored. For teachers, an overview and better understanding of the field can help in the decision-making process around the use of CALL in the classroom. However, it is the aim of this series to recognize and further the blur between teachers and researchers; increasingly, it is important that they are the same people.

CALL is a subject tied tightly to other areas of study within applied linguistics such as autonomy and other branches of knowledge such as computer science. In the worst cases, CALL is seen as little more than a tool mimicking a textbook, a learner's peer or a teacher. Research and practice in CALL that transcends the traditional and reaches the innovative is found in applications and practice that expand technological opportunities for teaching and learning new things in new ways.

CALL's history is brief enough to be well-documented but it points to an area of study which suffers from fragmentation and a lack of scientific rigour. Advances in understanding have not followed a linear set of steps stretching somewhere between ignorance and enlightenment. Rather, many researchers have pursued individual agendas that are often tied to soon-obsolescent software.

> **Quote 0.1** J. Fox on the intellectual isolation of CALL
>
> To a surprising degree, CALL seems uninfluenced by developments in applied linguistics, linguistics methodology, etc. Many CALL exercise types have changed little since the early 1960s. Conferences on CALL frequently permit papers of the type 'Me and my programs', which would not be accepted at other conferences. The essential conservatism and unimaginativeness of many of the programs is depressing.
>
> Fox (1991: 236)

CALL is a young branch of applied linguistics and is still establishing its directions. This book aims to help in this task not just by discussing what we know and do not know, but also ways in which classroom teachers as researchers can look for answers on their own.

This book is divided into four main sections. In writing this book, I was ironically faced with a problem that might have been solved through the application of one of its key ideas: hypertext. In making decisions about the ordering of chapters and explanations, it would have been far easier to use a hypertext structure in which the readers could ignore ideas with which they were already familiar and follow links to others for which they wished to see definitions, explanations and elaboration. In the case of this book, I encourage readers to use the Contents, Glossary of key terms and Index to help navigate among the ideas of most use to them.

Section I: Key concepts begins by defining CALL and includes both explanations of terminology and elaborations on ideas that have been important to the development of CALL. Throughout this and other sections, mention is made of those authors and researchers whose ideas have helped – and continue to help – to shape CALL and to whom the reader might turn for more in-depth information. As CALL is a relatively new field of study, these authors and researchers often represent multidisciplinary perspectives, including those of artificial intelligence, cognitive science, psychology, computer science, curriculum studies and fields of applied linguistics described in other books of this series.

Part of understanding the key concepts of this section is identifying terminology that is used in different ways by different authors. As much as possible, this book tries to define and make clear these differences with examples. The Glossary of key terms at the end of the book also provides further clarification.

An important part of this section is a historical perspective on CALL over the past 50 years; as we shall discuss, too much of CALL is involved in reinventing the wheel.

Section II: The place of CALL in research and teaching builds on the key concepts presented in Section I to show how ideas about CALL have been integrated into practical (and sometimes wildly impractical) curricular design, teaching and learning materials and testing. Special mention is made of computer adaptive testing. This section also explores the reasons why important ideas and innovations in CALL have not been integrated into classroom practice, including problems with technology, ideology, classroom conditions, cost and teacher training.

Theory that illuminates the ideas that guided the creation of such materials as well as illustrations and case studies, are included in this section through a review of the history of computers and their relationship to CALL from its earliest beginnings to the present day. Special attention is paid to how well a variety of CALL applications accommodate the needs of particular teachers and learners.

At the close of this section, gaps in the research – that *terra incognita* of the map of CALL – are elaborated with reference to a model of the teaching and learning processes. It is hoped that this section will help you define personal objectives in your own CALL teaching and research.

Section III: Researching CALL begins with an examination of current research interests in CALL. As is common in many other fields, research interests in CALL have tended to follow trends; for example, the focus of many early studies was quantitative rather than qualitative. That is, the emphasis was on classroom teaching. Such studies are still undertaken, but they are not as frequent, or perhaps even as necessary, as CALL is now perceived as something that is inherently different from and/or complementary to classroom teaching.

To help examine current research interests, this section reviews 145 recent publications in the field to outline some areas of current interest. Brief summaries of many of the publications are given. Reference is also made to a range of issues identified by individual researchers.

This section then highlights examples of different types of CALL research projects, each with a different approach to research and a different focus. Each research project is examined in terms of:

- Context
- Aims
- Procedure
- Evaluation
- Further reading

Together, the studies provide a range of methodologies for investigating issues in CALL.

Section IV: Resources provides specific tools for learning more about CALL and conducting research. These tools include a list of references, both traditional and virtual, that help you conduct research. Links in the form of postal addresses and websites provide easy access to bibliographies, professional associations, conferences, commercial organizations and publications concerned with CALL.

Following this section is a Glossary of key terms with definitions for ideas used throughout the book. The References at the end of the book include all publications and websites mentioned in the text as well as others for further reading.

A note on websites

While every effort has been made to ensure that the addresses for each of the websites was correct up to the moment of publication, website addresses are subject to change. If you cannot find the website at the address cited, typing in the keywords into a search engine such as *www.google.com* may help you find web pages that have moved to a new location. In doing so, you may also find more current websites on your area of interest.

Section

Key concepts

Chapter 1

The emergence of CALL

This chapter introduces computer-assisted language learning (CALL) and offers definitions of it and various related terms and concepts. It also briefly outlines what has not been included in the research agenda for CALL.

1.1 The emergence of CALL

Given the breadth of what may go on in computer-assisted language learning (CALL), a definition of CALL that accommodates its changing nature is *any process in which a learner uses a computer and, as a result, improves his or her language.* Although this definition might seem unworkably large, it at least encompasses a broad spectrum of current practice in the teaching and learning of language at the computer. An awareness of this spectrum allows learners, teachers and researchers to recognize appropriate materials and methodologies and adapt others to various teaching and learning styles.

Concept 1.1 **The teacher as researcher**

The division between teachers and researchers has narrowed. Teachers are now much more likely to be involved in some form of research, such as Action research (see Section 9.7 Action research) investigating issues in the classroom. Also more involved in research are the most common subjects of the research, learners. When learners participate in the research process, they bring insights that may otherwise be overlooked.

CALL covers a broad range of activities which makes it difficult to describe as a single idea or simple research agenda. CALL has come to encompass issues of materials design, technologies, pedagogical theories and modes of instruction. Materials for CALL can include those which are purpose-made for language learning and those which adapt existing computer-based materials, video and other materials. However, in the midst of so many directions, it is important to attempt to examine CALL practice in order to give a context to what has been tried and found wanting in the general area of language learning at the computer. It is also important to establish a sense of directions in which future practice and research might profitably venture.

Because of the changing nature of computers, CALL is an amorphous or unstructured discipline, constantly evolving both in terms of pedagogy and technological advances in hardware and software. Change is also occurring with advances in computer literacy among both teachers and learners.

CALL is employed in many ways, both in and out of the classroom. In some commercial applications meant to be used by individuals away from the home, CALL is promoted as a complete method of learning a language. In classrooms it can be used both as a reward for better learners or a remedial aid for weaker ones. Some language labs integrate CALL and some teachers use CALL activities based on email and the World Wide Web (WWW) to supplement student learning. Delivery methods for CALL include individual computers at home or in the classroom, classroom sets of computers, language labs into which computer functions have been incorporated, online instruction through the WWW and distance and networked learning through the use of email.

It is likely that in future, computer-based language-learning tools will become both pervasive and invisible; that is, they will be commonly included in other applications and computer interfaces will become almost completely intuitive, perhaps through computer software able to recognize and intelligently respond to speech. Computer-based language functions are already integrated into word processing and other software that corrects spelling and grammar.

Computer-based language functions have also been integrated into various learning toys. Examples include *Speak N Spell*, first developed in the 1980s. *Speak N Spell* is a stand-alone spelling bee program which randomly pronounces words that the learner then spells by typing onto a miniature keyboard. Versions with additional visual prompts are now common as software programs for personal computers.

More recently, interactive animatronic toys such as *Barney*, *Tickle Me Elmo* and *Furby* in the 1990s have extended the interactions. An advertising description for *Furby* reads in part:

> A loveable interactive animatronic pet. Furby responds to light, touch, sound and motion by speaking and moving his eyes, ears, mouth and foot. Has approximately a 200-word and sound dictionary of 'English' and 'Furbish'. Can learn tricks and speech as well as communicate with other Furbys (*www.pondsidegifts.com/Furby*).

For the children who play with them, these toys seem to listen and to learn; the children overlook the fact that it is often they who are learning. An area of CALL research and practice is the use of animatronic toys, games and other materials which are intended for other purposes but which may be incorporated into CALL activities.

CALL is related to several other terms, some of which have overlap and some of which differ. Some terms are disappearing, but it is important to be able to recognize them in the research literature.

Concept 1.2   **Terms peripheral to CALL**

CAI *Computer-aided instruction* refers to learning at the computer, but not necessarily with a language focus. Although it may not be the intention of all those who use the acronym, the term *instruction* suggests a teacher-centred approach.

CAL *Computer-assisted learning* similarly to CAI, CAL may refer to the learning of any subject (including language learning) using a computer. But in contrast to CAI, CAL emphasizes the learner.

CALI *Computer-assisted Language Instruction*, a term once commonly used in North America.

CALT *Computer-assisted Language Teaching* CALL but with emphasis on the teacher.

CALT *Computer-assisted Language Testing* or *Computer Adaptive Learning Testing*. Computer adaptive testing refers specifically to situations in which the computer considers the answer to each question and raises or lowers the level of difficulty accordingly.

CAT *Computer-adaptive Testing* using a computer, but not necessarily testing language.

CAT *Computer-assisted Teaching* refers to learning at the computer, but not necessarily with a language focus.

CBT *Computer-based Training* tends to refer to programs used for corporate training with narrow and short-term instructional goals but may refer more generally to any kind of training. The term is not often used in the language-learning context except where it refers to the teaching of some discrete language learning skills, such as listening training.

CMC *Computer-mediated Communication* refers to a situation in which computer-based discussion may take place but without necessarily involving learning. However, opportunities for learning are inherently present, especially in situations in which learners need to engage in negotiation of meaning with native speakers of the target language or even with peers of non-native proficiency.

CMI *Computer-mediated Instruction* refers to instruction that takes place through the use of a computer and may, for example, include learning that occurs when a learner communicates with a distant tutor through email or simply uses some form of computer hardware and software. Again, the term *instruction* shows a teacher-centred approach.

ICALL *Intelligent Computer-assisted Language Learning* describes software programs which attempt to customize feedback features that cater to individual learner's input.

TELL *Technology Enhanced Language Learning* refers to any technology used in the classroom such as video, tape recorders or even entire listening labs.

WELL *Web Enhanced Language Learning* refers to CALL that focuses on the WWW as the medium for instruction.

CALL is closely related to many other disciplines and the computer, as a tool to aid or study teaching and learning, is often subsumed within them. For example, CALL has become increasingly integrated into research and practice in the general skills of reading, writing, speaking and listening and more discrete fields, such as autonomy in learning.

> **Quote 1.1**   M.-M. Kenning and M.J. Kenning review early benefits of providing autonomous learning materials:
>
> The early CALL literature contains many statements on the benefits of privacy and individualization: 'The central concept of PLATO is individualization of learning. Each student proceeds through the material in privacy at his own pace' (Curtin *et al.*, 1972: 360); 'each student can use the computer to review the grammar at his own speed with special emphasis on areas where he is weak' (Nelson *et al.*, 1976: 37); and a few years later, 'the computer can ... correct mistakes privately and repeatedly without the *aggro* (i.e. *aggravation*) that sometimes accompanies such public correction' (Crispin, 1981: 134).
>
> Kenning and Kenning (1990: 114)

Autonomy is fostered by CALL in different ways. CALL can present opportunities for learners to study on their own, independent of a teacher. CALL can also offer opportunities for learners to direct their own learning (see Benson, 2001). But such assumptions may be questionable for many CALL software programs that follow a lock-step scope and sequence. Such programs give learners only limited opportunities to organize their own learning or tailor it to their special needs. On the other hand, most

CALL materials, regardless of their design, allow for endless revisiting that can help learners review those parts for which they need more practice.

Further reading

Benson, P. (2001) *Teaching and Researching Autonomy in Language Learning*. Harlow: Longman. – In this, another book from this ALiA series, Benson presents an overview of issues in autonomy.

Dias, J. (2000) Learner autonomy in Japan: transforming 'Help yourself' from threat to invitation. *Computer Assisted Language Learning*, 13(1): 49–64. – This paper discusses changing a culture of learning through the use of CALL.

Randall's ESL Cyber Listening Lab *www.esl-lab.com* – provides online listening resources in the form of passages of various lengths.

1.2 Technology driving CALL

In the last four decades, CALL materials have gone from an emphasis on basic textual gap-filling tasks and simple programming exercises (see Papert, 1984) to interactive multimedia presentations with sound, animation and full-motion video. But this progress has not been purely linear and, in terms of pedagogy, the new and improved have not always replaced the old and tired. Instead, many programs being produced today feature little more than visually stimulating variations on the same gap-filling exercises used 40 years ago. There are several reasons for this lack of concerted progress. Materials designers are often either teachers with limited technical skills or competent technicians with no experience in teaching. For both parties, software authoring programs often include simple ways to create gap-filling exercises that are seductively easy to use.

Another barrier to better CALL materials is the lack of ways to monitor and correct unpredictable student answers. It is easy for a computer to mark and give feedback to a multiple answer question; it is almost impossible to do so with answers set in sentences, although some programs try by having an answer field recognize several pre-designated key words. However, the problem with such an approach is the computer's difficulty in sorting out unexpected answers. For example, in a sentence in which the key word answers were designated as *talking* and *phone*, the computer would:

- overlook incorrect syntax (*Talking he telephone the on.)
- be confused by variations in grammar (He *talks* on the telephone.)
- fail to accept synonyms (The man is *speaking* on the *phone*.)
- fail to notice erroneous and extraneous words (*She* is *be* talking *and waiting* on the telephone *thing*.)

One solution to such problems is to have learners email or otherwise save answers for teachers who then mark them by hand.

Concept 1.3   **Interactive**

Interactive is a concept which has become vague from overuse. In its simplest sense, interactive refers to a software program in which the learner has some small degree of choice, perhaps only in selecting answers to multiple choice questions. Many software authoring programs such as Macromedia *Authorware* now allow teachers/programmers to choose other question types such as true/false, select an image or part of an image and move parts of a picture or a sentence to correct positions. In more elaborate interactive learning programs, the learner can enter into a simulated world and make choices which affect the direction of learning. For example, choosing to read a simulated newspaper or 'talk' with different characters.

Multimedia and speech recognition capabilities have attempted to extend the traditional reading and listening foci of CALL to include writing and speaking activities too. Each of these skills' place in CALL continues to

---

Concept 1.4   **Artificial intelligence, expert systems and natural-language processing**

The term *artificial intelligence* (AI) was first used in 1956 by John McCarthy of the Massachusetts Institute of Technology (MIT). Artificial intelligence includes *expert systems* and *natural-language processing* (NLP). *Expert systems* help make decisions based on a review of previous cases. For example, a doctor might list a series of symptoms and the computer would review all the cases that exhibit those symptoms and offer a diagnosis. In language learning, an expert system might examine a list of student errors and offer both solutions and exercises to ensure comprehension.

The eventual goal of natural-language processing is to allow people to interact with computers with speech, just as one would with another person. Some advances have been made on the simple command level (e.g. 'open file'; 'scroll up') but so far computers have great difficulty handling more complex speech. In the CALL context, students' imperfect command of the target language is likely to produce frustrating results that would perhaps lead to more trouble than the investment of time is worth.

NLP should not be confused with *speech recognition*. Speech recognition programs decode utterances and type what a speaker says but generally do not recognize the meaning of what they hear and write beyond the simple command level.

---

develop with the technology. For example, at this point, computers are still quite limited in terms of speech synthesis and voice recognition. Most commonly, computers present graphical representations of speech patterns which the learner can try to match, but decoding such displays and matching them to real speech is perhaps beyond most learners.

Many brave attempts have been made to have the computer teach writing, but the failure of such systems is always rooted in the computer's inability to accommodate unpredictable learner output. A sentence that may be grammatically correct may be semantically nonsensical, as Noam Chomsky pointed out with the example, *Colourless green ideas sleep furiously*. Work in artificial intelligence and natural-language processing attempts to address this problem but has so far had only limited success.

Murray (1995) suggests that there are severe limitations to the implementation of natural-language processing computer systems.

> **Quote 1.2**   J. Murray on the limitations of natural-language processing:
>
> Such pattern-matching programs have severe limitations. For machines to understand and produce language, they must be able to process natural language at the morpho-syntactic, semantic and discourse levels. For spoken language, the system also needs to process language at the phonetic and phonological level.
>
> Murray (1995: 146)

The recent history of rapid innovation in computer hardware and software suggests that what Murray labels severe limitations in 1995 are likely to be at least partially addressed by researchers and practitioners in coming years.

1.3   The changing focus of research in CALL

Although research in CALL is the focus of Section III, it is necessary to outline briefly what is no longer a concern of studies of CALL. One area of declining interest includes studies which focus on the need for computers in the classroom. Another area of less interest are those studies that attempt to make direct comparisons between CALL and traditional learning in terms of effectiveness.

> **Quote 1.3** C.M. Neuwirth and D.S. Kaufer on the dominant pattern of research in CALL:
>
> Thus far, the dominant pattern of (research) in computers and composition studies has involved empirical questions about existing software – asking, for example, *Do word processors improve writing quality or revision performance?* – usually by experimental comparison to some traditional technology for writing such as pen and paper.
>
> Neuwirth and Kaufer (1992: 173)

Neuwirth and Kaufer's (1992) description of research in CALL is still much practised but is of waning interest. Focus has instead shifted to other areas, which are outlined in greater detail in Section III of this book. Similarly, a focus of much research in the early years of CALL – whether or not computers should be used in the classroom for the learning of languages – is no longer pertinent. Computers appear to be here to stay. The presence of computers in educational contexts has grown from a single unit in one or more classrooms to computer labs and even to widespread individual ownership by students in some countries. In 2001, of 238 first and second-year university students in the author's classes at City University of Hong Kong, all had at least one computer at home. Several had laptop computers which they brought to class and one had a Personal Digital Assistant (PDA). Some university programs have made purchase of a computer a prerequisite to enrolment.

Accordingly, research is now directed into *how* computers should be used and *for what purposes* but a major challenge to many studies in CALL remains a lack of empirical research.

The timeline for the studies cited (see Quote 1.4) by Chapelle and Jamieson stretches over 15 years (1971 to 1986) during a time of many advances in computer hardware and software. A more recent review by Meich, Nave and Mosteller (1996) in an examination of 22 empirical CALL studies conducted between 1989 and 1994 concluded the opposite: CALL can '. . . substantially improve achievement as compared with traditional instruction' (p. 1).

Another factor that challenges the validity of early studies is the general increase in the average learner's computer literacy. Logan (1995) explores the importance of computer literacy when he suggests that computers represent the fifth in a series of languages which humans have mastered, the previous four being speech, writing, mathematics and science. He further suggests that a failure to recognize computers as a new language has led to the inappropriate teaching and uses of computers. While his conclusions are debatable, the importance of computers in general and the

Quote 1.4 C. Chapelle and J. Jamieson on the CALL versus traditional classroom instruction:

In CALL-versus-classroom studies, researchers typically investigate whether *CALL plus classroom* is superior to classroom instruction alone. In this case, the independent variable is the kind of instruction learners receive – from the computer and the teacher or from the teacher alone. A number of early studies have found that the CALL group slightly outperformed the teacher-only group (e.g., Buckley and Rauch, 1979; Freed, 1971; Oates, 1981; Reid, 1986; Saracho, 1982; Van Campden, 1981). However, in other studies no significant differences between the groups have been found (e.g., Brebner, Johnson and Mydlarski, 1984; Klienmann, 1987; Lysiak, Wallace and Evans, 1976; Murphy and Appel, 1977). These studies, which typically have investig-ated instruction in a number of language skill areas over a period of time lasting from one to at least several weeks, have not provided strong empir-ical evidence for the superiority of CALL over classroom instruction.

Chapelle and Jamieson (1991: 37)

increase in computer literacy among both teachers and students can hardly be ignored.

A general area of study is the advantages and disadvantages of computers in providing communicative tasks which foster language learning. These have been well documented in relation to traditional methods of instruc-tion (for examples, see Ingraham and Emery, 1992; Liu, 1992; Conrad, 1996). However, such studies inevitably ignore the special features of com-puters' organization and presentation of information, particularly learner-centred opportunities to explore different links (or paths of inquiry) and the appropriateness of multimedia models for accommodating different learners' learning styles and even gender. These differences will be explored in successive chapters through an investigation of the history of CALL and computers and aspects of hypertext, hypermedia and multimedia.

Summary

This chapter defined CALL and showed that there are many related terms. Much of CALL is technology-driven, with improvements in computers' power, speed, storage and software tools helping to define directions for pedagogy and research. One area that is no longer a focus of CALL is direct either/or comparisons between CALL and classroom teaching; CALL is now seen to be complementary to classroom activities.

Chapter 2

A brief history of CALL

Early first-person accounts of the history of CALL are something of an endangered species. Because advances in technology have made some parts of early books on CALL irrelevant, entire books have been discarded by publishers and valuable information lost except to those able to access university library collections. It is important to preserve such history not just to give a sense of the changing focus of CALL over time, but also to ensure that researchers do not overlook earlier issues and developments and waste time reinventing the wheel.

This chapter reviews some of the early developments in CALL and features some significant CALL programs which serve to illustrate what is both possible and desirable in CALL. Some of these possibilities and desires are simply a move from a behaviourist instructional design to a constructivist design. Although these terms are explained at length in Chapter 5, a summary is useful at this point.

A comparison of behaviourist and constructivist design features

Figure 2.1 narrows behaviourist and constructivist models of instruction into practical concerns for learning materials but, in both cases, the definitions are severe, and one is unlikely to find learning materials that exclusively adhere to one design. Still, the differences provide opportunities for examining a range of CALL materials in this and other chapters.

2.1   CALL in the 1950s and 1960s

The first computers used for language learning were large 1950s' mainframes that were only available at research facilities on university campuses. These

A behaviourist design . . .

- Eliminates extraneous information
- Simplifies for comprehensibility
- Uses a convergent, task-analysed model as a basis
- Reconstructs/replicates knowledge
- Abstracts instruction experiences
- Focuses on acquiring skills
- Offers prescriptive sequences of instruction
- Supports individual learning and competition

A constructivist design . . .

- Supports natural complexity and content
- Avoids oversimplification
- Presents multiple representations/perspectives
- Engages knowledge construction
- Presents instruction in real-world contexts (authentic tasks)
- Engages reflective practice
- Offers open learning environments
- Supports collaboration

Figure 2.1   **A summary of behaviourist and constructivist approaches to learning materials**
(after Jonnassen, Wilson, Wang and Grabinger, 1993)

presented particular organizational problems as learners had to leave the classroom and travel to a computer, or at least to a computer terminal, for instruction. The high cost of these early machines and demands upon them for pure research meant that time allocated for teaching and learning was limited. Nonetheless, the importance of finding ways efficiently and scientifically to teach language was perceived and time and funds made available for research. Parallel research also took place on subjects such as machine translation that would, in turn, provide insights that would influence CALL.

Concept 2.1   **Machine translation**

Machine translation (MT) is the application of computers to the task of translating texts from one natural language to another. The task is made difficult by the impreciseness of languages and the use of sarcasm, puns, innuendo, idiomatic expressions and rhetorical devices.

In many of these projects, Cold War (1945–91) political motivations may have been involved in funding, particularly those based on insecurities about the Union of Soviet Socialist Republics' (USSR) advances in science after the USSR's launch, on 4 October 1957, of Sputnik, Earth's first artificial satellite. The first CALL programs created at three pioneering institutions: Stanford University, Dartmouth University and the University of Essex (The Scientific Language Project) all focused on the teaching of Russian although, eventually, other languages were included as well (see Ahmad *et al.*, 1985 for a summary).

Note: CALL in other languages

Much of the research and software cited in this book is concerned with English language materials. For a review of CALL developments in other languages, see Conrad (1996). Also, use a search engine such as *www.google.com* on the WWW with the keywords *computer assisted language learning* + the language, e.g. *Japanese*.

Further reading

Arnold, D.J., Balkan, L.S., Meijer, S., Humphreys, R.L. and Sadler, L. (1994) *Machine Translation: an Introductory Guide*. London: Blackwells-NCC. *http://clwww.essex.ac.uk/MTbook/* – a good background to ideas behind machine translation.

Hatim, B. (2001) *Teaching and Researching Translation*. Harlow: Longman – Although Hatim does not address computer-based translation, his book is useful for a better understanding of the difficulties involved in translation.

2.1.1   PLATO

Among the first and most significant applications for the teaching and learning of language at the computer were those used on the Programmed Logic/Learning for Automated Teaching Operations (PLATO) system, developed in 1959 by the University of Illinois working with a business partner, Control Data Corporation (for a summary, see Merrill *et al.*, 1996). PLATO combined some of the best CALL features being developed at other universities but differed from many other attempts to use computers to teach language in that PLATO's computer and its programming language were custom-designed for the purpose of teaching language, as well as a range of other university-wide disciplines.

Much of PLATO's first language learning work was done in teaching Russian using a grammar translation approach. The focus was on translation of Russian documents, especially scientific documents. Curtin *et al.*'s (1972) work in Russian language teaching and learning included grammar explanations, vocabulary drills and other drills and translation tests over a course of sixteen lessons requiring 70 hours to complete. The system had so-called 'intelligent' (in this case, simply a system that offers *feedback* as tailored advice) features still used today, such as tests that were followed by directions to complete appropriate remedial work depending on the errors a learner had made. The system also included rudimentary spelling and grammar-checkers (Ahmad *et al.*, 1985). For a review of Intelligent CALL, or ICALL, see Bailin, 1995.

Richards and Rodgers (1994) note that, 'Grammar Translation dominated European and foreign language teaching from the 1840s to the 1940s, and in modified form it continues to be widely used in some parts of the world today' (p. 4). In terms of Second-language Acquisition (discussed in 5.1.1), the Grammar Translation approach probably appeared to work to a limited degree in early programs such as PLATO because the learner would have to adapt to the materials by creating personal learning strategies beyond those offered by the teacher or suggested by the learning materials. In some cases, these strategies might be quite crude, such as simple mnemonics, but others might include the use of more sophisticated approaches related to Schema theory (discussed in Section 5.6.1).

> **Quote 2.1**   T.G. Anderson helps to define a schema approach to teaching and learning by suggesting it is one in which knowledge is:
>
> ...not merely a collection of facts. Although we may be able to memorize isolated facts for a short while...meaningful learning demands that we internalize information; we break it down, digest it and locate it in our pre-existing highly complex web of interconnected knowledge and ideas, building fresh links and restructuring old ones.
>
> Anderson (1988: 197)

2.2 Simulations

The earliest language-learning programs were strictly linear, requiring each learner to follow the same steps in the same fashion with rewards in the form of points and advancement for correct answers. The tasks were essentially adaptations of traditional textbook exercises and did not take advantage of special features of the computer.

However, it was soon realized that the special nature of the computer could be brought into play to allow for branching choices, such as those found in simulations. This opportunity to make choices can be seen as a step toward an interface using a constructivist model of instruction in which learners bring what they understood about the world to the task(s).

The importance of simulations, with different avenues of exploration, is that they create challenges for learners to explore multiple links (over

Quote 2.2 M.J. Atkins notes the need for a design agenda in CALL:

... the cumulative impression left by such studies is that multimedia designers are adopting an eclectic 'pick 'n' mix' approach, which, while it has the virtue of complete flexibility, can slide into *post hoc, ergo propter hoc* (meaning *after this, therefore because of this*, criticizing the tendency to confuse sequence with consequence) justifications. What seem to be missing are models of learning appropriate for the design opportunities offered by the new technologies.

Atkins (1993: 251)

Quote 2.3 T. Friedman notes the structure of many games and simulations, which he calls *interactive fiction*:

Although production values may have vastly improved since the days of text-based 'interactive fiction', the problem that designers of contemporary 'interactive cinema' face remains the same: how to define 'interactive'? How can one give the player a sense of 'control' over the game while still propelling the player through a compelling narrative? The solution, dating back to *Adventure of Zork*, has always been to set up the game as a series of puzzles. The player must muddle through the universe of the game – exploring settings, talking to the characters, acquiring and using objects – until she or he has accomplished everything necessary to trigger the next stage of the plot. In the process, the player is expected to regularly make mistakes, die and restart the game in a previously saved position.

Friedman (1995: 78)

successive sessions) and see the consequences of different actions and inputs. This turns the classroom, or computer-based environment (e.g. a learner at a home computer), into a place where participants learn through the frequent making of errors in a non-threatening way. If learners are assigned to work together on a simulation or task, there is the advantage of encouraging exploration and collaboration as learners share their methods or so-called 'secrets' to succeeding in the program.

On the other hand, simulations in autonomous learning situations that allow for repeated attempts may lower the positive stress that often fuels learning; participants recognize that it does not matter if they make errors so they may become lackadaisical in their approach. This problem is partially alleviated by scoring systems that track learners' success within the program (sometimes comparing sequential attempts) but this, in turn, may only lead to a learner's pursuit of meaningless 'points' with little or no regard for learning. Some learning programs address this problem by offering ever-changing selections from a bank of questions. Another feature of some programs, such as the WebCT platform, is the opportunity for teachers to track automatically the number of minutes learners spend working. Of course, the learner can also circumvent this by simply leaving the computer on with the program in operation while doing other things.

These issues draw CALL into another area of applied linguistics, the study of motivation.

Further reading

Dörnyei, Z. (2001) *Teaching and Researching Motivation*. Harlow: Longman – In this book from this ALiA series, Dörnyei presents an overview of issues in motivation. However, he does not address motivation at the computer.

2.2.1   Possibilities and limitations in simulations

Higgins and Johns (1984) note that, in an early demonstration of language applications for PLATO, one of the authors was also shown simulations developed for other applications. These included a medical emergency in which one could play the part of an ambulance driver and make a series of choices. Higgins and Johns recognize that, although this ambulance program was not envisaged as something to foster language learning, it could certainly be used as such. Certainly, such use of scenarios coupled with authentic materials has become a common approach to learning since then. But what differs among such simulations is the extent to which each one mirrors reality.

Quote 2.4   P.F. Merrill *et al.* explain the idea of *fidelity* in simulations:

Because simulations and models are but an imitation of reality, their use requires a certain amount of imagination. The more realistic a simulation is, the less imagination is required. Conversely, the less realistic a simulation is, the more imagination is required. Simulations fall on a continuum of realism. Those that are near duplicates of the actual phenomenon are said to have high fidelity with reality, whereas those with few characteristics in common with reality are said to have low fidelity.

Merrill *et al.* (1996: 93)

Multimedia-enhanced CALL is easily capable of creating learning situations of great fidelity or authenticity, both through the presentation of images of realia and through audio and video input that can present real-world situations as realistically as television but with greater interaction.

I am not aware of any recent empirical studies dealing with the effect of fidelity of learner materials in CALL simulations, but it would seem a promising area of research to attempt to correlate the fidelity of a program with opportunities for second language acquisition. For example, such research might suggest that learners forced to use a greater degree of imagination engage in a greater degree of negotiation of meaning.

However, it must also be noted that there is a limit to the range of abstract ideas that may be dealt with through direct reference. There is also a narrow range of real-world situations which teachers and learners are able to simulate in a computer environment.

Quote 2.5 T. McArthur explains limitations of simulations:

The term *situation*, however, is Janus-faced: there are real situations out there and there are simulated situations in the classroom, embedded more or less artificially in the selected and graded material of a syllabus. The problem was how to make simulated situations resemble real situations more successfully, how to get a wooden dialogue to turn – magically – into what one would say, hear and do in a real café or hotel. Better, the problem began to be perceived as how to avoid simulation and get the teacher–learner ensemble to create authentic and appropriate language of its own.

McArthur (1983: 101)

Before it was retired from the institutions that first developed it in favour of smaller, less expensive and more efficient machines with more flexible architectures and programming languages, PLATO came to support a wide range of languages, including Chinese, which presents particular character display challenges. Initially, PLATO's interface consisted of teletype machines (the computer printer had been invented in 1953 and the dot-matrix printer in 1957) for inputting and outputting information. As display technology advanced, a screen and eventually even a touch-screen were used. For a survey of language learning work done with PLATO, see Hart (1981) and Chapelle and Jamieson (1983). Also, Merrill *et al.* (1996) report that PLATO is still in use in Japan where a version continues to be developed by the electronics conglomerate TDK.

Because the work on and with PLATO and similar large systems was so well funded and available to an academic elite, developments to do with miniaturizing computer components (often at the cost of computing power) tended to offer only limited improvements in pedagogy. As a pioneering platform, PLATO set a standard for educational computing, influencing a generation of educational software developers.

2.3   CALL in the 1970s and 1980s

Concept 2.2   **Classifying computers**

During the period in discussion, computers were classified into mainframe computers, mini-computers and microcomputers. *Mainframe computers* were room-sized machines. *Mini-computers* were closer to what we now call *servers*. *Microcomputers* are what we would now call *desktop computers* or *personal computers*. *Portable*, or *laptop*, computers are included in this last category, but were introduced much later and are now far more powerful than the first mainframe computers.

In 1975, microcomputers were first sold in kit form (Merrill *et al.*, 1996). This spurred the development of small applications on computers such as the *Timex-Sinclair* and the *Commodore Pet*. Many of these platforms were extremely limited by their processing power. The *Timex-Sinclair*, for example, had a processing capacity of 16K; for purposes of comparison, currently, a standard computer diskette used today has a capacity 90 times larger and the processors (not to mention the memory) of current laptop computers are a minimum of 2,000 times more powerful and as high as 30,000 times more powerful.

High-end mainframe computers continued to be available and used for CALL research throughout the 1970s and 1980s at university laboratories and commercial institutions. One focus of CALL research during this period was videodisc technology, a high-volume storage system. Unlike videotape, videodisc players featured rapid access to multiple points or 'chapters' on a disk and had better pause, or freeze frame, features along with the possibility of advancing one frame at a time through a set of video or still (e.g. photographic) images or images/pages of text.

The format has been largely replaced with Compact Disk Read-Only Memory (CD-ROMs) as they have a greater installed base in personal computers and feature a format that is smaller, more convenient and less prone to warping. However, CD-ROMs do not carry as much information as videodiscs and, in turn, are likely soon to be replaced by larger volume media such as Digital Videodiscs (DVD).

The high speed and storage capacity of videodisc technology made it possible for computers to go beyond behaviourist models of instruction on less powerful computers that generally relied upon textual exercises.

> **Quote 2.6** M.D. Bush and J. Crotty compare videodisc instruction to traditional instruction and suggest the former has several advantages
>
> The use of video-based exercises makes practice inherently more meaningful than traditional text-based exercises. Video gives students an understandable context in which to work while providing many extralinguistic clues. The control options built into the interactive lesson allow students an array of problem-solving strategies to choose from.
>
> Bush and Crotty (1991: 86–7)

Bush and Crotty (1991) list several possible features of videodisc learning: priority of listening over speaking; exclusive use of the target language; implicit rather than explicit grammar; correction/corroboration through modelling and special efforts to create a low-anxiety atmosphere. To illustrate what has become possible with videodisc technology three early examples, *Macario*, *Montevidisco* and *Interactive Dígame*, are discussed below.

2.3.1 Macario

Gale (1989) describes *Macario* as an early videodisc program for learning Spanish. It was developed at Brigham Young University and was an attempt to create learning materials by adapting existing materials, in this case a feature-length commercial video. The video was made into an interactive format by adding a pedagogical layer and using it to teach listening skills. Such materials can be considered authentic as they were originally intended to be used for non-educational purposes by native speakers of the target language.

This approach of building on existing materials has the advantage of avoiding the high cost of video production while allowing the freedom to tailor associated learning materials to a specific group of learners. In some ways, this approach is similar to creating a literary study guide, but differs in that the focus is on language learning, particularly the paralinguistic aspects. Each scene of the *Macario* video was given annotations, footnotes, questions and/or comments. Learner control consisted of being able to start and stop the video as necessary to answer questions and ensure comprehension or simply to learn more about what was going on. In a semi-immersion approach, questions were available in English, but all responses were given in Spanish.

Gale (1989) does not mention if *Macario* was used individually or in a classroom situation (a common approach with early materials), but presumably there would have been no reason it could not have been used by individual learners. In a classroom, small group or pairwork situation, the program would have presented opportunities for negotiation of meaning, particularly as the answers were only available in the target language.

In terms of model of interface, *Macario* parts may be considered to be based on a constructivist model of instruction because the aim of the program was to allow learners to construct the meaning of the film from a range of visual and linguistic clues. These clues were presented in the form of hints, annotations, footnotes, comments and the film itself, which the learners could choose to use or ignore.

On the other hand, to answer the questions set for them, learners had to try to understand the teacher's interpretation of the meaning through correctly answering a set of questions which may have driven the learners toward one (possibly narrow) interpretation of the film. In this way, the program's interface may be closer to a behaviourist model of instruction.

2.3.2   Montevidisco and Interactive Dígame

As with early versions of PLATO, Macario is essentially a linear program; in this case, one follows the course of a film and cannot vary from it. Gale (1989) (also see Stevens, 1992) mentions two similar videodisc programs that featured non-linear opportunities for learning, *Montevidisco* and *Interactive Dígame*. These two programs pioneered the idea of learners making greater choices about what is to be learned at the computer.

Interactive Dígame differed from previous programs in that it was a teacher-controlled situation in which on-screen video provided visual and listening opportunities that were intended to be followed up with in-class conversation in the target language. In this way, it foreshadowed the approach of many teacher-led video-based learning lab activities. The program had constructivist elements in that it left the learners free to discuss their own interpretations of the reality on the screen, but the provision of teacher direction in the delivery now seems unnecessary; learners are able to control the course of events themselves.

In *Montevidisco*, the videodisc introduces a plaza where the learner is confronted with a local citizen. The citizen speaks and then the video frame freezes and presents several choices of response. Based on the selected response, 1,100 branching choices allow the learner to pursue different links or lines of enquiry. For example, when the on-screen character asks what the learner is looking for, the learner might choose one of several pre-set options, including going for coffee; at the coffee shop, the learner might choose to use language skills to order a coffee or just read the newspaper. Each choice presents different links/opportunities for learning and only through repeating the program several times can all the choices and language opportunities be fully exploited.

This non-linear approach is an essential element of many current interactive software learning programs and serves to differentiate them from paper learning materials which generally require learners to begin on page one and proceed page by page until they reach the end of the book. Such programs essentially feature a constructivist model of instruction in that the learner needs to understand the realities of the plaza and its many characters through investigation of peripheral elements such as signs, overheard conversations and articles on-screen in a newspaper. The learner needs to make decisions based on what he or she encounters and, in this way, the program encourages negotiation of meaning.

A non-linear approach in computer-based learning materials is attractive because it allows for greater learner autonomy and encourages critical thinking. However, it also brings with it specific concerns such as a reassessment of the place of scope and sequence in language learning: how does a materials developer deal with *scope* when she cannot be sure of the learner covering all the materials? How can a materials developer deal with *sequence* when the learner can choose among many links and series of links?

2.3.3   ALLP

The Athena (after the Greek goddess of wisdom) Language Learning Project (ALLP) (see Murray, Morgenstern and Furstenberg, 1991; McConnell, 1994; Murray, 1991, 1995) began in 1983 as part of a heavily funded long-term Massachusetts Institute of Technology (MIT) project exploring the role of the computer in education. For the project, Digital Equipment Corporation (DEC) and International Business Machines (IBM) contributed staff for five years as well as US$50 million; Massachusetts Institute of Technology (MIT) contributed a further US$20 million (McConnell, 1994: 161).

Instead of relying on large mainframe computers or independent videodisc technology, ALLP worked with UNiversal Interactive eXecutive (UNIX) (*or* UNiversal Inter-eXchange *or* UNIversity eXchange; the etymology is anecdotal) workstations that, at that time, were then a little less powerful than common laptop computers today. These UNIX machines were connected to each other and to textual and visual databases through a local area network (LAN).

Murray, Morgenstern and Furstenberg's (1991) list of three advantages of the ALLP system (see Quote 2.7) includes one point, *interactivity usually*

> **Quote 2.7** The advantages of ALLP are noted by J. Murray, D. Morgenstern and G. Furstenberg as being:
>
> 1. The encyclopedic information usually associated with print that can be recalled with the speed of the computer
> 2. The extensive models of the language provided by multiple speakers (including native speech in its appropriate cultural context) usually associated with television or film materials, and
> 3. The engagement of interactivity usually associated with more primitive drill-and-practice routines.
>
> Murray, Morgenstern and Furstenberg (1991: 101)

associated with more primitive drill-and-practice routines, that might be trying to portray a typical behaviourist drawback as an advantage by putting together the behaviourist idea of *engagement* and with the more constructivist idea of *interactivity*. In a behaviourist model of instruction, engagement is more likely to stem from extrinsic rewards such as points. In a constructivist interface, intrinsic rewards are likely to engage learners to participate based on the interactivity of the program's responses to their interests.

Murray, Morgenstern and Furstenberg's third point serves to demonstrate the fact that few software programs are exclusively behaviourist or constructivist. Instead, programs are likely to benefit from a combination of the two so as to appeal to learners at different stages of cognitive development.

Two projects to come out of ALLP merit special mention, *No Recuerdos* (*I Don't Remember*) and *À la rencontre de Phillippe* (*Recognizing Phillippe*). In both these programs, learners enter into computer simulations that require realistic responses to the main characters. The programs also both include what has now become a standard aspect of adventure games and many language-learning simulations: branching sets of events with visual responses that can be selected with a mouse click, as opposed to *Montevidisco*'s multiple textual choices.

2.3.4 No Recuerdos

No Recuerdos features a strong narrative in which Gonzalo, an amnesiac scientist, cannot recall the location of a biological hazard that threatens to destroy the whole of Latin America. This literal *deadline* in helping Gonzalo to recall what has happened fuels the learner's urgency and sets the pace of the program.

Concept 2.3   Near-impossible objectives

A near-impossible objective is a feature of many multimedia learning programs, particularly those with a game focus. Essentially, a near-impossible objective is some goal that is difficult to reach so as to encourage repeated attempts, perhaps forcing the learner to adapt new strategies and make use of what has been learned in successive failures. In other cases, a near-impossible objective is heightened by increasing the difficulty or changing the goal with each failed attempt.

A learner's initial failure to achieve a near-impossible objective adds to the motivation to attempt the program repeatedly. This near-impossible objective, representing a heightened level of difficulty involved in completing the task or tasks, is a feature of many computer games and simulations. If the level of difficulty is too low, then the user only explores a limited number of links or options within the program and, having reached the goal, grows bored and loses out on the learning benefits of repeated attempts.

The inclusion of a near-impossible objective essentially turns a behaviourist product-orientated approach into a constructivist process approach in which the artificial purpose (to achieve some goal or collect a certain number of points) remains, but the learner, in attempting to achieve it, engages in constant review. The best learning programs are those in which the strategies for meeting the objectives mirror real-world language tasks such as searching for information on a menu. Also, learners working alone or in groups to review what has been done and what might be done alone, or in a collaborative situation, helps foster negotiation of meaning.

Quote 2.8   P.F. Merrill, K. Hammons *et al.* suggest essential problem-solving skills:

1. A desire to solve the problem
2. A base knowledge of possible actions and solutions
3. The ability to take action
4. The resources to monitor and assess the mental and physical actions or solutions as they unfold
5. The controls to effect changes in those actions as the need arises

Merrill, Hammons *et al.* (1996: 88)

In order to complete the task(s) in *No Recuerdos*, the learner gathers information by questioning the main character, Gonzalo (i.e. the program).

However, a problem with this type of scenario is that computers are generally unable to process ambiguous or erroneous input. Three solutions in the case of this program is to deal with the problem by having Gonzalo:

- say he cannot remember
- develop a headache so that he is unable to respond, or
- seek clarification

This clarification algorithm is rather sophisticated compared with many later software programs that, instead, simply seize up when confronted by unorthodox learner input and responses. In many programs, the ability to accommodate even the simplest of unexpected responses is the dividing line between behaviourist pre-programmed instruction and a more constructivist model of instruction. Such programs are usually distinguished by their inability to confront ambiguity because their behaviourist interfaces feature only a limited range of virtual buttons to push.

2.3.5   Eliza

Part of the simulated or artificial intelligence aspect of *No Recuerdos* is based on earlier work done by Weizenbaum (1976), who created a program called *Eliza* (after George Bernard Shaw's character in *Pygmalion* who is taught how to speak 'properly'). The *Eliza* software program seeks clarification and simulates a sympathetic listener through a series of general comments, requests for explanations and paraphrases/rephrasings of the learners' comments with additional question tags.

Example 2.1   A discussion might begin in the following way (phrases in *italics* showing how *Eliza* adapts the learner's utterances):

Eliza: How are you today?
Learner: I'm feeling tired.
Eliza: Why are you *feeling tired*?
Learner: I watched the football game last night.
Eliza: Tell me more about *the football game last night*.
And so on.

This program and later, more sophisticated versions (in various languages) have often been combined with large databases of information (e.g. an extensive number of facts about a pop music group). Variations on Eliza programs have also been used in order to challenge the Turing Test, a measure of how closely a computer can simulate human intelligence.

Concept 2.4   **Alan Turing and the Turing Test**

The Turing Test is named after the computer pioneer Alan Turing (1912–54) who, in arguments over machine intelligence, decided that an experiment would be necessary to settle the matter.

The Turing Test features a terminal in one room and a computer set up in another. Through typed discussion, the human is required to determine whether the interlocutor is a human or a machine. The work is important in that it leads toward the still distant goal of constructing a superior interface in which computers can be said to simulate the intelligence of a real teacher. It also provides insights into the nature of artificial intelligence, language learning and discourse.

Turing has an interesting connection to computers and language; in 1937 he published his influential paper *On Computable Numbers*, outlining the theoretical abilities and limits of a computer. His ideas were soon put to the test during the Second World War when, in 1943, he helped to build the *Colossus*, the first British mainframe computer, used to assist in deciphering German Enigma cryptograms. Also intended for cryptography, but built too late to be of use in the Second World War, was the American *Electronic Numerical Integrator And Calculator* (*ENIAC*) computer, completed in 1945.

Higgins and Johns (1984) outline two early applications of *Eliza*, neither of which was intended as a language learning program, but both of which could offer reading and writing practice for learners. These programs, *Doctor* and *Parry*, were intended to help train doctors, but could easily be adapted to language learning.

Quote 2.9   Higgins and Johns on two early applications of *Eliza*:

In *Doctor*, the machine takes on the role of a 'non-directive' psychiatrist, and issues noncommittal responses to the user's input sentences. In Colby's *Parry*, an extension of the same idea, the computer assumes the role of a psychopath responding to a psychiatrist and issues aggressive messages. It's fairly easy to make these programs talk nonsense so they don't pass the Turing Test. However, it is also possible to sustain a very plausible connected discourse over a lengthy set of exchanges.

Higgins and Johns (1984: 75)

It is perhaps the possibility of a high degree of nonsensical responses that have discouraged extensive CALL work using *Eliza*, but it seems a promising avenue for future CALL research and learning materials development.

Already, *Eliza*-like programs are being used for applications that address common queries, such as computer-based help-lines which must attend to a large set of frequently asked questions (see _____. A killer app for computer chat, *Economist*, 10 April 1999, pp. 79–80). When confronted with unpredictable and unorthodox questions, the solution is to connect the questioner to a human operator.

2.3.6 À la rencontre de Phillippe

Like *No Recuerdos* another program, *À la rencontre de Phillippe*, also allows the learner to enter into a semi-authentic language environment. The narrative is fictional but, like *No Recuerdos*, it offers opportunities to explore documentary style depictions of reality, in this case, the city of Paris. And like *No Recuerdos* it adds a sense of urgency; Phillippe has just lost his apartment and must find some place to stay.

The narrative revolves around learners helping the central character Phillippe find a new apartment, a task that can be accomplished in many ways or, if the learners choose to simply explore the program, not at all. Finding an apartment in the program requires using on-screen telephones and fax machines and paying attention to written clues such as notes posted on walls and telephone poles. Another part of the program allows learners the opportunity to create their own documentaries using information on the same neighborhood explored in the scenario (Murray, Morgenstern and Furstenberg, 1991).

Concept 2.5 **Learners as authors**

Many programs allow learners to manipulate materials to create on-screen narratives or even design their own learning materials. For example, HyperCard-type applications are not too sophisticated for even young students to master and many learners are able to create their own web pages using programs such as Microsoft *FrontPage* and simpler versions available free on the WWW. Some programs such as *Story Book Weaver Deluxe* allow young learners to write stories on-screen and illustrate them with custom designed clip-art. Hutchings *et al.* (1992), talking of learners authoring, suggest, 'Those who prepare the course material may learn much more than those who receive it' (p. 171).

The above approaches serve to promote language acquisition and awareness as learners are driven to explore and interpret the information necessary to complete the selected tasks. *À la rencontre de Phillippe* (recently re-released as a CD-ROM) was contained within a larger program that featured 60 minutes of full video.

Kenning and Kenning (1990) suggest CALL does not necessarily feature greater authenticity than printed text but, since the publication of their book in 1990, the technological capabilities of the computer to store (e.g. on CD-ROMs), display (colour monitors and printers) and share a range of information and media (e.g. using the WWW) is far greater.

Concept 2.6   The folly of definitive conclusions

Kenning and Kenning's (1990) book *Computers and language learning: current theory and practice* provides a serious caution to anyone hoping to make definitive statements on quickly evolving technologies. So much has changed in computing since their book's publication that some of their conclusions are now quite out of date. For example, they conclude that the computer's display of information is severely limited on the printed page because of the lack of right ragged edge and paragraph indentations and problems with typography (see pp. 96–8).

They little realized that within five years the computer would all but replace and revolutionize traditional typography and provide far more flexible editing and graphical display options for the printed page than any mechanical innovation in printing since the illuminated manuscript.

In another route to authenticity, some commercial software packages allow teachers to copy WWW materials such as online WWW newspapers and quickly adapt them into annotated lessons and computer-based cloze and multiple choice tests. However, it must be noted that such programs might challenge some countries' copyright laws.

À la rencontre de Phillippe features both real-world authentic materials (e.g. apartment listings) and authentic tasks (e.g. looking for an apartment) that could be reproduced in a textbook format, but part of the authenticity of such programs is the process the learner engages in looking for the materials in a situation rich in contextual details – some of which are significant, many of which are not.

A related project, by Gilberte Furstenberg, *Dans le quartier Saint-Gervais* (In the neighborhood of Saint-Gervais), features a documentary approach to allow learners to explore an old Parisian neighbourhood and follow various links to explore 200 years of history. Like *À la rencontre de Phillippe* the program offers learners opportunities to make their own documentaries and multimedia documents from the resource materials used in the program. *À la rencontre de Phillippe* and *Dans le quartier Saint-Gervais* both feature constructivist aspects in their interfaces as the learner is given many relatively unstructured opportunities to explore the resources and to solve problems. In *À la rencontre de Phillippe* in particular, learners build language awareness and skills through the need to negotiate meaning from disparate sources of information. Negotiation of meaning with the computer, not simply with another learner, is both possible and encouraged.

The above examples show well-funded applications from university-based research on improving language teaching. Changes to the field of CALL in the 1970s and 1980s were marked by a shift from mainframe computers and computer workstations such as UNIX machines to desktop models with applications that were more easily available for classroom use. Even though these machines were limited in power, it meant that classroom teachers could begin experimenting with creating their own, often simple, CALL applications to address local language teaching and learning concerns in a broad range of languages. At the same time, the move to a more affordable platform with a larger installed base of computers within schools began to encourage and influence the production of commercial software programs.

Concept 2.7   Commercial providers of software

In conversations with large commercial publishers in Hong Kong and Australia, I have often asked about the threat of teacher-created materials freely available on the WWW. Generally, publishers are dismissive of such efforts. The consensus seems to be that publishers add enormous value to their products and bring together a number of skilled individuals to create materials, not the least being editors who check the quality and veracity of the content. Other participants in the publishing process include language experts, graphic designers, computer programmers to create custom software and marketing staff who research market demand. Teachers considering creating CALL software should first ensure that they have the skilled help they need to create worthwhile materials.

On the other hand, some commercial publishers, such as Clarity Consultants Ltd (*www.clarity.com.hk*) have a history of partnering with teachers to develop commercial materials.

2.3.7   HyperCard

In 1984, Apple Computer introduced a new style of computer, the *Macintosh*. It differed from earlier domestic-use or personal computers in that it offered a graphical user interface (GUI). A computer with a GUI uses icons to summarize and take the place of lines of typed code and arcane commands. One of the major innovations in this environment was *HyperCard*, a materials authoring program that was developed by Apple Computer. HyperCard provides an influential metaphor for CALL. As the name suggests, it works by creating a set of virtual index cards that can be extensively cross-referenced. On these cards, text, images, audio, animations and video can be added, along with questions and buttons to take users to other cards that might feature further questions, information and/or answers.

The importance of HyperCard is that it was among the first applications to take advantage of the theoretical hypertext and hypermedia (see Chapter 3) capabilities of computers and allowed teachers and learners easily to create their own CALL applications. Various, more flexible and feature-laden, versions of HyperCard have since been developed under various brand names.

Concept 2.8   Metaphors for authoring

HyperCard takes as its inspiration a shuffled set of index cards. Other software authoring programs have embraced other metaphors including books (Asymetrix *Toolbook*) and movies (Macromedia *Director*). The development of new metaphors might free the creation of CALL software from the confines of traditional learning materials. For example, an aquarium, with its ever-changing displays and interactions of information (moving fish), might inspire a new kind of program in which learning occurs as learners observe screensavers. Instead of fish, the computer might mingle words and sounds that attract and avoid each other.

2.4 CALL in the 1990s

Thousands of new CALL programs have been published since the few mentioned above, but the ones cited so far provide an overview of the types of features likely to be offered in a multimedia CALL environment. Murray, Morgenstern and Furstenberg (1991: 97–118) provide guidelines as to what might be usefully included in multimedia learning environments. The guidelines (paraphrased below) also serve to suggest how narrative-driven multimedia learning environments might be evaluated:

1. *Multiplicity of protagonists*: allows for the story to be told from different points of view. This then creates learning gaps requiring the learners to fill in information.

2. *Multiplicity of plot events*: creates variety based on learner choices that influence the development of the narrative.

3. *Knowledge-based choice points*: allow for learning tasks that are necessary to the continuation of the narrative.

4. *Choice-points based on temperament of the learner*: allow learners to pursue the narrative according to the depth of their own interests or abilities to complete more practical or narrative tasks which, nonetheless, cover the same materials.

5. *Whimsical surprises*: offer unexpected enjoyment thus allowing for momentary diversion and encouraging exploration. In many newer programs, this has been encapsulated in programs called *Easter Eggs* that, like the elegant jewelled Fabergé eggs created for the Russian aristocracy, contain unexpected surprises.

6. *Multimedia for presentation*: offers different methods of output (aural, textual) but also, in the case of the ALLP projects, in different realistic contexts, such as a radio, telephone or newspaper.

7. *Intrinsic rather than extrinsic rewards*: motivate learners to progress through the program because completing the tasks and acquiring language are the same objective. This can be contrasted to embedded quizzes that must be completed as an irrelevant test before the learner progresses through the narrative.

There are many non-narrative multimedia materials that do not accommodate many of the above points but the list is a useful starting point for deciding what is possible and desirable within a multimedia context.

Example 2.2   Who is Oscar Lake

A popular contemporary program is *Who is Oscar Lake*, available in multiple languages. The highly interactive program features live action video as well as clever animation. The live action video is situated within the program and most often features native speakers offering answers, comments and advice that helps the learners solve the mystery of Oscar Lake. The program features a 1,200-word vocabulary list and 33 separate language-learning activities. Objects within the program can be identified by pointing and clicking on them for their target language word or a translation into English, Spanish, French, German or Italian. The program is also available in those languages. Learners can record and play back their own voices. Within the simulation, there are opportunities to collect clues and follow branching multiple possible endings to encourage revisiting and the user can also save the game at any point.

Summary

This chapter looked at the history of CALL, highlighting several developments of hardware and software and noted how the arrival of desktop computers prompted more teacher-led research. In general, a lot of CALL software is stuck in a behaviourist rut partly because offering a behaviourist mode of instruction is easy for computers to do.

Further reading

Fertig, S., Freeman, E. and Gelernter, D. (1996) Lifestreams: an alternative to the desktop metaphor. *Computer–Human Interaction* 96 Electronic Proceedings. *http://www.acm.org/sigchi/chi96/proceedings/videos/Fertig/etf.htm* – This paper presents one alternative to the desktop metaphor.

Chapter 3

Hypertext, hypermedia and multimedia

Chapter 2 has already pointed to several examples of computer programs with specific applications to the teaching and learning of language. In this chapter, more attention is paid to the special features of the computer that give it the potential to offer something different (if not better) than traditional teaching and learning materials. These features include hypertext, hypermedia and multimedia.

3.1 Hypertext

Hypertext refers to links among textual items, often indicated by key words set in underlined blue type that, when highlighted by a pointer device (e.g. mouse, trackball, finger on a touch-sensitive screen) and selected or clicked, takes the reader to the referent. These links are usually defined in terms of their activity and are referred to as *hotlinks* or *hyperlinks*. The referent at the end of the hyperlink might be a separate screen or so-called 'page' that obscures or replaces the first page, or simply a small box of text that appears to float above the initial page. For example, in a language-learning program, one might click on a hypertext link to go to one of several choices in a branching story and arrive at that link on another page, or simply click on a word to get a floating box offering its dictionary definition. Hypertext is often used to link text to materials traditionally contained in footnotes and annotations but may also include much more.

Bolter (1991) explains the significance of hypertext: 'Electronic text is the first text in which the elements of meaning, of structure, and of visual display are fundamentally unstable' (p. 31). By this he means that electronic texts are subject to rearrangement and reordering by the user beyond the traditional linear organization of books. This has countless implications to the

> **Quote 3.1** J.D. Bolter on footnotes:
>
> In a printed book, it would be intolerably pedantic to write footnotes to foot-notes. But in the computer, writing in layers is quite natural, and reading in layers is effortless. All the individual paragraphs may be of equal importance in the whole text, which then becomes a network of interconnected writings. The network is designed by the author to be explored by the reader in precisely this peripatetic fashion.
>
> Bolter (1991: 15)

creation of language-learning materials where the sequence of learning is so often strictly pre-determined, based on research as to the order of complexity of lexical items and structures (see Nunan, 1987).

The development of hypertext has been associated most closely with a constructivist (see Section 5.6) model of learning and aspects of schema theory. But while the behaviourist model might use hypertext's special features only to link text with explanations, tests and answers, the constructivist model might consider the same features and use them to encourage learners to collaborate over the structure and the sequence of their own learning. This latter approach is more likely to accommodate collaboration and negotiation of meaning as it involves a greater degree of decision-making.

3.2   Hypermedia

Hypermedia refers to similar links as those used in hypertext, but instead of simply linking text to text, hypermedia involves linking various media, such as sound, images, animation and/or video. For example, a word or picture might have a link to a sound file giving its pronunciation. A video of a language-learning opportunity, such as a shopping excursion, might be linked to an animation that shows the same exchanges simplified, omitting the distracting elements around the interactions between the shopper and the sales clerk. Or, an animation might focus on a related aspect, such as a review of the value of different denominations of money.

The projects mentioned in the ALLP (see Section 2.3.3) would be classified as hypermedia systems, although their creators (see Murray, 1995) classify them as Intelligent Computer Assisted Language Learning (ICALL). ICALL differs from CALL in that it offers often dubiously labelled 'intelligent' feedback features that customize responses to learner input through subroutines similar to the already mentioned *Eliza* program (see Section 2.3.5).

> **Quote 3.2** J.D. Bolter on dismissing so-called 'intelligent' aspects of the computer:
>
> Computer-assisted instruction . . . is nothing more than a hypertext in which the author has restricted the ways in which the student/reader can proceed. In typical computer-assisted instruction, the program poses a question and awaits an answer from the student. If the student gives the correct answer, the program may present another question. If the student's answer is wrong, the program may explain the student's error. If the student makes the same error repeatedly, the program may present a review of the point that the student has failed to grasp. In most cases, these questions and explanations are texts that the teacher/programmer has composed and stored in advance. However, good programming can make these simple programs seem uncannily clever in replying to the student.
>
> Bolter (1991: 30)

Differences in positions on computer intelligence are only a matter of semantics. While we do not expect a computer to think and converse intelligently, it can have some features that appear to simulate intelligence.

3.3 Multimedia

Multimedia usually refers to many of the same ideas associated with hypermedia, but where hypermedia might only make use of two types of media (e.g. *text + sound* or *text + photographs*) multimedia tends to feature several media types including text, images, sound, video and/or animations. Current language-learning programs classified by their vendors as multimedia

> **Quote 3.3** A.D. Thompson, M.R. Simonson and C.P. Hargrave on terminology:
>
> . . . many educators are confusing hypermedia with multimedia and ignoring the differences between the two. Whereas multimedia refers to the use of a variety of media, hypermedia can be defined from the two words that make up the term. *Hyper* means *non-linear* or *random* and *media* refers to *information represented in many formats*. Educational technology futurist Dede (1987) defined hypermedia as a framework for non-linear representation of symbols. He considered hypermedia an external associational memory where the technology provides assistance in organizing and accessing information.
>
> Thompson, Simonson and Hargrave (1992: 57)

generally fall into this broad definition. On the other hand, Thompson, Simonson and Hargrave (1992) offer a slightly different definition of hypermedia contrasting it to multimedia and suggest that the former has a pedagogical perspective while the latter is simply a mode of presentation. This definition also accords with the structure of many of the multimedia programs on the market, most of which tend to dictate a set path of instruction.

A type of program more likely to match Thompson, Simonson and Hargrave's (1992) interpretation of hypermedia would be a software reference tool such as Microsoft's CD-ROM encyclopedia *Encarta*. In this, as in traditional paper encyclopedias, one is not expected to read through the materials in a linear fashion but rather jump from topic to topic as need or interest dictates. Also, within each of *Encarta*'s topics and definitions, one may well choose to follow separate hyperlinks that lead to distinct areas of inquiry just as one would follow a paper encyclopedia's linked subjects, often indicated through words set in small capitals or bold.

The difference, or advantage, of hypermedia is the possibility for easy access to various links within a program; selected referents are only a keystroke away. The word *possibility* has to be emphasized here; the design of interfaces differ from program to program affecting their ease of use. Similarly, multimedia links are selected and based on the perceptions of the program designer and may not mirror the needs of the learner. A multimedia program, by Thompson, Simonson and Hargrave's (1992) definition, would be a program that uses several media, but only a fixed linear path. For example, a children's storybook in which learners must start at the first page and continue reading to the end may only use extra media to provide incidental sound and visual effects to enhance the text. In a multimedia version, one might read the story of Peter and the Wolf and have opportunities to follow links and learn more about wolves or hear the Sergei Prokofiev musical adaptation.

However, these small (and perhaps dated) distinctions are largely lost in the current literature on multimedia so, for the purposes of this book, the term *multimedia* is used to encompass the non-linear organization of text in *hypertext* and the non-linear and multiple information formats referred to in *hypermedia*.

Quote 3.4 N. Williams suggests that multimedia and the computer need no longer be differentiated:

both the hardware and the software of these technologies are converging, such that there is little point in trying to discriminate between them. Everything on the 1997 computer can be called 'multimedia'.

Williams (1998: 153)

In the following discussion, many of the references to the theoretical basis and application of hypertext and hypermedia apply equally well to this definition of multimedia.

3.4 Antecedents of multimedia

Chapter 2 has already provided some examples of multimedia CALL programs from past decades, but in understanding multimedia, it is useful to examine the ideas that led to its formation.

The idea of multimedia learning resources is not new. Some wistfully trace multimedia back to hypertext aspirations of Mr Casaubon in George Eliot's novel *Middlemarch*; his life's work is creating a textual set of grand connections among all knowledge. In 1945, Vannever Bush published an article titled *As we may think* in which he outlined plans for a desk-sized *Memex* (MEMory EXtension) *System* which would access and organize large amounts of information (Bush, 1945). Bush had built a mechanical computer at Massachusetts Institute of Technology (MIT) and had been Director of Scientific Research for the American War Office during the Second World War, so he was already familiar with British and American efforts in constructing the first modern computers, the already mentioned *Colossus* and ENIAC machines. In the article, he notes that, after witnessing worldwide conflict, he was eager to turn the intellectual resources applied to warfare to more humanitarian and educational pursuits.

Further reading

Bush, V. (1945) As we may think. *Atlantic Monthly* (July) 176 (1): 101–8. *http://www.theatlantic.com/unbound/flashbks/computer/bushf.htm* – This article is concerned with the development of the *Memex* machine but deals more generally with issues about the organization of information.

Although Bush's *Memex* was never built, the article describing it directly influenced Douglas Engelbart whose Stanford Institute laboratory developed many of the tools which would eventually make multimedia possible: the mouse pointing device; a windows interface; word processing and electronic mail were all developed there in the 1950s and 1960s. In the 1960s, Ted Nelson coined the terms *hypertext* and *hypermedia* although the concepts had already been established and were in general use by those with access to computers. Around the same time, a research scientist working in the area of computers, Alan Kay, introduced the idea of the graphical user interface (GUI) made up of icons to represent chains of textual commands, and the portable computer, which he called the Dynabook (Cotton and Oliver, 1993).

Biography: Ted Nelson and Xanadu

Theodor Holm Nelson (1937–), studied philosophy before pursuing a Master's degree in Sociology at Harvard. In 1960, after enrolling on a computer course, he tried to invent a word-processing program but was unsuccessful in part because of the primitive computing facilities available to him. He began promoting the idea of hypertext which he saw as being applicable to a wide range of media, including maps and movies. His influential ideas included his plans for Xanadu, a system of web-based copyright in which micro payments could be made for using text and images, each of which would be tagged with detailed copyright information and permissions. The system has had influential backers but has not yet been released.

For more information on Xanadu, visit *http://xanadu.com/*

3.5 Science fiction and CALL

Science fiction has long been a rich ground for speculation about the use of the computers and, in many ways, serves to offer idealized visions of learning without concern for the constraints of technology that lag behind imagination. Many concepts that first appeared in science fiction have inspired developments in computing.

Quote 3.5 J. Gunn

One of the techniques of science fiction is to analyze concepts for their irreducible meanings and then to synthesize new and sometimes surprising combinations of ideas out of that basic material.

Gunn (1995: 26)

Author William Gibson created the metaphor *cyberspace* in his 1984 science fiction novel *Neuromancer. Cyberspace* retains its original (although poetic) definition as 'a consensual hallucination' and 'a graphic representation of data (i.e. hypertext, hypermedia and multimedia)' (Gibson, 1984: 51). The basic idea is that when interactions take place online, such as within a simulated environment (see Section 2.3.5), they are taking place within cyberspace.

The sense of cyberspace as a meeting place has been developed in other novels by Gibson (1986, 1988, 1996) and Neal Stephenson (1995, 2000). In their virtual venues, simulated worlds are created and machines given avatars, or online personalities that might be based on human forms, fanciful animals or even machines. In the novel *Snowcrash*, based on ideas of the fall of a modern Tower of Babel, a vast information/library database is given the appearance of a rumpled, friendly but almost infinitely knowledgeable librarian (Stephenson, 2000). Humans in the novel project themselves, or artistic interpretations of themselves, and interact as they would in the real world.

The use of human-like avatars is not far-fetched; the technology, although sometimes clumsy to manipulate with a keyboard or mouse, is already in place and widely used in gaming situations. The applications to CALL, however, have not been widely exploited.

Conceptual ideas along with electronic networks featuring services such as the World Wide Web (WWW) and physical collections of data in CD-ROMs, has fostered the growth of multimedia as new learning

Example 3.1 Virtual worlds and avatars

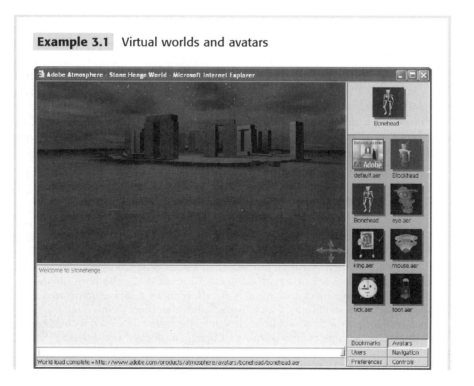

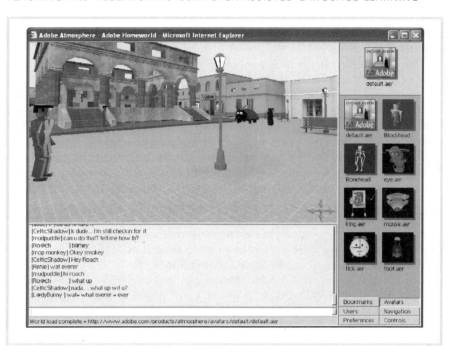

resources, particularly for language learning. The principal qualities of multimedia that have made it useful are the types of information (text, images, sound, animation, video) that can be stored and, more importantly, the useful ways that multimedia can be used to search information, electronically developing Dr Johnson's second quality of knowledge after actually knowing a thing itself: knowing where to find it (Boswell, 1791). The contrary argument is that the extensiveness of data available on media such as the WWW has made searching more, not less, difficult.

Concept 3.1   **Affordances and misaffordances**

Affordances are the visual clues that an object gives to its use as well as what it is capable of doing in terms of both intended and unintended functions. A chair is for sitting on and the size of the seat suggests that it might be comfortable for that purpose, but the chair can also be stood upon or used as a weapon; these are other affordances. Affordances can be both obvious and learned. An object can have both affordances and *misaffordances*. A misaffordance is something which distracts from an object's intended use. A misaffordance for a chair would be design features that disguised its purpose or interfered with its central purpose of being comfortably sat upon.

Misaffordances are common in software programs where, for example, flashing words or pictures distract from the purpose of reading.

Concept 3.2 **Interface**

Interface has already been mentioned in terms of graphical user interface (GUI). In pedagogical terms, an interface is the aspects of a computer that allow the user to have visual interaction with a program. The screen can present an interface in many different ways, most of them controlled by a mouse cursor or by keyboard commands. On screen, one can use a mouse and keyboard commands to press buttons, turn dials, move sliders and drag images and text from one place to another. Drop down menus, such as on the Microsoft *Windows* interface, are a widely used interface tool.

Further reading

Murray, J. (1997) *Hamlet on the Holodeck: the future narrative of cyberspace*. New York: Simon & Schuster. – This book provides an excellent overview of science fiction and other writings concerning the computer.

Curious Labs' homepage *http://www.curiouslabs.com/worlds/curiousworld.html* – This website offers examples of virtual words and avatars. To view the worlds, you need to download and install a free software application from Adobe: *Atmosphere http://www.adobe.com/products/atmosphere*

3.6 The printed book and CALL

Like modern multimedia, the printed book changed the nature of information through the ways in which ideas could be shared, recorded and explored. The increased access to information made possible by the book shifted the focus of education from an apprenticeship model of learning towards classroom-based instruction and increased opportunities for autonomous self-directed learning.

Concept 3.3 **The print and computer revolutions**

Johannes Gutenberg's (1400–68) invention of the moveable type printing press led to a proliferation of books that changed the world by changing the ways in which education could take place. In words that could equally well apply to the WWW today, information became more portable, cheaper and generally more accessible. Postman (1993) writes, 'Forty years after Gutenberg converted an old winepress into a printing machine with moveable type, there were presses in 110 cities in six countries. Fifty years after the press was invented, more than eight million books had been printed, almost all of them filled with information that had previously been unavailable to the average person' (p. 61).

Several authors (McLuhan 1962 – focusing on television; Birkerts, 1995; Hanson-Smith, n.d.) have linked current innovations in electronic publishing, and multimedia learning materials development occurred as the printed book changed the nature of information and knowledge established by the illuminated manuscript.

Some are critical of such comparisons, such as Johnson (1991) who mocks those who imagine, 'grandiose schemes of software/hardware interrelationships that resemble the cosmic attractions of the Middle Ages: layers of hierarchically related strata of reality teeming with agents of all kinds' (p. 272). However, since Johnson wrote the above, the WWW has begun to 'teem' with agents such as automated 'bots' which search and compare different kinds of information, such as the price of goods and services and 'spiders' which look throughout the entire web, documenting web pages for the use of search engines.

An increasingly important role of schools is to encourage learner autonomy to enable and encourage learning outside the classroom. In other words, schools provide learners with not just a body of knowledge, but the tools to modify and expand that knowledge beyond their formal classroom education. A concern of teachers has always been to push learners along a continuum of knowledge from novice to expert through transmitting critical thinking skills and strategies for learning as well as exploring ways in which learners may educate themselves. CALL helps in this process by increasing the resources available to learners outside the classroom, the search tools for finding that information and the presentation of that information in multiple media.

Quote 3.6 S.A. Weyer outlines the organization of the traditional book:

A book may be written in a linear, page-oriented order that may be alphabetical, chronological, geographical or pedagogical in its organization. Pieces of information are related to each other by their physical proximity in a paragraph, on a page or on neighboring pages. A subject index provides access to parts of the book in some other order. A good teacher, a set of questions or the authors can help provide connections and cross references to seemingly distinct sections and ideas; footnotes (and parenthetical remarks) refer to details of minor interest, named references to figures and chapters lead to other pages, and bibliographic citations point to other books or articles.

Weyer (1982: 88)

Weyer (1982) points out that the organizing devices of a book make it a useful tool for a reader whose needs match its organization. But Weyer (1982) also outlines the problems that occur when there is a mismatch between the learner's mental model of a body of a text and its organization and organizing devices.

> **Quote 3.7** S.A. Weyer on mismatches between learner needs and the organization of a text:
>
> What happens, however, when your vocabulary, organization or perception of a subject domain does not match the ones provided? In deciding to read footnotes as soon as they are referenced, you may suffer minor inconvenience by losing your place in the main narrative. You may have more difficulty in trying to find a word in a dictionary if you have misspelled it, know only to look for a synonym for it or know only how it sounds. How do you locate work 'related' to your own: by reading through everything about man–machine interfaces (for example), asking a colleague or attempting to specify a set of keywords or commonly used free-text terms for retrieval from some information system?
>
> Weyer (1982: 88)

Weyer's (1982) questions about mismatches in the organization of a text and learner's needs are largely solved by the use of hypertext references. The ways in which multimedia provides hypertextuality are outlined below.

To take Weyer's (1982) example of looking for a synonym, in some computer programs, a thesaurus link is explicitly indicated for the learner, such as the already mentioned hypertext underlined blue mark-up hyperlinks that might connect a word to not just its dictionary definition, but also synonyms and antonyms. But, in other cases, such as a misspelling, the hypertext function is buried within a program. If, for example, a learner misspells phone as *fone, a computerized word-processing software program such as that in Microsoft *Word* underscores the word in red jagged line and offers possible correct spellings such as *one, foe, phone, fond* and *font*. Four of these words (*one, foe, fond* and *font*) have been pre-selected based on the likelihood of the learner making a typing mistake and, looking through a traditional paper dictionary, one might indeed find the latter three variations.

However, for both *one* and *phone* (the latter being phonetically closest to the misspelling), the learner would never find the correct spelling in the *f* section of the dictionary. In other cases, such integrated hypertext systems are also used for checking grammar, for example suggesting an additional *s* to complete subject–verb agreement or to change a clause from the passive to the active tense.

There are many other more advanced applications to which hypertext and multimedia are applicable. Several are noted in the following section.

3.7 Applications to general learning

The above examples point out a few of the remedial aspects of hypertext in reading and writing. Hypertext, hypermedia and multimedia also overcome other limitations of the book by making use of the computer's ability to search through vast databases of text and images and form new and unexpected links in the material. In an approach perhaps modelled on earlier cognitive approaches to learning, this is similar to the way that a learner fills out mental schema adding successive thoughts and ideas.

From the point of view of the learner, there are three main advantages to hypertext:

1. A hypertext footnote can be traced backwards and forwards to the referent or reference respectively.

2. A hypertext section can be referenced in several places within the text reducing the need for paraphrasing ideas that are used repetitively and ensuring consistency of information.

3. A hypertext reference can be visible at the same time as the text to which it refers; in a book, one might need to turn to an appendix or even another book.

Conklin (1987) lists other beneficial features, but these mostly pertain to authors of hypertext, for example: ease of creating new references and the ability to structure information and customize documents. He also includes *collaboration* as a beneficial function of hypertext authoring. Traditionally, authoring was considered the domain of the professional/commercial materials developer or the teacher acting as a materials developer. However, most of these functions can also be useful for learners if they are given the opportunity to create multimedia materials as part of their exploration of

---

Concept 3.4 **Database and search engine**

A database is a corpus of information that is accessible for selection and reorganization by predetermined criteria, as simple as alphanumeric ordering or by more complicated searches, such as by semantic field. The information can be in the form of text, numbers, images, sounds or any other media. From the point of view of the user, the World Wide Web (WWW) is essentially a single database which one investigates with a search engine such as *www.google.com*. Search engines used to rely on organizing principles and efforts of teams of librarians but with the exponential growth of the WWW, search engines are now generally automated with computer programs that look for the highest incidence of one's search words or, in the case of *www.google.com*, for the number of other websites linked to websites featuring the search words.

a knowledge base. An already mentioned application of this is the ALLP project, *Dans le quartier Saint Gervais* (In the neighbourhood of Saint Gervais), that allows learners to make their own documentaries and multimedia documents from the source materials.

3.8 Applications of multimedia to language learning

Most of the above points that favour hypertext and hypermedia also favour multimedia. Key writings on *hypertext* were mainly published in the 1970s and 1980s. After this period, the focus and terminology shifts to *multimedia* even though much of the content and many of the issues remain the same. The advantages to general learning are much the same for language learning. But there are also additional advantages more central to language learning. For example, Montali and Lewandowski (1996) review studies conducted with first language secondary school students favouring multimedia as a way of improving reading skills among average and less-skilled readers. They suggest that readers who enjoy reading tend to read more and are more motivated to read and that a computer can be useful in promoting interest.

> **Quote 3.8** J. Montali and L. Lewandowski discuss poor readers and the benefits of bimodal reading as a type of computer-based learning:
>
> According to Paris and Winograd (1991), poor readers may harbor such anxiety about their abilities and expected failure that many will intentionally and effortfully avoid reading. Bimodal reading instruction may increase a child's motivation by providing a more successful reading experience for youngsters with disabilities. Moreover, (Montali and Lewandowski, 1996) demonstrated that poor readers not only feel more successful with bimodal presentation, but are more successful in terms of comprehending content. This type of reading program delivered via computer may offer one solution to some of the problems educators encounter with students who display reading difficulties.
>
> Montali and Lewandowski (1996: 278)

Other advantages of hypertext and multimedia are in the promotion of autonomous language learning (see Benson, 2001, Benson and Lor, 1998, Benson and Voller, 1997). Learners who can take advantage of multimedia links to explore explanations and peripheral information can somewhat lower the teacher-centredness of the classroom (i.e. learner dependence on the teacher as the sole source or arbitrator of information). A well-formed multimedia database of materials can also assist those young and second-language learners who lack dictionary and library search skills.

Examples of multimedia which distract the learner from the task are too common: inappropriate and unnecessary interruptions, such as flashing screens and senseless noises are what Hoogeveen would label *incongruent*. Hoogeveen (1995) suggests that learners' responses to multimedia interact in a complex way giving learners the feeling of experiencing information instead of simply acquiring it and improve:

1. learning (retention, understanding, knowledge acquisition), but also
2. the user-friendliness of user interfaces and thus man–machine interaction
3. the entertainment value of systems (i.e. more fun)
4. the impact of messages (e.g. during business presentations or commercials) (p. 351)

Many of these advantages can be seen as following constructivist models of instruction but, as will be seen in Chapter 8 in a discussion of models of learning, there are more complex dimensions to their place within both behaviourist and constructivist models of instruction in the classroom.

Quote 3.9 M. Hoogeveen suggests that quality multimedia, featuring a high degree of interactivity, congruence (the degree to which different information types are used redundantly to express the same ideas) and visual references lead to:

1. a high level of stimulation of the senses, at least with regard to the auditory and visual perception systems
2. a high level of involvement, attention, concentration
3. emotional arousal, e.g., fun; the word arousal is used in the psychophysiological sense of emotional, internal arousal, related to arousal of the nervous system
4. strong recognition effects, using mental reference models.

Hoogeveen (1995: 350)

Summary

Hypertext, hypermedia and multimedia (now usually subsumed under the term multimedia) are among the special features of the computer that give it the potential to offer something different (if not better) than traditional teaching and learning materials. An extension of these is the creation of virtual worlds using avatars to represent people in MOO-like situations.

Further reading

Alessi, S. and T.S. (2001) *Multimedia for Learning: methods and development*. Harlow: Allyn & Bacon/Longman. – This comprehensive book, now in its third edition, offers new approaches to multimedia instruction as well as updating established methods such as tutorials, drills, simulations, games, and computer-based tests as well as constructivist and what the authors call 'instructivist' approaches.

Shirley, Veenema and Gardner, Howard (1996) Multimedia and multiple intelligences. *The American Prospect* 7 (29), 1 November 1996–1 December 1996. – This article uses the example of a CD-ROM created around an American Civil War battle to illustrate how such technology can offer multiple entry points to the same materials.

Chapter 4

Eight CALL applications

Chapters 2 and 3 outlined CALL applications using simulations. Simulations are ideal for immersive environments that offer exposure to the target language in various media but sometimes lack the focus of other approaches. This chapter features eight current CALL applications that together illustrate the breadth of what is available to CALL practitioners. While not intended to be exhaustive, this chapter includes sections on:

- Word processing
- Games
- Literature
- Corpus linguistics
- Computer-mediated communication (CMC)
- WWW resources
- Adapting other materials for CALL
- Personal Digital Assistants

4.1 Word processing

Word processing is the poor cousin of CALL. Most computers are now sold with some version of word processing already installed and such programs are widely used in the composition process. Within such word-processing packages, spelling and grammar checkers are standard tools.

There used to be only one way for learners to correct spelling on their own: using a dictionary. Now, as learners increasingly use computers in the composition process, they frequently do their spelling corrections with computer-based spelling checkers and seldom refer to a dictionary.

Spelling checkers are also included in other applications such as database programs because as many as one in ten database queries fail because of spelling mistakes either in the query or within the database index itself (Smith, 1991).

After much research in the 1980s and early 1990s, attention has shifted away from the influence of spelling checkers and grammar checkers. However, it is an area which continues to merit attention as learners turn away from writing on paper to computer-based composition.

Further reading

Wong, C.J. (1996) Computer Grammar Checkers and Teaching ESL Writing. Paper presented at the 9th Annual Midlands Conference on Language and Literature, Omaha, NE. *http://www.coe.missouri.edu/~cjw/portfolio/grammar-checker.htm* – This article summarizes the history of grammar checkers, explains with examples how grammar checkers work and points out advantages and disadvantages.

Although computer software manufacturers may consult educators, most word-processing programs and other applications are designed not for school use, with attendant pedagogical concerns, but for business environments where learning is less important, or even completely unimportant. In business, the focus is on the completion of tasks. This is particularly seen in programs that offer spelling correction but do not provide any definitions. Learners frequently misspell a word then choose the first correction offered, without considering whether it is appropriate or not. Moreover, word-processing programs do not record misspellings and give no feedback to learners interested in reviewing their errors. Even worse, spelling checker programs allow learners to add new words to standard dictionaries and sometimes these words are simply misspellings.

It may be that spelling checkers assist in fluency by relieving learners of undue concern over their spelling during the composition process. However, when learners look through a traditional or even online dictionary to correct a word in response to uncertainty or a teacher remark or correction, it may help their acquisition of vocabulary to wade through dozens of related words, practising alphabet skills in using the guide words at the head of the page, and scanning through several entries, sometimes coming upon an illustration which shows the hyponyms and associated words to the target word. It is a slower, but far richer process.

Word-processing programs also provide grammar support, although such support is sometimes of questionable worth. The grammar checker included with various versions of Microsoft *Word*, for example, is programmed to object to the use of the passive voice, even though the passive voice is appropriate in some situations. This and other rules can be suppressed within the program but it may be difficult for learners to do so.

Beyond word processing, software such as Microsoft *Word* is increasingly multi-purpose. For example, it is commonly used by teachers (and sometimes learners) for creating semi-authentic learning materials featuring text, tables and illustrations as well as simple websites.

Further reading

Tuzi, F. (1997) Using Microsoft Word to generate computerized tests. *The Internet TESL Journal* III(11) – Although written for an earlier version of *Word*, the general principles of this article still apply to later versions.

4.2   Games

Most educational games or games used for pedagogical purposes make use of a form of subversive teaching; learners are unaware of the objectives or, rather, do not share the same objectives as the teacher. Instead, learning takes place as an activity peripheral to play. Learners asked to play the board game *Monopoly*, for example, may not be aware that they are learning a few rudimentary concepts about the value of money and real estate, nor will they associate these concepts as part of learning objectives.

A research question in this area is concerned with transfer: to what degree are skills learned in a game of use in the real world? The peripheral learning benefits in a game are likely to be small but are hopefully greater in a program devoted to some specific educational objective. The best educational games are those which embed the pedagogical objectives so that the learners' perceptions are of play, while the teachers' hidden objectives are still achieved.

Quote 4.1 A.C. Derycke, C. Smith and L. Hemery suggest:

Some of the highest pedagogical objectives can only be achieved by employing group learning activities such as group problem solving, games, case studies, exchanges with real experts.

Derycke, Smith and Hemery (1995: 182)

In other cases, learning materials which are not perceived as being game-like by the teacher may be perceived as such by the learner. For example, Nord describes an exchange with his students at Nanzan University in Nagoya, Japan in which they asked for another session in the computer-assisted language learning (CALL) laboratory using a particular game. Nord was confused until he realized that the game they were referring to was actually a traditional grammar drill (J.R. Nord, private communication, 1998). The idea of *game* rests in the perception of the user, not the description of the developer, the pedagogical model or the label used by the teacher.

Among computers' most popular uses today are as platforms for arcade-style computer games. While such entertainment applications have certainly increased general computer literacy and served to make computers more familiar and less threatening to the average young person, a question that needs to be addressed is: To what degree do young learners transfer their computer skills and enthusiasm to learning other approaches? It may be that young learners' familiarity with the possibility of what computers are capable of makes them less tolerant of educational applications that do not match the average computer game's exciting presentation of information.

A degree of excitement is necessary in computer-based learning materials, particularly in the case of young learners who lack motivation for learning. Young learners seldom see beyond the moment to consider the consequences of their learning (or not learning) something. Young learners can perhaps be cajoled into learning through the threat of tests, but cannot easily assess the importance of year-end grades, distant graduation or future employment. Within the classroom environment, computers can help in motivation through the organization of learning into game-like formats.

Quote 4.2 Z. Dörnyei and K. Czizér's 10 Commandments for motivating language learners

1. Set a personal example with your own behavior.
2. Create a pleasant, relaxed atmosphere in the classroom.
3. Present the tasks properly.
4. Develop a good relationship with the learners.
5. Increase the learners' linguistic self-confidence.
6. Make the language classes interesting.
7. Promote learner autonomy.
8. Personalize the learning process.
9. Increase the learners' goal-orientedness.
10. Familiarize learners with the target language culture.

Dörnyei and Czizér (1998: 215)

On the simplest level, the computer is a suitable game player as it can provide clues, levels of difficulty and rewards for solutions through points or visual stimulation. Most importantly, the computer is endlessly patient and never grows bored. Simple computer games include variations of many of those found in the real world.

Example 4.1 Hangman

Hangman is a game that has long had a slightly morbid fascination for children learning English. In the paper-based version, a scaffold for a public hanging is drawn over a series of dashes representing the number and positions of letters in the target word. As the learner playing the game guesses, letters are filled in their correct places or body parts (head, torso, arms, legs) are drawn on a person in the hangman's noose. Players who can complete the word before the entire body is completed win, those who can't, lose. In computer-based versions of this game, the hanging is animated with a walk to the scaffold and loser messages such as 'Sorry! You failed to save him.'

Despite the popularity of this game, teachers need to consider its appropriateness in the second-language classroom where some immigrant students may be fleeing repressive governments where public hangings, perhaps of relatives, were commonplace.

http://www.allmixedup.com/hangman/
http://kids.ot.com/cgi/kids/hangman

4.2.1 Commercial quiz software

Games are often in the form of quizzes which test knowledge more than they teach it. Like games, quizzes are very motivating for learners as they appear to illustrate a learner's progress and give some security against fear of more formal exams. As computer-based quizzes are often done outside of class and not marked by teachers, learners may feel less threatened.

A popular quiz format is that used in cloze programs such as *Clozewrite* and *Clozemaster*. In *Clozewrite*, learners choose a text from a menu on the computer screen and delete words at any point in the text (for example, after an introductory paragraph) at selected intervals; every second to every ninth word. Deleted words are replaced with numbered blanks. Learners can request clues in the form of single letters. Such programs encourage careful reading but frustration may occur as they do not accept synonyms; learners must guess the exact word that has been deleted.

Other quiz software includes programs to check spelling, listening, speed reading, knowledge of synonyms and antonyms, general knowledge and other English skills.

4.3   Literature

One of the ways in which learners are presented with opportunities to acquire language is through activities peripheral to the study of literature and other disciplines. A work of literature is not a simulation, but it has a high degree of fidelity, or authenticity, in that the learning materials are both extensive and taken from real-world sources. Literature forms the basis of many CALL programs.

Collie and Slater (1987) offer four main justifications for the use of literature in the language classroom: valuable authentic material, cultural enrichment, language enrichment and personal involvement. They also note the place of non-fictional authentic materials, such as bus schedules.

Quote 4.3   J. Collie and S. Slater suggest:

Literature is a valuable complement to (other classroom) materials, especially once the initial 'survival' level has been passed. In reading literary texts, students have also to cope with language intended for native speakers and thus they gain additional familiarity with many different linguistic uses, forms and conventions, and so on. And, although it may not be confined within a specific social network in the same way that a bus ticket or an advertisement might be, literature can nonetheless incorporate a great deal of cultural information.

Collie and Slater (1987: 4)

Quote 4.4   J. Collie and S. Slater on the use of literature in language learning:

While there is little doubt that extensive reading increases a learner's receptive vocabulary and facilitates transfer to a more active form of knowledge ... literature provides a rich context in which individual lexical or syntactical items are made more memorable. Reading a substantial and conceptualized body of text, students gain familiarity with many features of the written language – the formation and function of sentences, the variety of possible structures, the different ways of connecting ideas – which broaden their own writing skills. The extensive reading required in tackling a novel or long play develops the student's ability to make inferences from linguistic clues, and to deduce meaning from context, both useful tools in reading other sorts of material as well.

Collie and Slater (1987: 4–5)

Collie and Slater (1987) use the term cultural enrichment to refer to the wealth of insights about other cultures (particularly the target language culture) that literature offers.

Skills in making inferences and deductions can be taught in different ways, but literature tends to teach them more naturally. In fact, the best CALL programs offer learning in the same way as good literature, presenting a narrative in which the reader/learner draws a more general understanding of themes.

Quote 4.5 J. Collie and S. Slater speak of personal involvement:

Core language teaching materials must concentrate on how a language operates both as a rule-based system and as a socio-semantic system. Very often, the process of learning is essentially analytic, piecemeal, and, at the level of the personality, fairly superficial. Engaging imaginatively with literature enables learners to shift the focus of their attention beyond the more mechanical aspects of the foreign language system.

Collie and Slater (1987: 5)

In addition to the arguments raised above, there is also the fact that a simple love of literature supports autonomous language learning (see Falvey and Kennedy, 1997; Montali and Lewandowski, 1996). Learners who are exposed to literature in the classroom and enjoy it are likely to expand their exposure to literature in various forms and provide themselves with associated opportunities for language learning outside of the classroom.

Further reading

Brumfit, C.J. and Carter, R. (eds) (1986) *Literature and Language Teaching*. Oxford, Oxford University Press. – Although this book does not focus on CALL, it does provide a wealth of insights into the use of literature as a path to teaching language.

4.3.1 The relationship of literature to computer-based learning materials

Although Collie and Slater's (1987) observations on the link between language learning and literature were written with reference to traditional paper-based learning materials they also hold true for computer-based learning materials. However, there is a principal difference: computer-based learning materials easily bridge the gap between fictional and non-fictional resources by routinely offering multimedia links between the two. In paper-based materials, this is sometimes found to a lesser degree in heavily annotated editions of literary works such as Shakespeare plays. A Shakespeare play presented on the computer is likely to offer video of plays being performed, diagrams of costumes, virtual tours of a theatre, interactive dictionaries and other tools for literary and language enrichment.

4.3.2   Hypertext and literature

Deegan and Sutherland (1990) note advantages of hypertext for both the study and writing of literature, arguing that texts and non-textual material are essentially fluid and easily manipulated, making it an ideal tool for showing the interconnection of ideas.

> **Quote 4.6** G.P. Landow on the advantages of hypertext as a tool for learning *connectiveness* in literature:
>
> The sheeplike behavior displayed by many freshmen is often due to their having little information and little idea of what to do with it. One cannot make connections between fact A and six other facts if one knows only fact A. This lack of factual knowledge leads to reductive thinking. Additional information, however, will not help students think critically unless they have techniques for relating facts to each other. College liberates because it provides students with facts and offers examples of the way they can make connections for themselves. Intellectual freedom derives from an ability to make choices. Anything that can help teachers communicate information to students as well as provide them with techniques to relate it to what they already know provides a model for education. The habits of mind, thus encouraged, apply to all kinds of activities, inside the classroom and out, and they remind us that education and thinking are active procedures.
>
> Landow (1989: 176)

Whether or not learners use hypertext to make their own connections in literature and whether it helps in their learning is an area of research worth investigating.

4.4   Corpus linguistics

Corpus linguistics is an important area in its own right within applied linguistics, but it is also a useful tool for the teaching and learning of language at the computer. This section outlines some of the key aspects of corpus linguistics and concordancing before going on to explain their applications to CALL.

The *corpus* in *corpus linguistics* refers to a body of text. The text can be made up of different examples of spoken or written language or a combination of both. Corpora (corpora = plural of corpus) can be based on simple and brief texts on a narrow topic or run into the millions of words, such as the British National Corpus, a 100-million word corpus of British English. Corpora can be unformatted text made up of individual words or formations. Alternatively, these can be tagged for grammatical functions or for other functions. Simple searches can be used to count the frequency of different words and structures.

To access, or make use of, a corpus, one uses a concordancer to look at language patterns. A concordancer is a tool that looks at individual words (nodes) or groups of words and lists them with their immediate contexts; usually the seven or eight words that come before and after but in some cases the entire sentence for each word. The term for describing this approach is *key word in context* (KWIK).

Using corpora in the classroom involves making use of a concordancing program's ability to spot patterns and differences in language use.

Quote 4.7   M.H. Wu on the importance of learning from corpus linguistics:

Only when words are in their habitual environments, presented in their most frequent forms and their relational patterns and structures, can they be learnt effectively, interpreted properly and used appropriately.

Wu (1992: 32)

Further reading

Leech, G., Myers, G. and Thomas, J. (eds) (1995) *Spoken English on Computer: transcription, mark-up and application.* Harlow: Longman. – A useful collection of papers on issues related to working with spoken English and the computer.

Thurston, J. and Candlin, C.N. (1998) Concordancing and the teaching of the vocabulary of academic English. *English for Specific Purposes* 17: 267–80. – This paper focuses on the use of concordancing to build learner vocabulary.

Tribble, C. (1997) Improvising corpora for ELT: quick-and-dirty ways of developing corpora for language teaching. *http://web.bham.ac.uk/johnstf/palc.htm* – In this paper, Tribble proposes 'that small, informally produced corpora can be a useful resource in the language learning/teaching project' (n.p.).

Kennedy, G. (1998) *An Introduction to Corpus Linguistics.* Harlow: Addison Wesley Longman. – This book provides a good overview of the field.

4.4.1   Corpus linguistics in the classroom

Both teachers and learners can use corpus linguistics in various ways within the classroom.

A teacher might collect a set of student assignments and use a concordancing program to analyse examples of learners' language looking for typical error patterns. Systematic errors in learners' writing can be used as a basis for the development of learning materials. Alternatively, a teacher might look through established corpora of texts by native speakers of the target language and find examples for patterns and present these to learners as examples or adapt them into exercises.

Learners themselves can be trained in the use of a concordancing program (St John, 2001) and corpora, then become their own researchers finding examples and developing their own rules for grammatical structures, idioms and general usage, for example, investigating the differences between *look* and *see*. This approach is often called Data Driven Learning (DDL).

Concept 4.1   **Data Driven Learning (DDL)**

Data Driven Learning (DDL) is an inductive approach to learning in which learners acquire an understanding of language patterns and rules by becoming more involved researching corpora, usually through the use of a computer-based concordancing program. Instead of studying patterns and rules, learners naturally internalize them. This approach can stimulate learners' interest in language and give them a sense of empowerment and responsibility for their own language education.

Further reading

St John, E. (2001) A case for using a parallel corpus and concordancer for beginners of a foreign language. *Language Learning and Technology* 5(3) *http://llt.msu.edu/vol5num3/stjohn/default.html*

Thomas, J. and Short, M. (eds) (1996) *Using Corpora for Language Research*. London: Longman. – This book focuses on how the researcher can make use of corpora.

Tribble, C. and Jones, G. (1990) *Concordances in the Classroom*. London: Longman. – This is a seminal book in the use of concordancing as a teaching and learning tool.

Wichmann, A., Fligelstone, S., McEnery, A. and Knowles, G. (eds) (1997) *Teaching and Language Corpora*. London: Longman. – This book provides a general overview of many issues in concordancing.

4.5   Computer-mediated communication

Communicating using the computer is often referred to as computer-mediated communication (CMC) and is one of the more popular activities associated with CALL. CMC encompasses communication by email, bulletin boards, chatlines and within MOO (Multi-user domains, Object Oriented) environments.

CMC refers to a situation in which computer-based discussion may take place but without necessarily involving learning. Of course, opportunities for learning are inherently present, especially in situations in which learners need to engage in negotiation of meaning with native speakers of the target language or even with peers of non-native proficiency.

It is common for teachers in different countries to create assignments for their students to communicate in a common target language, for example, students in Korea and Brazil both learning English working together to collect information about each other's interests and studies.

Further reading

Coski C. and Kinginger, C. (1996) *Computer-Mediated Communication in Foreign Language Education: An Annotated Bibliography* *http://nflrc.hawaii.edu/NetWorks/NW03/*

McLaughlin, M. and Rafaeli, S. (eds) *Journal of Computer-mediated Communication* available online at *http://www.ascusc.org/jcmc/*

Swaffar, J., Romano, S., Arens, K. and Markley, P. (eds) (1998) *Language Learning On-line Theory and Practice in the ESL and L2 Computer Classroom*. Austin, TX: Labyrinth Publications. – The entire book is also available as a .pdf format at *http://labyrinth.daedalus.com/llo/*

Warschauer, M. (1997) Computer-mediated collaborative learning: theory and practice. *The Modern Language Journal*, 81(iv): 470–81. – This paper touches on themes in CMC which Warschauer has developed over several papers and books.

4.5.1   Email

Email is among the most popular of activities on the WWW and is an easy way to enhance learning. One of the great advantages of email is the record of both one's own messages and the messages one receives.

Using email, learners can communicate with peers, teachers and native speakers. The messages can be structured as an assignment in which the learner solicits special information, shares information about assignments (especially in a jigsaw format) or submits thoughts, questions and assignments with a teacher. However, communication with native speakers can be difficult if the learner provides input with substantial spelling and grammatical errors. Some email programs now come with rudimentary spelling checkers but teachers concerned with the quality of their students' writing may encourage them to compose their messages in a word-processing software program then copy and paste it into their email messages.

Concept 4.2   Asynchronous and synchronous communication

Communication using the computer is either asynchronous or synchronous.

Asynchronous refers to communication that takes place at different times, for example, through email in which a message is sent and may be read at leisure by the recipient. Synchronous refers to communication that takes place at the same time, such as through chatlines. There are advantages to both modes. An asynchronous email allows the writer to take time to consider and compose a message, and messages can be processed when the interlocutor is ready – an important consideration when the communication is in different time zones.

4.5.1.1   Net pals

One informal use of email is for the establishment of email penpal arrangements. Such penpals or penfriends are sometimes called *net pals*. Ideally, net pal communication is between someone learning the target language and a native speaker of the target language living in the culture of the target language. For example, a Nepalese student learning German corresponding with a native German-speaker living in Berlin. The advantages to the learner is that the native speaker is likely to offer extensive examples of authentic language, probably pitched at the appropriate age level of the language learner.

In practice, however, both parties can find net pals a frustrating experience. Native speakers may feel they cannot communicate effectively with the learner and may feel the learner has nothing to offer in return for the exchange. The language learner may find that slang, idioms, misspellings and typos interfere with comprehension. Net pals are best done level at a level where both parties have extrinsic motivation (e.g., a common interest in football or visiting one another's countries) and where the language learner has good clarification strategies and/or the support of a language teacher.

Further reading

Warschauer, M. (1995) *E-mail for English teaching: bringing the Internet and computer learning networks into the language classroom*. Alexandria, VA: Teachers of English to Speakers of Other Languages. – This is a practical book and even though some of the web addresses are no longer valid, they point directions for the researcher/teacher to find equivalent websites.

4.5.2   Chatlines

A chatline refers to *Internet Relay Chat* (IRC) and appears on-screen as a window that presents what the learner is writing in one pane while general discussion among other participants continues in another. Once the learner has completed a message and presses the *send* command, the message is queued and appears in the main pane as quickly as the modem and host computer allow. In some older programs, it is necessary to press the *reload* or *refresh* button to update to the latest message.

Concept 4.3   R U ready 2 GA?

The speed of discussion on chatlines challenges many learners' typing skills, so a series of abbreviations and emotives (sideways faces made through the use of type characters) are used to take the place of commonly used phrases. An online conversation might follow along these lines.

John, IMHO, it's NBD that I can't CU tonite. We had FTF yesterday and U were:). If you were:) B4, you shouldn't be :'-(now. TTYL. Janet.

:)	a happy face
:'-(	a crying face
2	to
4	for
ABT	about
B4	before
BW	best wishes
CU	see you
FTF	face to face
FYR	for your reference
GA	go ahead
IMHO	in my humble opinion
IOW	in other words
NBD	no big deal
POV	point of view
R	are
TTYL	talk to you later
U	you

4.5.2.1   Bulletin boards

Bulletin boards in which learners (both teachers and users) can post messages to be read later by others are built into some CALL environments and more general learning platforms such as WebCT, a learning environment developed at the University of British Columbia, Canada. In WebCT, users can post messages and comment on the original posting and subsequent comments ad infinitum (see Concept 9.2).

Example 4.2 Bulletin board

The advantage of bulletin boards over email is that the messages are shared with a broader community (a few select people, a class or the whole world) and comment can be more considered as readers have more time.

Concept 4.4 **Netiquette, flaming and emotives**

In online chatline discussions, email and on bulletin boards, there are certain rules of etiquette, or *netiquette*, to be followed. These rules cover issues such as the length of postings and technical issues (such as not including the entire message to which you are responding), privacy issues (such as posting other people's email addresses without permission) and so on.

One of the most commonly abused of these netiquette rules is *flaming*. Flaming is responding inappropriately to others. Flaming can include the use of ALL CAPS (the equivalent of online shouting), personal insults, excessive sarcasm and other behaviours that one might avoid, or at least temper with ironic expressions or tones, were one speaking in person. One way of tempering one's comments online is through the use of emotives, symbols made up of alphanumeric characters to form sideways-viewed faces: a smiling face :) a face sticking out a tongue :! A face expressing surprise :o

However, in some cases, when two or more people are actively responding to the same posting, communication can resemble a chatline.

4.5.3   MOO, MUA, MUD, MUSH, MUG

> Concept 4.5   **MOO, MUA, MUD, MUSH, MUG**
>
> MOO: Multi-User domains, Object Oriented
> MUA: Multi-User Adventure
> MUD: Multi-User Domains/Dungeons
> MUSH: Multi-User Shared Hallucination
> MUG Multi-User Game

MOO, MUA, MUD, MUSH and MUG generally refer to the same thing (and will be referred to hereafter as *MOO*), an online environment where moveable objects represent things and people. MOO objects may be photo-realistic 3-D manipulated models or 2-D flat representations. This environment is a synchronous online multi-user space, that is, action takes place in real time among several participants who put their characters into the same scene on a computer screen. These scenes are usually referred to as rooms and can have great visual interest. For example, 'rooms' can be seaside settings featuring lighthouses and surprisingly active sea life or depictions of castles in the air.

MUDs were originally developed in 1978 by Roy Trubshaw, a student at Essex University, for playing games online (particularly versions of *Dungeons and Dragons*) and socializing. Richard Bartle developed the game and helped to promote it internationally. A version of the game is still available at the commercial website *Compuserve*.

Many such environments are enhanced chatrooms where participants find it easier to identify everyone online by seeing whether or not there is a representation of them in the room. Academic and learning applications soon became obvious and a MOO environment was developed by Pavel Curtis in 1996.

> **Example 4.3**   Getting learners involved in conferencing on a MOO
>
> Frizler (1997) suggests the first step in getting learners involved in learning on a MOO is to get them involved in a conference, which allows both the teacher and student to keep files of what has been said. She offers the following procedure:

1. Introduce the students to the basics of MOOing. Take the class to a MOO in small groups and have them communicate with each other so they get used to the unique environment.
2. Collect the first drafts of an essay from the students (via hard copy or email). Have a copy of the draft with you for reference during the conference (either printed out or on-screen in a separate window).
3. Set up conferences for each student. Ask the students to bring three questions regarding their essay to the conference.
4. Meet each student at the MOO to discuss the draft, focusing on the questions they bring.
5. Through non-verbal gestures, encourage the student to do most of the 'talking'.
6. Lead the students to state clearly by the end of the conference what they will focus on during the revision process.
7. Have the students save a log of the conversation to their hard drive or a floppy disk, or do it yourself and send it to the student in an email message.

The advantages of such environments to learning a language is that a learner can enter into an environment where a target language is being spoken and be forced to react to others' words and actions. MOOs seem a promising direction for further research and materials development although the cognitive overhead of learning how to operate within such an environment may be daunting for some teachers and learners.

Quote 4.8 Cynthia Haynes on the value of writing in MOO:

this kind of writing is something teachers may have trouble seeing as productive discourse, but if students can see how much they write, and if it *counts* as writing, which I think it should, then we begin to value other genres of writing and interactivity equally. Plus we encourage teachers to build into their assessment of the student the notion of 'activity' as much as the 'writing products' we are used to grading.

http://www.dartmouth.edu/~webteach/cases/linguamoo.html

Further reading

Boswood, T. (ed.) (1997) *New Ways of Using Computers in Language Teaching.* Arlington, VA: TESOL – This book provides an overview of good pedagogical approaches to using technology, rather than just focusing on the latest technologies.

Haynes, C. and Holmevik, J.R. (eds) (1998) *High Wired: On the Design, Use, and Theory of Educational MOOs*. Ann Arbor, MI: University of Michigan Press. – This book is intended for the teacher, rather than the student and is of interest to those who want to set up a MOO, or just learn more about them.

Holmevik, J.R. and Haynes, C. (2000) *MOOniversity: A Student's Guide to Online Learning Environments*. New York: Longman. – This book is intended for the student, rather than the teacher, and features relatively current examples of MOO environments. However, MOOs are constantly evolving in complexity according to what is technically possible.

4.6   WWW resources

Example 4.4   Dave Sperling's ESL Café

One of the more popular language-learning sites on the WWW was created by Dave Sperling, a California-based teacher who started Dave Sperling's ESL Café as a class project in 1995. His students' efforts attracted the attention of other learners and their queries lead naturally into providing information. The website now serves as a kind of portal, providing a directory of other CALL websites and attracts more than one million visits a month.

Dave Sperling's ESL Café: *http://www.eslcafe.com/*

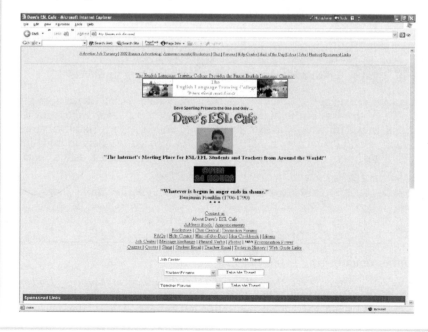

Several examples have already been given of opportunities for learning language using the WWW. The WWW has also presented opportunities for the creation of commercial websites dedicated to the teaching and learning of English. Such sites may have different foci in terms of age, level or even profession. For example, websites for improving business writing are popular.

Many such websites are driven by commercial concerns. Typically, the learner pays a fee for enrolling and taking online lessons or endures advertising, much of which will be targeted at the learners by, for example, textbook publishers, language schools and language testing services. Several publishers also maintain educational websites featuring portions of their work or extra study materials for their work.

Example 4.5   **Augmenting a textbook**

Expressions, a book series by David Nunan (with one book, *Expressions Intro* co-authored by the author of this book), has an interactive website with additional materials and interactive quizzes tied to each chapter of the series. The website provides extra tests that students using the book – or anyone else – can make use of. The tests are computer-corrected and the results are returned to the students on-screen, almost immediately.
http://expressions.heinle.com

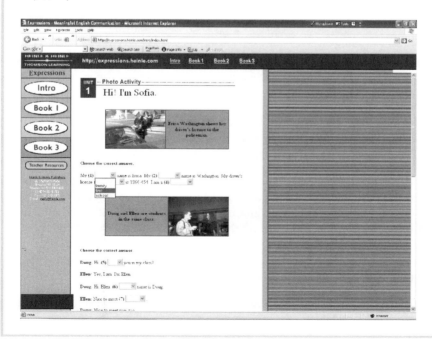

Other resources commonly found on the WWW include those created by learners and teachers. These include everything from software to class handouts and presentations in the form of PowerPoint files. These resources vary in quality and extent but at least have the virtues of being free and easy to find with a search engine.

Many websites, especially those associated with government and non-profit organizations, such as Greenpeace (*www.greenpeace.org*) create associated websites to cater to students and language learners. These may also have professional and informative free materials included for teachers.

Example 4.6   KAHooTZ

KAHooTZ is based on a CD-ROM developed by the Australian Children's Television Foundation. The CD-ROM, linked to the WWW, makes for a creative and secure online children's community that allows children to share and exchange the multimedia content they make using construction tools that come with the KAHooTZ CD-Rom. KAHooTZ offers a library of animated fonts, clip-art, drawing tools, background images, sound bytes, music bytes and audio editor, along with sequencing controls and a hyperlink editor. Members can chat online in real-time, publish their work or mail either simple messages or rich multimedia stories directly to each other. *http://www.kahootz.com/*

Further reading

Kid's On-line Resources *http://www.kidsolr.com/kidswww/* – Kid's On-line Resources is a clearinghouse of websites for children. It features translation software and international learning websites.

4.7   Adapting other materials for CALL

Besides materials especially targeted for language learning, there are many materials which can be adapted. Many games and simulations not intended for language learning can be adapted for such a purpose, particularly for advanced learners, as they are likely to be rich in authentic language.

Example 4.7   SimCity

SimCity (i.e. simulated city) is one of many programs from Maxis which offer interactive simulations.

The first *SimCity* was created in 1989 and has influenced many other so-called 'god games' in which one organizes and influences events in a simulated world. In the case of *SimCity*, the user is a mayor or city manager who makes decisions on how a city should be built. The game teaches some basic economics as the user reconciles additions to the community which generate income (e.g. a toxic waste dump) with problems (e.g. increased pollution). Each solution seems to have an attendant disadvantage and the user is constantly petitioned by fictional citizens protesting and making requests. There are also virtual newspapers which influence events and various meetings one must attend.

Maxis has produced many Sim games for environments ranging from jungles to other planets. The most interesting recent development has been the release of a program called *The Sims*. In this game, users create characters and their families, build homes and cater to their needs (e.g. hunger). If one clicks on a fridge, the character on screen will go to the fridge and prepare a meal for himself/herself. Many users model their own families and homes in the program.

Maxis: *http://simcity.ea.com/us/guide/*

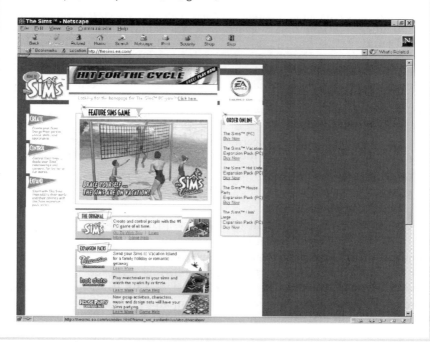

Many other materials on the WWW are easy to adapt for classroom learning and offer a rich source of authentic text, images, sound and video. For example, a learner studying Japanese can go to countless websites on different topics of interest related to Japan to learn more about culture or information related to Japanese for Specific Purposes. Learners can also visit online newspapers for the target language they are studying.

Virtual treasure hunts are activities in which the teacher assigns learners to collect images or explanations on a variety of topics. For example, a Spanish teacher might give hints to ask learners to find an image and description of a famous Spanish mosque; most learners might arrive at pages related to the Mosque at Córdoba, but learners might also find further examples. The purpose of the treasure hunt is not so much to find the answers but to expose learners to the target language in the course of the hunt.

4.8   Personal Digital Assistants (PDA)

Concept 4.6   **Bleeding Edge**

Bleeding Edge is a pun on *Leading Edge* and refers to a concern in educational computing and computing in general: the cost of buying the latest hardware and software.

New hardware and software is constantly being introduced and short-term profit is often a greater consideration than reliability. This is especially true in the case of untried products which may not gain wide acceptance. Apple introduced the Newton PDA in 1993 but discontinued production five years later. Although it was the first PDA, it did not endure. Essentially, it was a bleeding edge development.

Teachers need to be concerned about investing time and money in unproven technology but, at the same time, want to have current software and hardware that will not be soon outdated.

A Personal Digital Assistant (PDA) is a small hand-held computer for downloading and storing information such as documents, databases and calendar entries. It is less powerful than a desktop or laptop computer, but less expensive and more portable. Portability is achieved by eliminating the keyboard and minimizing the screen size. The PDA market consists of several models created by different companies using different software systems by Palm, Microsoft and, most recently, Linux.

4.8.1   Teaching and Learning with PDAs

PDAs are not yet widely used in education, but their portability and expense could make them a popular choice in classrooms, especially when combined with accessories such as collapsible keyboards, digital cameras and modems that allow for WWW and email access. PDAs generally feature an infrared port that allows users to share information with each other and receive information, such as class notes, pictures and small software applications. PDAs can only work with specially adapted files.

One of the advantages of a PDA is that it is easy to back up on one's computer. A one-button *hotsync* operation generally allows the user to synchronize and update files from their PDA to a larger laptop or desktop computer.

Example 4.8   Benefits of PDA learning from an East Carolina State University study:

1. Students are able to receive and send their assignments wirelessly through modems and wireless cards with the corridor (backbone) that ECU has established on campus.
2. Instructors have immediate/round-the-clock access to their students.
3. It provides a viable way to manage information technology resources allowing for mobility.
4. Students have an intensive learning environment.
5. There is greater involvement in the class atmosphere and preparation of learning materials.
6. Faculty and staff have become trained on hand-held computer devices and wireless technology.
7. There is greater flexibility in when and where assignments are posted and completed.

http://www.ecu.edu/handheld/

4.8.2   Graffiti handwriting software

In Ray Bradbury's (1958) collection of science fiction short stories, *The Martian Chronicles*, one tale tells of a man who finds an alien's deserted home that miraculously adapts to his needs for water and shelter. However, the home soon grows tired of adapting and instead transforms the man into one of its original occupants: an overgrown lizard. It is a suitable metaphor for the computer's tendency to impose its style and affordances (i.e. what the program is or appears to be capable of doing in terms of both intended and unintended functions) on users and this has been the route taken by the designers of Graffiti, a handwriting recognition system.

In the absence of a keyboard, a major challenge to PDAs has been recognition of handwriting. Early models struggled to recognize individual handwriting but the creators of the Graffiti system realized it would be easier to make users adapt their handwriting to the PDA.

Graffiti uses a modified and simplified punctuation, numbers and upper-case letters. Each character must be unconnected; one cannot write on the screen without lifting the stylus between letters. However, each character is a continuous line. The system is quickly and easily learned and games are available to help develop fluency.

The future success of PDAs will depend on their ability to accommodate reliable and convenient voice recognition and to remain significantly less expensive than laptop computers.

Summary

This chapter looked at different CALL applications. The main point is that there are many diverse ways of approaching CALL and new ways, such as the use of PDAs, are being developed. One measure of the success of any of the applications mentioned in this chapter is the amount of work they require on the part of the teacher and learner before language learning begins. If the cognitive overhead is too high, then the technology, however wonderful, may not be worth the investment of time by teachers and learners.

Further reading

Mann, S. and Rischpater, R. (2001) *Advanced Palm programming*. New York: Wiley.
– This book is aimed at those creating programs for the Palm interface.
Pogue, D. (1999) *PalmPilot: the ultimate guide*. Sebastopol, CA: O'Reilly & Associates.
– This book is a kind of enhanced user's manual, giving background, instructions and resources for PalmPilot computing.
The following three websites are worth visiting for those interested in education applications for hand-held computing.
Palm Education Site
http://www.palm.com/education/
Handheld Education
http://handheldeducation.com/
The Educator's Palm
http://educatorspalm.org/palm12/teachlearn/teachlearn.html

II The place of CALL in research and teaching

▬▬▬▬

Chapter 5

Second-language Acquisition and models of instruction

This chapter looks at Second-language Acquisition (SLA) based on hypotheses of how second languages are learned. Models of instruction based on behaviourism and constructivism have already been briefly mentioned and in this chapter more background is given before defining their role in the design of computer-based learning materials.

The principal concern of this chapter can be summarized as an attempt to define the meanings of and relevance to CALL of the following terms:

• Second-language Acquisition (SLA)
• Comprehensible input
• Comprehensible output
• Behaviourism
• Programmed instruction
• Mastery learning
• Constructivism

5.1 Concepts in SLA, behaviourism and constructivism

This chapter begins by offering a brief overview of Second-language Acquisition (SLA) then introduces the complementary constructs of comprehensible input and comprehensible output. With reference to CALL, this chapter discusses behaviourism as a model of instruction, two outcomes of behaviourist pedagogy: programmed instruction and mastery learning. This chapter also discusses constructivism and its role in a constructivist model of instruction, and then contrasted with behaviourism and a behaviourist model of instruction in terms of the development and design of learning materials.

5.1.1   Second-language Acquisition (SLA)

Concept 5.1   **Second-language Acquisition (SLA)**

Second-language Acquisition (SLA) refers to the study of the processes through which learners acquire a new language. However, various hypotheses about how such acquisition occurs have been subject to intense debate with some researchers critical of a lack of empirical evidence.

Concept 5.2   **Negotiation of meaning**

Nunan (1993) offers a concise definition of *negotiation of meaning*, 'The inter-actional work done by speakers and listeners to ensure they have a common understanding of the ongoing meanings of the discourse' (p. 122). Offering a further explanation of negotiation of meaning, Ellis (1998) provides a brief summary of a theoretical account of how discourse affects language acquisition: 'acquisition is promoted when the input to which learners are exposed is made comprehensible as a result of interactional modifications that arise from a communication breakdown – a process known as the negotiation of meaning' (p. 160).

Essentially, if two learners are assigned a so-called second-language collaborative task and *do not* need to speak, they are often in agreement about how to complete the task and probably do not need to collaborate. That is, the learners are either merely cooperating (each completing a part of the task without need for interaction) or the task is so simple that all decisions are obvious.

However, when the task requires that the learners communicate, grappling with words, expressions and new ideas that surround the task as well as the technology of the computer's interface and input and display devices, the act of negotiation of meaning may assist in the acquisition of the target language. Of course, negotiation of meaning is not SLA's sole route or complete means for SLA. Pica (1998), for example, notes that learner negotiation of meaning can be quite simple and not cover some important aspects of language learning.

However, Pica's ideas do not address issues related to CALL programs that may improve learners' morphology and syntax. There is also room for negotiation of meaning through collaboration where discourse is both

Quote 5.1 T. Pica on negotiation of meaning

In spite of the evidence that negotiation serves as a social process that interacts with cognitive and psycholinguistic processes of L2 learning, and that addresses interlanguage change, learners have been observed to negotiate more frequently over lexis than over morphosyntax. For example, learners and interlocutors give more attention to the physical features and attributes of the people and objects in their discourse than to the time and activities in which they engage (see Pica, 1994; Pica *et al.*, 1995). Although negotiation has been observed over grammatical morphology, this has not been shown in impressive amounts (Pica, 1994). In light of these production-related contributions of negotiation, and the input feedback contributions discussed above, it would appear that as a social process, we see that negotiation for meaning can contribute to L2 learning, but that additional contributions are needed to support the psycholinguistic process of L2 learning.

Pica (1998: 19)

between the two learners as well as with the computer software program. A computer program can provide a high level of comprehensible input in various media.

Opportunities for Second-language Acquisition (SLA) can be offered at the computer as learners are exposed to new language and when learners are prompted to engage in collaboration that promotes negotiation of meaning. Negotiation of meaning and collaboration can occur regardless of the program; ironically, some of the worst programs may present more opportunities for SLA as learners struggle – and discuss their struggles – to make sense of the content and interface.

However, exactly how SLA occurs remains a mystery, or rather, some theories of how SLA occurs explain some levels of acquisition, but not others.

Quote 5.2 T. Pica on theory in SLA:

Since its inception, the field of second-language acquisition (SLA) has been both theory-less and theory-laden. It has been theory-less in that, as most major textbooks remind us, there has yet to emerge a single, coherent theory that can describe, explain and predict second-language learning. Yet it is theory-laden in that there are at least forty claims, arguments, theories, and perspectives that attempt to describe and explain the learning process and predict its outcomes (see Larsen-Freeman and Long, 1991 p. 227).

Pica (1998: 9)

> **Quote 5.3** A. Bailin on why SLA theory can still be considered to be in its infancy:
>
> One major reason may be that available second-language theories such as that of Krashen (Krashen, 1981; Dualy et al., 1982; Krashen and Terrell, 1983) are simply too informal to be of much use. On the other hand, psychological and linguistic theories (e.g., MacWhinney, 1987) generally do not take into account the social context in which this learning takes place. However, we use language appropriately not only in relation to the grammar of a language but also in relation to textual and social factors. Learning a language is a matter of not just learning the grammar for a language but also learning the rules for contexts. Whether or not a theory of acquisition of grammar must take into account the social context of learning, it is difficult to see how a theory that incorporates the acquisition of rules for appropriate use can avoid the context in which the acquisition occurs.
>
> Bailin (1995: 335)

Bailin (1995) suggests that an SLA theory may be possible, but hints that it may need to incorporate so many variables as to make it too general to be of use. And, although we may observe what goes on in the language classroom and try to interpret those observations in theory and models of instruction, the rules that learners are internalizing may not be visible and are seldom fixed. This is because teachers may make use of portions of a variety of theories over the course of a semester or even within the course of a single class. Good teachers make use of this flexibility to bolster their own teaching styles and to adapt to their learners' learning styles. Both teachers and learners tend to draw on a wide range of experiences, including their own backgrounds learning language(s). Language learning and teaching is a fluid process in which different learner and teacher learning styles need to be accommodated on an almost individual basis.

In terms of CALL, the individualization of instruction makes for even greater opportunities for SLA to be promoted through software designs that assess learners' learning styles and track their acquisition through tests which remember and revisit individual items with which each learner has difficulty. However, although this is both possible and desirable, I am not aware of commercial software that does so.

One of the key contentions within SLA is the role of comprehensible input and comprehensible output. These terms are explained and discussed in the following section.

Further reading

Cohen, A. and Oxford, R. (in preparation) *Teaching and Researching Learning Strategies.* London: Longman.

5.2   Comprehensible input and output

Comprehensible input is an idea that originated with Terrell and Krashen (Krashen, 1981; Krashen and Terrell, 1983) but several others, including Ellis (1985), have defined it in their own ways.

Quote 5.4   R. Ellis on comprehensible input:

The input refers to the language which learners are exposed to. This can be 'comprehensible' (i.e. input that they can understand) or 'incomprehensible' (i.e. input that they cannot understand). When native speakers speak to L2 learners, they frequently adjust their speech to make it more comprehensible. Access to comprehensible input may be a necessary condition for acquisition to take place.

Ellis (1985: 294–5)

However, Ellis (1994) notes that Krashen did not see comprehensible input coming from other learners, 'Interaction also provides learners with the opportunity to talk in the L2. According to Krashen (1985), this has no direct effect on acquisition.' However, other researchers (Li, 1989; Loschky, 1989; Tanaka, 1991; Yamazaki, 1991) have argued differently,

---

Quote 5.5   A.B.M. Tsui on comprehensible output:

when students respond to the teacher's or their fellow students' questions, raise queries and give comments, they are actively involved in the negotiation of comprehensible input, which is essential to language acquisition. And when students produce the target language and try to make themselves understood, they are in fact testing out the hypotheses they are forming about the language. Swain (1985) points out that the production of comprehensible output is also essential to the acquisition of the target language.

Tsui (1985: 81)

viewing learner output as contributing to interlanguage development (the stage between one's first language and acquisition of one's second language) (p. 280). Swain (1983) calls learner output, *comprehensible output*, and suggests that it is not enough for learners to see and hear language in use; to truly understand they need to have opportunities to use the target language.

Quote 5.6 D. Nunan on comprehensible input:

Messages addressed to the learner that, while they may contain structures and grammar that are beyond the learner's current competence, are made understandable by the context in which they are uttered. According to Krashen's Comprehensible Input Hypothesis, acquisition occurs when learners understand messages that are just beyond their current stage of development.

Nunan (1999: 303–4)

In terms of CALL, Krashen (cited in Kenning and Kenning, 1990) describes optimal input for acquisition as having four characteristics:

1. it is comprehensible
2. it is interesting and/or relevant to the acquirer
3. it is not grammatically sequenced
4. it is provided in sufficient quantity (p. 87)

CALL can generally deal with all of these criteria, including adding a wide range of extra-linguistic clues through sound, images, animation and video. But a concern with CALL is how the computer ensures that the input for the program is neither too easy nor too difficult for the learner. Such decisions are relatively simple for a well-trained teacher to make, but are difficult for a computer. Three ways in which computer programs deal with this problem are: by offering learner-prompted extra-linguistic elements as clues; by having learners select their own level of comprehension; and/or through computer-adaptive testing (CAT) in which the learner is directed along easier or more difficult tasks or links depending on answers to questions at key points of the program.

Concept 5.3   **Computer-adaptive testing (CAT)**

Computer-adaptive testing (CAT) uses a database of questions to match the difficulty of each test item to the abilities of the learners being tested. Learners take a CAT test at the computer and because the computer can instantly mark each answer, the following answer can be tailored or adapted.

If a learner correctly answers a question, the computer will ensure that the next question will be more difficult. If a learner incorrectly answers a question, the next question will be easier.

One of the great advantages of CAT testing is that randomization of test items can ensure that learners of a large class taking a test in the same room may all take slightly different tests as their correct and incorrect answers prompt the computer to take them to different levels. However, the effort in setting up CAT testing is also difficult and learners may not like the fact that they cannot review or change the answers to any questions they have already answered.

Further reading

Chalhoub-Deville, M. (ed.) (1999) *Development and research in computer adaptive language testing*. Cambridge: University of Cambridge Examinations Syndicate/ Cambridge University Press. – This book provides a recent overview of CAT, which is constantly changing with developments in computer technology.

5.3   Criticism of comprehensible input and output theory

The theories behind the Comprehensible Input and Comprehensible Output hypotheses have been criticized.

Quote 5.7 R. Oxford on comprehensible input:

the concept that any single methodology focusing on fluency at the expense of accuracy can apply to all students, such as the Natural Approach of Krashen and Terrell (1983), must be seriously questioned (Oxford, 1990; Scarcella and Oxford, 1992).

Oxford (1995: 359)

But, while the hypotheses have been challenged, they do carry several intuitive aspects that may not be quantitatively measured; although we may not be able empirically to measure the extent of acquisition and clearly relate it to a particular input, it would seem a given that acquisition is encouraged when learners are confronted with a target language task and the need to struggle to make sense of it through negotiation of the meaning of both the task and the ways of addressing it. It may be that, while the hypotheses are not perfect, they may be the best way of explaining what we understand about SLA.

Quote 5.8 C.B. Cazden on progress in language development:

Confrontation with alternative ideas, whether from adults or peers, cannot be expected to produce immediate change. Language development is a case in point. . . . At those moments, the child seems impervious to contradiction, and no amount of correction has any obvious effect. Yet progress does occur, and we have to assume that exposure to alternatives plays a part, even though we can't track their influence in the silent processes of the child's mind.

Cazden (1988: 128)

A difficult issue in CALL, and one that sets computers clearly apart from human teachers, is the idea that errors in early efforts might be tolerated; it is a nearly impossible challenge for a computer to make complex decisions on what should be tolerated and what should be corrected. Also, it may be difficult for learners to understand that a computer program may be subjective and selective in its corrections.

Further reading

Larsen-Freeman, D. and Long, M. (1991) *An introduction to second language acquisition research*. London: Longman. – Although this book does not focus on CALL, it provides concise and useful background to the field.

5.4   Behaviourist and constructivist models of instruction

Quote 5.9 E.G. Rozycki on behaviourism and marketing:

behaviorist theory has provided the rationale for a variety of marketable although short-lived teaching devices. Educational budgets have long proven to be easy prey for scientific-sounding entrepreneurs.

Rozycki (1996: 54)

A central defining characteristic of many CALL materials is their heavy reliance on behaviourist methods of instruction, making use of behaviour modification principles in their design. These principles include features that are so ingrained in standard classroom practice that many teachers may assume there is no alternative. In general, these principles include ideas that lessons should proceed along strictly sequenced lines, that learners need to be given incentives such as marks and grades in order to motivate them to learn and that these individual grades must be measured against standardized tests.

Within the area of CALL, behaviourist aspects generally include stating the purpose of the program or task, offering reinforcement through text, images, audio, animations and/or video and providing a marks system for each task summarized at the end with grades or some other statement of progress. Much of this approach is perceived as endemic to the nature of the computer through the limited ways in which it is able to simulate interactions with the learner.

The next sections of this chapter offer a background for theories of behaviourism and constructivism, compare the ways in which they inform models of instruction and consider implications of their different models to computer-based instructional design.

5.5   Behaviourism

As mentioned earlier in relation to methods and approaches, theories of learning do not appear in a vacuum. They are influenced by earlier practices (e.g. observations of classroom behaviour) and theories from other disciplines (e.g. mathematics, philosophy, psychology). In the case of behaviourism, there is a great deal of earlier practice in teaching methods dating back to the ancient Greeks. More recent and empirical influences include Ivan Pavlov (1849–1936: dates are given for some authors to give a sense of the chronology of their contributions) whose experiments observing dogs salivating as a *conditioned reflex* (response) to the ringing of their dinner bell, the bell being considered a *conditioned stimulus*.

Pavlov's ideas are now called *classical conditioning*, as opposed to *operant conditioning* (explained below). Ideas of stimuli and responses working to modify behaviour were expanded upon and refined by John Broadus Watson (1878–1958), Edward L. Thorndike (1874–1949), Clark L. Hull (1884–1942) and others (see Chambliss, 1996). But the person most associated with behaviourism in the classroom is B. F. Skinner (1904–90) whose approach (Skinner, 1954, 1957, 1968) emphasizes rote learning, along with the techniques of mimicry and memorization through repetitive drills in which learners are rewarded by small positive responses, often including the right to move to a new level of drill, as is now common in computer-adaptive testing (see Concept 5.3 above).

The behaviourist theories of Skinner are based upon the idea that learning is a function of change in overt behaviour. Changes in behaviour are the result of an individual's response to events (stimuli) that occur in his or her environment. Skinner advanced previous behaviourist theories by showing how a response produces a consequence such as defining a word, hitting a ball or solving a maths problem. When a particular stimulus and response pattern is reinforced through rewards, the individual has been *conditioned* to respond. Skinner called this approach *operant conditioning* and it differs from earlier forms of behaviourism (now called *classical conditioning*) in that it recognizes that a person (or animal) can *emit* responses and not only *elicit* responses in reaction to a stimulus.

Another important feature of Skinner's theory is the role of reinforcement: things or actions that strengthen a desired response by making the learners feel better about themselves. He also suggests a role for *negative reinforcers* or reduced rewards for inappropriate responses; Skinner did not believe in punishment, which he suggested only reduced responses (Skinner, 1968: 57–8).

Quote 5.10 C.T. Fosnot on ways in which educators incorporate behaviourism in the classroom:

Pre-planning a curriculum by breaking a content area (usually seen as a finite body of predetermined knowledge) into assumed component parts – 'skills' – and then sequencing these parts into a hierarchy ranging from simple to more complex. It is assumed (1) that observations, listening to explanations from teachers who communicate clearly, or engaging in experiences, activities, or practice sessions with feedback will result in learning and (2) that proficient skills will quantify to produce the whole, or more encompassing concept (Bloom, 1956; Gagne, 1965). Further, learners are viewed as passive, in need of external motivation, and affected by reinforcement (Skinner, 1953).

Fosnot (1996: 8–9)

Many will recognize Fosnot's (1996) behaviourist assumptions as an accurate description of much classroom experience over the past few decades and in keeping with the model used in many classrooms today.

In terms of a practical application to classroom teaching and learning, as well as CALL, behaviourism was developed into two methods: programmed instruction and mastery learning. These are discussed below before moving on to a discussion of constructivism and a comparison of behaviourism and constructivism.

5.5.1   Programmed instruction

One of the practical applications of the behaviourist approach is the design of *programmed instruction* or *programmed learning* on which Skinner's behaviourist contributions to CALL centre. A behaviourist model of instruction suggests that learners can be taught a wide variety of subjects if presented with information in small steps, each step requiring appropriate responses (e.g. correct answers to questions) from the learner before going on to more difficult or more advanced steps. Such an idea seems machine-like and, in fact, Thorndike put the idea of an automated book forward in 1912: 'If, by a miracle of mechanical ingenuity, a book could be so arranged so that only to him who had done what was directed on page one would page two become visible, and so on, much that now requires personal instruction could be accomplished by print (cited in Merrill *et al.*, 1996: 54).'

Example 5.1   Programmed instruction

A set of frames to teach the spelling of 'manufacture' to third-graders
Frame 1. Manufacture means to make or build. Chair factories manufacture chairs. Copy the word here: _ _ _ _ _ _ _ _ _ _ _
2. Part of the word is like part of the word factory. Both parts come from an old word meaning make or build. m a n u _ _ _ _ u r e
3. Part of the word is like part of the word manual. Both parts come from an old word for hand. Many things used to be made by hand. _ _ _ _ f a c t u r e
4. The same letter goes in both spaces: m _ n u f _ c t u r e
5. The same letter goes in both spaces: m a n _ f a c t _ r e
6. Chair factories _ _ _ _ _ _ _ _ chairs.

(from Skinnner (1958: 969–77))

Skinner, B.F. (1958) Teaching machines. *Science 128* (3330), 969–77.

Merrill notes that Thorndike's automated book was constructed as early as 1926 by Sidney L. Pressey (1888–1969) and explains that Pressey's machine 'presented multiple-choice questions on a rotating cylindrical drum. Students responded by pressing one of four keys, each of which represented one of the answer choices. In the drill mode, all keys except the one representing the correct answer were locked; in the test mode, no clues of correctness were given. The machine recorded all responses and was capable of giving the user a piece of candy when a programmable number of correct responses had been made' (p. 54).

Skinner (1968) promotes Pressey's work, suggesting that Pressey was ahead of his time, and supports the idea of machine instruction as a way of increasing learner autonomy to avoid an essential problem in classroom instruction, the pace of instruction in a group of learners whose comprehension and learning rates are at different levels.

Quote 5.11   **B.F. Skinner on the challenge of teaching different levels in the same class:**

Even in a small classroom the teacher usually knows that he is going too slowly for some students and too fast for others. Those who could go faster are penalized, and those who should go slower are poorly taught and unnecessarily punished by criticism and failure. Machine instruction would permit each student to proceed at his own rate.

Skinner (1968: 30)

Skinner and others designed more mechanical and electrical machines that tried to put behaviourist ideas into practice but it was not until the arrival of the computer that an ideal technology was presented for such lockstep learning. In his book, *The Technology of Teaching* (1968), Skinner includes several photographs of his and others' mechanical and electric (but not electronic) teaching machines and explains the ways in which they 'taught' users.

Quote 5.12   **T. McArthur on two variations on programmed instruction:**

Programs can be linear, in which all students go through the same sequence of frames, or branching, in which a variety of paths through the program is provided. Linear programs tend to use constructed responses, while branching programs conventionally use a multiple-choice format. These structures were closely followed in the first CAL (computer-assisted learning) programs, and, as has been said, both types are still in use today.

McArthur (1983: 76–7)

Many features of programmed instruction are found in CALL such as the use of multiple-choice questions, constructed response answers and hotlinks. But critics soon saw that programmed instruction had its faults. Rivers (1981) pointed out that programmed instruction tended to teach details about language but not communication.

Despite these criticisms, programmed instruction continues to be pervasive in CALL, sometimes combined with other, less behaviourist, features. The reason for its enduring appeal is simply that programmed instruction is an easy – if not pedagogically ideal – thing for the computer to do.

5.5.2 Mastery learning

Aspects of programmed instruction are also seen in another approach, mastery learning.

> **Quote 5.13** P. Lai and J. Biggs on mastery learning:
>
> (Mastery learning) is based on the assumption that learning is a function of time (Bloom, Hastings and Madaus, 1971; Carroll, 1963). In theory, by varying time for learning, nearly all students are able to learn a subject to the point of 'mastery' (Guskey, 1985). In implementing mastery learning, it is thus necessary to establish a criterion, and to provide corrective instruction in the event of failure. Learners failing to reach the objectives initially are given more time in which to pass in subsequent attempts. The content to be learned is divided into units, with a formative test on each unit.
>
> Lai and Biggs (1994: 13)

> **Quote 5.14** C.J. Fosnot on mastery learning:
>
> This model assumes that wholes can be broken into parts, that skills can be broken into subskills. Learners are diagnosed in terms of deficiencies, called 'needs', then taught until 'mastery' – defined as behavioral competence – is achieved at each level. Further, it is assumed that if mastery is achieved at each level, then the more general concept, defined by the accumulation of the skills, has also been taught.
>
> Fosnot (1996: 9)

The challenge of mastery learning in CALL is the necessity of providing new material or new approaches when a learner fails to accomplish the initial goals. It is important that, in a restricted time frame, learners do not abrogate the task of thinking and take advantage of a software program's willingness to supply default answers. Like a good teacher, a computer should prod and stimulate learners to consider an answer rather than just giving in to the first 'I don't know' and supplying the answer.

Learner motivation is a key consideration in the creation of CALL materials many of which, like electronic versions of Pressey's mechanical candy-dispensing testing machine, are set up as adventure games or include positive reinforcement in the form of points, and virtual items to be collected by the learner/player. In many cases, learners learn more about how to acquire points than the knowledge intended to be imparted by the game's creator. For example, learners quickly discover that, in some programs, repeatedly selecting random answers prompts a default sub-routine giving the correct answers. Learners can proceed through a program making numerous errors then try the program again, apparently showing remarkable progress and attainment of 'mastery'. In fact, they *have* learned, but only how to manipulate the system, not to understand the content.

Despite these problems, it is easy to understand the attraction of the computer as a vehicle for a mastery learning model. Two of the computer's principal defining characteristics are consistency and patience; the computer can provide uniform repetitive lessons to the same learner or a group of learners and test indefinitely. But this requires a behaviourist/mechanistic view of the learner quite at odds with current humanistic thinking. Mastery learning also tends to assume that, once a learner has demonstrated the ability to answer a question or complete a task, he or she knows it forever. But, in reality, something may be only stored in a learner's short-term memory; learners not only learn, they also forget.

5.5.3   Summarizing behaviourism

Behaviourism takes the view that the learner comes to the learning process with little or no background knowledge. Strict objectives of what is to be learned are broken into instructional steps and rules. Learning activities are sequenced from simple to complex with frequent reviews and tests of key points. Failures or mistakes lead the learner to repetitions of key parts of the program or remedial activities. The control of the sequence or program is usually with the program, not the learner.

Behaviourist machines, mechanical, electric and electronic, in the form of computers, are suited to the strict guidelines set down by the behaviourist model of instruction. In a behaviourist model, the software program or teacher – not the learner – is assumed to be the expert and the source of the learning materials.

It should be noted that not all the above behaviourist features are present in all CALL applications, but a greater proportion will be found on the behaviourist end of the continuum stretching toward a constructivist model.

In terms of its appropriateness as a model of SLA, behaviourism has been criticized for its simplistic approach. For example, Oxford (1995) notes that Skinner's behaviourist theory of learning 'does not seem to me to fit with the highly complex activity of learning a second or foreign language' (p. 359). But a principal reason cited for a failure of behaviourist learning systems is that their focus on repetitive drills is boring and demotivating for learners. Also, it is argued that behaviourism, with its focus on stimulus of an organism leading to a response behaviour that was either reinforced or not, is not a true picture of the workings of the mind or an accurate description of the learning of language. Attempts to provide a better picture of mental processes are provided by Noam Chomsky (1965) and his ideas have influenced some methodologies, although Fox (1991) suggests that his work on language universals has not affected computer-assisted learning. Of peripheral interest to CALL is work done in 1943 by Emil Post who defined computation based on generalized grammar rules. This in turn influenced Chomsky whose work on context-free grammars would eventually complete a circle and influence the development of modern computer languages.

Reactions to the failures of behaviourism, programmed instruction and mastery learning were in part responsible for a move towards another model of instruction, known as constructivism. This chapter now turns to a discussion of constructivism.

5.6   Constructivism

Constructivism is a humanistic model that differs radically from behaviourism, suggesting that learning is a process by which learners construct new ideas or concepts by making use of their own knowledge and experiences. The learner has greater control and responsibility over what he or she learns and relies on schema (mental models; the plural of *schema* is *schemata*) to select and transform information, create hypotheses and make decisions. The following section briefly outlines schema theory before going on to compare behaviourism and constructivism in terms of various learning materials.

5.6.1   Schema theory

Schema theory is important to CALL because it provides an idea of how knowledge is organized. Psychologist F.C. Bartlett (1886–1969) first proposed the idea of schema theory in 1932. Nunan (1993) defines schema theory as 'A theory of language processing which suggests that discourse is interpreted with reference to the background knowledge of the reader or listener' (p. 124). Nunan also notes 'schema theory suggests that the knowledge we carry around in our heads is organized into interrelated patterns. These are constructed from all our previous experiences and they enable us to make predictions about future experience' (p. 71).

Quote 5.15 T.G. Anderson helps to define a schema approach to teaching and learning:

[Knowledge is] not merely a collection of facts. Although we may be able to memorize isolated facts for a short while...meaningful learning demands that we internalize information; we break it down, digest it and locate it in our pre-existing highly complex web of interconnected knowledge and ideas, building fresh links and restructuring old ones.

Anderson (1988: 197)

Anderson (1988) notes that among the differences between experts and novices is the fact that an expert will break down new information into more relevant chunks than a novice will and an expert has more knowledge to which it may be connected. That is, experts will deal more efficiently with new information because their schemata are more developed and, in a sense, more accommodating. Two common ways of creating such schematic maps are word association (e.g. making semantic connections) and pattern noting (examining ideas and the real world and drawing inferences about the relationships).

Schema theory is important to CALL because many aspects of schema mirror the organization of hypertext, hypermedia and multimedia.

Quote 5.16 A. Dillon, C. McKnight and J. Richardson suggest that:

Some hypertext researchers and designers believe that hypertext information structures should reflect the structures of human memory and that by empirically deriving and then mapping the semantic structure of information onto hypertext and explicitly illustrating that structure in the hypertext interfacer will result in greater changes in the knowledge structures of the users (Jonassen, 1990, 1991b; Lambiotte et al., 1989; McAleese, 1990; McDonald, Paap and McDonald, 1990).

Dillon, McKnight and Richardson (1993: 165)

While Dillon, McKnight and Richardson (1993) draw parallels between interface and schema building, they also suggest that hypertext alone is not sufficient to help learners in their acquisition of a second language, although it may help them process tasks. Moreover, when learners collaborate at the computer, their individual semantic structures of the information may differ from each other and that of the hypertext author.

Example 5.2   Mind map software

Mind maps are visual representations of schemata. They are usually presented as a series of branching lines radiating from a central circle containing the main idea. The lines terminate in circles of related ideas which may branch off to further ideas. A commercial application that makes creating mind maps easy is Inspiration Software's *Inspiration* and a simpler version for young children *Kidspiration http://www.inspiration.com* These programs provide templates to build on as well as a variety of tools in the form of symbols and shapes to help build mind maps.

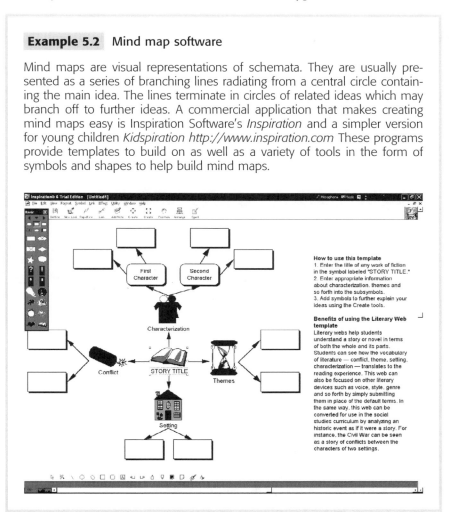

5.6.2   How constructivism differs from behaviourism

Schema theory offers a dividing line between behaviourism and constructivism in that it is largely ignored by the former but is integral to the latter. Behaviourism often assumes that the learner's state of mind is that of a blank slate, waiting to be written on; constructivism assumes that the learner comes to the classroom with a rich set of ideas and experiences.

Constructivism differs from behaviourism in that it allows and encourages learners to build on what they already know and go beyond the simple collection and memorization of information to develop individualized internalized principles. Constructivism supports key constructs of CALL, collaboration and negotiation of meaning. Collaboration provides opportunities for negotiation of meaning as learners struggle to build new schemata and extend existing ones. The role of the teacher in a constructivist model includes presenting opportunities for learning (repeating and rephrasing some elements in spiral fashion) and encouraging reflective thinking in learners, partly through collaborative peer activities.

Constructivism may be traced back to humanist thinkers such as René Descartes (1595–1650), but it is largely associated with the cognitive scientist George Kelly (1905–67).

Quote 5.17 R. Oxford on constructivism:

Constructivism is partly based on Kelly's (1955) theory of personal constructs. Kelly suggested that people understand experience by grouping according to similarity and opposites. A construct is a distinction between opposites, such as short–tall, fat–thin, black–white, pleasant–unpleasant, that is used to understand events, things and people.

Oxford (1955: 362–3)

Other cognitive scientists who were involved in related ideas include Jean Piaget (1896–1980), Lev Vygotsky (1896–1934) and J.S. Bruner. Bruner was a President of the American Psychological Association and a student of Piaget who followed Piaget's methods but differed in the conclusions he arrived at.

Quote 5.18 J.S. Bruner on the constructivist model:

To instruct someone in a discipline is not a matter of getting him to commit results to mind. Rather, it is to teach him to participate in the process that makes possible the establishment of knowledge. We teach a subject not to produce little living libraries on the subject, but rather to get a student to think mathematically for himself, to consider matters as an historian does, to take part in the process of knowledge-getting. Knowing is a process, not a product.

Bruner (1966: 72)

This process orientation of constructivism assumes that good methods for structuring knowledge should result in simplifying, generating new propositions and increasing the manipulation of information.

Biography: Seymour Papert

Seymour Papert, another student of Piaget, turned to the question of making a machine think. His team worked with children and developed a computer language called Logo which aimed to have the learner teach the computer rather than vice versa (Merrill *et al.*, 1996). Because his methods of instruction focused on having learners learn by constructing things, he called his brand of constructivism *constructionism*. His more influential books include: *Mindstorms: Children, Computers and Powerful Ideas* (1980), *Microworlds: Transforming Education* (1984) and *The Children's Machine: Rethinking School in the Age of the Computer* (1992).

5.6.3   Contributions of Vygotsky

Closely associated with constructivism is the *Social Development Theory* of Vygotsky. Vygotsky stressed the importance of social interaction, such as peer collaboration, in developing cognition.

Quote 5.19   L.S. Vygotsky on cultural development:

Every function in the child's cultural development appears twice: first, on the social level, and later, on the individual level; first, between people (interpsychological) and then inside the child (intrapsychological). This applies equally to voluntary attention, to logical memory, and to the formation of concepts. All the higher functions originate as actual relationships between individuals.

Vygotsky (1978: 57)

An important aspect of Vygotsky's theory is the idea that the potential for cognitive development is limited to a certain gap, which he calls the *zone of proximal development* (ZPD). Learning during the ZPD depends upon full social interaction. Vygotsky felt that the range of skills that would be developed with teacher guidance or through peer collaboration would exceed those that might be achieved by a learner working alone.

Like behaviourism, constructivism has also had a close connection with CALL. Atkins (1993) reviews several software packages built on a

> **Quote 5.20** J.S. Gould on characteristics of constructivist-orientated teachers:
>
> They focus on big ideas rather than facts; they encourage and empower students to follow their own interests, to make connections, to reformulate ideas, and to reach unique conclusions. Teachers and students in these classrooms are aware that the world is a complex place in which multiple perspectives exist and truth is often a matter of interpretation, and they acknowledge that learning and the process of assessing learning are intricate and require student and teacher interaction as well as time, documentation, and analyses by both teacher and students.
>
> Gould (1996: 93)

constructivist model and notes a common belief that such software merely follows the most recent trend. However, he adds this assertion:

> **Quote 5.21** M.J. Atkins on studies of CALL materials following the latest trend:
>
> It ignores the contribution of changes in the interactive technologies themselves, changes which had considerable design implications for learning and training applications. For example, the increase in cognitive approaches in the 1980s may be due as much to the arrival of object-oriented programming, hypermedia, and interactive video as to the growing ascendancy within psychology of the cognitive theorists. To ignore the history of the technological developments and their design implications is to present only half the picture.
>
> Atkins (1993: 253)

As with behaviourism, many teachers would recognize aspects of constructivism in both classroom practice and some CALL programs. As mentioned earlier, it is likely that many teachers make use of such models of instruction on the basis of their own experiences and training, as well as what works for the moment, rather than on deep-rooted ideological passions for one theory over the other.

5.6.4 Summarizing constructivism

In a constructivist model, the learner is assumed to come to the classroom with a range of experiences and a wealth of (sometimes imperfect) knowledge. It is assumed that knowledge is an objective interpretation of ideas

Quote 5.22 M. Pennington on the components of an ideal teaching system:

- Helps learners develop and elaborate their increasingly specified cognitive representation for the second language
- Allows learners to experiment and take risks in a psychologically favorable and motivating environment
- Offers input to both conscious and unconscious learning processes
- Offers learners opportunities to practice and to receive feedback on performance
- Allows learners to learn according to their own purposes and goals
- Puts learners in touch with other learners
- Promotes cultural and social learning
- Promotes interactivity in learning and communication
- Exposes the learner to appropriate contexts for learning
- Expands the learner's 'zone of proximal development'
- Builds to learner independence

Pennington (1996: 7)

and that such interpretations are best developed through the learner discovering and struggling with ideas.

Constructivism is a problem-orientated learning approach in which the learner is expected to construct his or her own reality based on a personalized understanding of the learning materials, often through analysis and synthesis of ideas. The role of the teacher is as a facilitator of learning, rather than as an expert. Instead, expert advice is culled from a variety of authentic sources, including knowledgeable individuals. Mistakes are encouraged if they help with learning.

As with behaviourism, not all aspects of constructivism are likely to be found in all learning materials labelled *constructivist* nor is constructivism likely to be completely pervasive in any teacher's daily classroom practice. The next section looks at the role of collaboration and negotiation of meaning.

5.7 The role of collaboration and negotiation of meaning in the two models

Collaboration and negotiation of meaning are dealt with in greater detail in the following chapter but it would seem, on surface examination, that the constructs of collaboration and negotiation of meaning fall solely within the constructivist model.

In fact, the constructivist model does openly support these constructs, but there is room within the behaviourist model for them as well. For example, Susman (1998) looks at factors that increase the effectiveness of cooperative learning in CALL programs. In the 36 studies she reviews, conducted between 1980 and 1998, 16 are classed as tutorial, 10 are drill and practice and 10 are defined as problem-solving. That is, the 26 studies in the first two categories could be considered behaviourist and the 10 in the last category could be considered constructivist, yet all 36 studies were regarded as cooperative. The terms *cooperative* and *collaborative* are used interchangeably by some authors without reference to their differences. This seems to be the case with Susman who does not differentiate between tasks which can be subdivided and completed by two or more learners (cooperative) and tasks which require that two or more learners work together on all parts of a task.

The implication is that cooperation/collaboration and negotiation of meaning may exist as features of both behaviourist and constructivist models of instruction. However, the degree to which they are effective within each model needs to be examined.

Summary

In this chapter, historical ideas behind behaviourism were outlined along with resulting methods, including programmed instruction and mastery learning. The advantages and disadvantages of each were considered in terms of CALL software programs and second-language acquisition (SLA). The computer, with its binary logic, provides a natural environment for behaviourist models of learning. Constructivism, making use of schema theory, differs from behaviourism, partly on the former's suitability for facilitating collaboration and negotiation of meaning, the topic of Chapter 6.

Further reading

Kohonen, V., Jaatinen, R. Kaikkonen, P. and Lehtovaara, J. (2001) *Experiential Learning in Foreign Language Education*. Harlow: Longman. – This collection of papers provides a useful perspective on experiential and intercultural learning and autobiographical knowledge in teaching and learning.
The following two books are key readings for understanding constructivism:
Vygotsky, L.S. (1962) *Thought and Language*. Cambridge, MA: MIT Press.
Vygotsky, L.S. (1978) *Mind in Society*. Cambridge, MA: Harvard University Press.

Chapter 6

Collaboration and negotiation of meaning

Collaboration is among the most useful ways in which learners acquire language at the computer. When two or more learners sit at a computer and discuss process and content in the target language, they often engage in scaffolded learning, helping each other improve their language.

This chapter focuses on collaboration, exploring the differences between it and similar terms such as teamwork and cooperation. It then goes on to define collaboration in the context of CALL and show how collaboration supports negotiation of meaning through scaffolded instruction. When learners negotiate meaning, their discourse often indicates their collaborative (and non-collaborative) intentions. This chapter ends with a brief explanation of discourse analysis. Particular concern is paid to how collaborative intentions might be evidenced through discourse.

The principal concerns of this chapter can be summarized by the following five questions:

- What is collaboration?
- What are the differences between collaboration and related terms?
- How does collaboration support negotiation of meaning through scaffolded instruction?
- What challenges exist to collaboration at the computer?
- How are such challenges evidenced through discourse?

6.1 The place of collaboration in CALL

Learners often collaborate, either on their own initiative or as an assigned activity. Collaboration is an important activity in the classroom because it

Quote 6.1 P. Dunkel on small-group work:

Does small-group work at a computer terminal generate conversational interactions among group participants, and if so, what is the quality and what are
the constituents of the discourse generated?

Dunkel (1991: 6)

encourages social skills and thinking skills and mirrors the way in which
learners often need to work once they leave an academic setting. From the
point of view of learning a language, there is an additional benefit; in the
process of negotiating the meaning of a task and the means by which it
may be addressed, learners make decisions about the learning materials
they study and the ways in which they should study.

Quote 6.2 C.N. Candlin on a context for a social dimension for
materials:

It would seem then, to be indispensable that language-teaching materials
provide adequate context so that pragmatic and discoursal meaning can be
reasonably 'worked' on. The same need exists for a clear social dimension
where learners can investigate the presuppositions and shared knowledge
and beliefs of interlocutors. What is taken-for-granted has to be open to investigation by learners.

Candlin (1981: 34)

To negotiate meaning, learners engage in discourse that provides opportunities for comprehensible input and encourages comprehensible output.
Together, opportunities for comprehensible input and output help learners
build vocabulary, skills and language awareness. That is, learners learn by
talking about problems, the content of the learning materials and other
information necessary to solve the problems.

Although computers do not take an active part in discourse, in some
cases they appear to respond intelligently to learner inquiries and actions
and, in doing so, provide comprehensible input. They also offer opportunities for comprehensible output when they prompt learners to undertake
tasks and answer questions.

6.1.2   Collaboration and negotiation of meaning

> **Quote 6.3** V. Stevens on groupwork at the computer:
>
> Students engaged in computer-based activities often form groups around the computer. This is in part because computers promote brainstorming in resolving the outcome of interactional sequences, and in part because exploratory interaction creates opportunities for using language to discuss with teachers and peers the nature of discoveries made in the course of completing computer-based tasks.
>
> Stevens (1992: 28)

Collaboration has already been mentioned in earlier chapters but it is necessary to define collaboration in terms of a set of behaviours that encourage and discourage learning goals within a CALL context, especially those behaviours that influence negotiation of meaning.

> **Quote 6.4** C. Chaudron on scaffolded instruction:
>
> the provision through conversation of linguistic structures that promote a learner's recognition or production of those structures or associated forms. The import of this concept is that in various conversational or other task-related interaction, the 'vertical discourse' – the sequence of turns taken with conversants – aids learners in gradually incorporating portions of sentences, lexical items, reproducing sounds, etc., in meaningful ways rather than in mechanical repetition or lengthy monologues.
>
> Chaudron (1988: 10)

Stevens (1992) differentiates conversation between the learner and peers, conversation between the learner and a teacher and conversation between a learner and the computer, or rather the exchanges that take place when a learner interacts with a computer. But clearly, all three present opportunities for negotiation of meaning and SLA as a result of scaffolded instruction.

Ellis (1998) suggests that scaffolding describes a situation in which a learner interacts with someone who can guide, support and shape his or her learning.

Although computers do not take an active part in discourse, in some cases they appear to respond intelligently to learner inquiries and actions

Quote 6.5 R. Ellis on aspects of scaffolded learning:

1. recruiting interest in a task
2. simplifying the task
3. maintaining pursuit of a goal
4. marking critical features and discrepancies between what has been produced and the ideal solution
5. controlling frustrations during problems solving, and
6. demonstrating an idealized version of the act to be performed

Ellis (1998: 161)

through mimicking the above six aspects of scaffolded instruction and, in doing so, provide comprehensible input. They also offer opportunities for comprehensible output when they prompt learners to undertake tasks and answer questions (see Section 5.2).

6.1.3   Defining collaboration

Collaboration is defined as a process in which two or more learners need to work together to achieve a common goal, usually the completion of a task or the answering of a question. Collaboration is manifested in the actions a learner takes when working with others and can be evidenced, for example, as a willingness to listen to others' ideas, suggestions and opinions so that they can be discussed and integrated into further actions, such as decisions about how to complete a task.

Collaborative objectives can be defined in contrast to two other types of goals found in group learning: individualistic and competitive goals. Johnson and Johnson (1990) suggest that there are three basic types of goal structure that can be used to motivate classroom learning:

- individualistic, where a learner believes his or her chances of reaching the goal are unrelated to what others do
- competitive, where a learner believes he or she can reach the goal only when others cannot
- cooperative, where a learner believes that he or she can reach the goal only if others can too

Collaboration and related terms have been used to encompass a wide range of ideas about learners working together. This presents problems as researchers cannot properly examine the outcomes of collaboration if the scope of the term is not agreed upon beforehand.

> **Quote 6.6** P. Dillenbourg on fashion in terminology:
>
> When a word becomes fashionable – as is the case with 'collaboration' – it is often used abusively for more or less anything. The problem with such an over-general usage is two-fold. First, it is nonsense to talk about the cognitive effects ('learning') of 'collaborative' situations if any situation can be labeled 'collaborative'. Second, it is difficult to articulate the contributions of various authors who use the same word very differently.
>
> Dillenbourg (1999: 1)

Collaboration in the classroom begins with an activity that facilitates real communication, for example, verbal, written or electronic discussion in the course of solving a problem. But a true collaborative activity also requires that two or more learners engage in discourse over the decisions about the task, discussing what is most important, discussing the sequence of discrete problems within the task and deciding how to approach solving the problems within the task. Collaboration essentially puts learners into a semi-autonomous situation in which they are faced with a task, question or problem and must use discourse to negotiate each participant's separate learning strategies and make joint decisions about what is (and is not) worth investigating and learning.

But in many cases, collaboration is not a clearly defined phenomenon beyond a sense of *two or more individuals working together*. Several authors and researchers define collaboration in contrast to other terms, such as *cooperation*, while others list aspects of collaboration that help to define its parameters.

Further reading

Resources for Cooperative Learning, University of Miami, Oxford, OH. *http://miavx1.muohio.edu/~iascewis/resource.htmlx* – This website is a useful collection of websites, texts and contacts for cooperative learning.

Nunan, D. (ed.) (1992a) *Collaborative language learning and teaching*. Cambridge: Cambridge University Press. – Although not concerned exclusively with CALL, this provides a variety of useful perspectives on collaboration.

6.1.4   Promoting awareness and skill development

Nunan (1992) suggests that collaboration supports a communicative approach to learning.

> **Quote 6.7** D. Nunan on collaboration encouraging both learner awareness and skill development:
>
> - to learn about learning, to learn better and
> - to increase their awareness about language, and about self, and hence about learning
> - to develop, as a result, metacommunicative as well as communicative skills
> - to confront, and come to terms with, the conflicts between individual needs and group needs, both in social, procedural terms as well as linguistic, content terms
> - to realize that content and method are inextricably linked, and
> - to recognize the decision-making tasks themselves as genuine communicative activities
>
> Nunan (1992a: 3)

6.1.5   Achieving pedagogical objectives

Teachers have a variety of pedagogical objectives. Some of these objectives are best achieved through teacher-fronted modelling, but others might be best achieved by other means. Derycke, Smith and Hemery (1995) offer a justification for the use of collaborative learning.

> **Quote 6.8** A.C. Derycke, C. Smith and Hemery on pedagogical objectives:
>
> some of the highest pedagogical objectives can only be achieved by employing group learning activities such as group problem-solving, games, case studies and exchanges with real experts. In all of these activities and skills, language is explored, exercised and developed in ways supported by collaboration at the computer.
>
> Derycke, Smith and Hemery (1995: 182)

What Derycke, Smith and Hemery (1995) add to Nunan's (1992) justification of collaboration is the suggestion that a collaborative approach can be supported by the computer.

6.1.6   Improving literacy

Gould (1996) (see Quote 6.9) writes of young children in a native-language situation and, while her ideas are more likely to be concerned with literacy, there is no reason to believe that the same benefits are not also available to older native speakers as well as second-language speaking learners. Gould (1996) ascribes some of the same advantages to collaboration as raised by Nunan (1992) and Derycke, Smith and Hemery (1995) but focuses on the benefits to literacy.

> **Quote 6.9** J.S. Gould on the benefits of collaboration to literacy:
>
> Social activities integrated into the language arts processes can actually lead to better writing, reading and spelling (Graves, 1993), for the talking, sharing and listening that occur pull down the challenges to communication and enhance the child's literacy growth (Amarel, 1987).
>
> Gould (1996: 93)

6.1.7   Promoting language acquisition

O'Neil (1994) uses the term teamwork for what may also be defined as collaboration, and suggests that such skills involve the complex production of language. These include *adaptability*: recognizing problems and responding appropriately; *coordination*: organizing team activities to complete a task on time; *decision making*: using available information to make decisions; *interpersonal*: interacting cooperatively with other team members; *leadership*: providing direction for the team and *communication*: encouraging the overall exchange of clear and accurate information.

> **Quote 6.10** G. Jacobs summarizes ten potential advantages of group activities in language instruction:
>
> 1. The quantity of learner speech can increase
> 2. The variety of speech acts can increase
> 3. There can be more individualization of instruction
> 4. Anxiety can be reduced
> 5. Motivation can increase
> 6. Enjoyment can increase
> 7. Independence can increase
> 8. Social integration can increase
> 9. Students can learn how to work with others
> 10. Learning can increase

Several of Jacobs's (1998) points are identical to the advantages Hoogeveen (1995) (see Quote 3.9) ascribes to multimedia learning. This is perhaps because the computer naturally invites collaboration through its various affordances (i.e. what the program is or appears to be capable of doing in terms of both intended and unintended functions) including the *public* nature of the display or screen versus the relatively *private* nature of the textbook and sheet of writing paper.

Quote 6.11   C.B. Cazden on the public nature of the computer:

There may be several reasons why placing computers in classrooms seems to result in increased collaboration among peers. One reason is a permanent feature of the technology: work in progress on the screen is public in a way that paper on a desk is not. Other reasons may be more temporary. Most classrooms today have one computer at most, and that makes it a scarce resource whose use can be doubled by asking children to work at terminals in pairs. Expertise in the new technology is also a scarce resource, and student experts can supplement the limited availability of the teacher.

Cazden (1988: 148)

Cazden would seem to outline a paradox: a limited number of computers might in some cases be preferable to a class sets as more limited access is likely to promote collaborative language learning and associated benefits.

Collectively, the concerns of the above authors point to a wide range of benefits of collaboration. The following sections examine the need for structure in collaboration.

6.2   Structuring collaboration

Quote 6.12   M. Hamm suggests that the teacher must structure collaboration at computers through:

1. assigning students to mixed-ability teams
2. establishing positive interdependence
3. teaching cooperative social skills
4. insuring individual accountability
5. helping groups process information

Hamm (1992: 95)

One debate within collaboration studies is the degree to which a teacher should structure collaborative activities and offer skills training.

Hamm (1992) suggests that an aim of successful collaboration is to promote feelings that 'no one is successful unless everyone is successful' (p. 96).

Quote 6.13 M. Hamm on interdependence in collaboration:

1. Goal interdependence – stating clearly what each member of the group should know how to do upon completion of the task
2. Task interdependence – clearly defining the group goal, and what the team should agree on or be able to produce
3. Resource interdependence – specifying parameters, materials, the team's task
4. Role interdependence – reviewing the individual roles for the group members: keyboarder, checker, reporter, summarizer, encourager, and so on. Set up the expectation that everyone is responsible for explaining how they came up with the answer. Explain the grading procedures, group credit as well as credit for how well each student performs his or her group job

Hamm (1992: 96)

However, in the context of CALL, some of Hamm's (1992) suggestions for interdependence are taken over by the computer program. For example, the computer program often defines the task and the resources, although,

---

Quote 6.14 E.B. Susman on integrating interaction into software:

Software can be designed to give some interaction support features. CBIs (Computer-Based Instruction materials) can support 1. reflection, 2. exploration of multiple perspectives, and 3. the integrated use of multiple resources. These supports can be accomplished by a note-taking section or frame and providing links to a variety of media presentations and sources (e.g. links on the World Wide Web). Rysavy and Sales suggest pauses in the materials that direct group members to interact on their understanding. They also suggest that CBIs could remind students to monitor their performance. Even though CBIs cannot assure a cooperative environment, CBIs can help stimulate group processing by encouraging the group to analyze their progress and by teaching them how to effectively communicate.

Susman (1998: 317)

of course, the learners are free to deviate from what is suggested. The disadvantage of the computer program making decisions about the task and resources is that it lowers the opportunities learners have to negotiate meaning for themselves.

CALL programs should also provide ways to make motivation implicit instead of explicit. It is certainly true that some learners (especially younger ones) may need training in the skills necessary for working in a group, but many of the advantages of collaboration are lost if learners lose their autonomy and the task becomes purely teacher-centred and teacher-directed, adopting a behaviourist model of instruction.

Quote 6.15   R. Ellis on implicit versus explicit learning

Implicit learning is acquisition of knowledge about the underlying structure of a complex stimulus environment by a process which takes place naturally, simply and without conscious operations. Explicit learning is a more conscious operation where the individual makes and tests hypotheses in a search for structure. Knowledge attainment can thus take place implicitly (a nonconscious and automatic abstraction of the structural nature of the material arrived at from experience of instances), explicitly through selective learning (the learner searching for information and building then testing hypotheses), or, because we can communicate using language, explicitly via given rules (assimilation of a rule following explicit instruction).

Ellis (1994: 1)

In particular, Hamm's (1992) assignment of individual roles for each learner discourages the collaborative advantages of a learning activity. Learners are likely to be more concerned with being involved in fulfilling their individual roles and tasks rather than the overall process of socially engaging in a process of solving a problem through negotiation of meaning and the eventual benefits it might provide through fostering SLA.

Dillenbourg (1999) suggests forced roles inhibit collaboration or deny the benefits of collaboration. Similarly, trivial tasks can inhibit negotiation of meaning as there may be nothing 'to disagree upon, and in which there is nothing to misunderstand. The boundary between misunderstanding and disagreement is shallow. If we do not understand each other, we cannot say that we properly agreed' (p. 15).

From the point of the view of the learner engaged in a learning task, a conversation is partly about creating roles for each person. If a teacher assigns collaborative roles to learners, the learners are deprived of the opportunities to develop appropriate conversational and negotiation skills.

> **Quote 6.16** P. Dillenbourg on the impact of forcing roles upon learners:
>
> Negotiation can occur only if there is *space for negotiation* (Dillenbourg and Baker, 1996), i.e. if something can actually be negotiated. Negotiation at the meta-communicative level can be inhibited by forcing partners to play well-defined roles (a growing trend in research in collaborative learning).
>
> Dillenbourg (1999: 16)

> **Quote 6.17** J.C. Richards and R.W. Schmidt on the function of conversation:
>
> Conversation is more than merely the exchange of information. When people take part in conversation, they bring to the conversational process shared assumptions and expectations about what conversation is, how conversation develops, and the sort of contribution they are each expected to make.
>
> Richards and Schmidt (1983: 119–20)

The above descriptions and ideas serve to explain features, parameters and advantages of collaborative activities, but none provides a definition or shows the difference between *collaboration, cooperation* and other terms, such as *teamwork*. These definitions and differences are discussed in the following section.

> **Further reading**
>
> Dörnyei, Z. (2001) *Teaching and Researching Motivation*. Harlow: Longman. – In this book, another in the ALiA series, Dörnyei does not focus on CALL, but many of the issues are still applicable.

6.3 Differences between collaboration and other terms

The difference between collaborative learning and cooperative learning is not well defined and both have many shades of meaning. Biggs and Moore (1993), for example, suggest cooperative learning is an activity set by the teacher while collaborative activities are ones spontaneously set up by the learners. Kohonen (1992) uses *cooperative* and *collaborative* interchangeably. Nunan (1992a) defines collaboration as an activity in which learners have greater control over the design of their learning while cooperative learning is merely a mode of instruction. Other authors, such as O'Neil (1994) avoid the use of *cooperation* or *collaboration* and use the term *teamwork*.

Dillenbourgh *et al.* (1995) explain the difference between cooperation and collaboration as being not whether or not the task is distributed, but how it is divided:

> in cooperation the task is split (hierarchically) into independent subtasks; in collaboration cognitive processes may be (heterarchically) divided into intertwined layers. In cooperation, coordination is only required when assembling partial results, while collaboration is . . . a coordinated, synchronous activity that is the result of a continued attempt to construct and maintain a shared conception of a problem (p. 189).

This difference between collaboration and cooperation is made plain in Hamm's earlier suggestion for teacher-imposed division of roles among learners in a group engaged in a common task. Such an imposed division places Hamm's suggestions within the definition for cooperation. For this book, the definition used to define collaboration will be based on what Dillenbourgh *et al.* (1995) consider to be collaborative practices and situations, regardless of the terms used by other authors in describing pair or group learning. However, various authors' quoted texts retain their original choice of terms.

6.4   The range of collaboration and CALL

CALL programs, or other computer programs that can be used to encourage language learning, often address several of the cooperative, teamwork or collaborative skills mentioned above by various researchers. *Adaptability* (recognizing problems and responding appropriately) is found in various software programs that present learning as a quest. This is particularly appropriate in materials developed for younger learners in which a series of correct answers move one along a map or serve to save a creature in danger. This requires coordination and decision-making and interpersonal and communication skills. Such activities often work best with group members of different language and cultural backgrounds, such as in a mixed ESL classroom where English (however limited) is the only common language. In such situations, collaborative interpersonal skills such as consensus and queuing must be negotiated as well as the target content.

In recent years, much research has been done on computer-mediated learner collaboration in the area of computer-based instruction (CBI) and CALL via email (for a current summary, see Warschauer, 1995a, 1997). But most of this research has focused on individual learners using computers to collaborate over distance with other learners (for examples, see Kaye, 1992; Druin and Solomon, 1996). In one version of this approach, collaboration takes place through local area networks within a classroom or among different classrooms in a school. Using programs such as the Lotus software program *Notes for Workgroups*, learners can share data, questions and comments, work individually or in small groups on discrete parts of a task, or contribute ideas to the exploration of a larger task.

Another approach is to offer opportunities for learners to use email and the World Wide Web (WWW) to communicate with the wider world. This approach is particularly appropriate for distance-learning situations dictated by geographical isolation in which learners need to communicate with their teachers at greater regularity than is practical through correspondence-course mail and less expensively than by telephone. It is also common for learners to collaborate with other learners in distant places and search sources of authentic information. Other forms of collaboration include learning through a quasi-apprentice approach, for example, where learners assist scientists in the collection of meteorological or biological data (for examples, see Serim and Koch, 1996; Crook, 1994; Cummins and Sayers, 1995).

However, often overlooked is the commonly observed collaborative phenomenon: oral/aural collaborative language use among pairs or small groups of learners working at a single computer to complete a task or a series of tasks.

6.5   Collaboration at the computer

Many authors worry that working at a computer can be a socially isolating experience for learners as they work alone at separate terminals. However, Crook (1994) notes that the computer facilitates socially organized learning in the classroom rather than inhibits it. A commonly observed collaborative phenomenon is pairs or small groups of learners working on their own outside of a class at a single computer to complete a task or a series of tasks. This type of collaboration is sometimes teacher-initiated but is more often learner-initiated. In some cases, such collaboration may be a prelude to broader international communication or collaboration through email, chatlines and MOO environments (see Section 4.5.3).

In collaborating, learners sometimes work together at one computer because of limited access to enough computers. But my own observations over the past ten years of learner use of computers in computer centres, computer lab areas and design studios (for the past ten years, the author has taught desktop publishing and WWW-based courses at City University of Hong Kong) suggest learners commonly and naturally work together at the computer despite an abundance of computers that would allow them to work individually.

Argyle (1991) suggests three possible reasons, or motivations, for people to collaborate: for external rewards; to form and further relationships; and to share activities they are involved in (cited in McConnell, 1994: 13). Argyle's term *external rewards* suggest collaboration simply for extrinsically motivated reasons such as classroom marks. But Argyle's second and third seasons suggest more intrinsic motivations. These include the desire to offer assistance where one learner of the pair has already completed an assignment, to help with problems tangential to the assignments such as the operation of unfamiliar hardware/software or, less nobly, simply to plagiarize assignments (see Section 8.8).

But, perhaps the greatest reason for collaboration at the computer is the simple human desire for social contact; learners like to explore together and work together. Working together is an aspect of education consistent with one of the goals of modern schools: fostering the socialization of learners. The following section explores other benefits.

Further reading

Dillenbourg, P. (ed.) (1999) *Collaborative learning: cognitive and computational approaches*. Amsterdam: Pergamon. – This book brings together several perspectives on collaborative learning, including work on artificial intelligence.

6.6   Benefits of collaborative learning at the computer

The greatest single benefit of collaborative learning at the computer is in the way in which it serves to reveal information and ideas, not just to the learners' collaborative partners, but to the learners themselves.

McConnell (1994) suggests that cooperative learning (for which, as previously noted, we can substitute collaborative learning) serves to make public what individuals and group members know

> This 'making public' works as a central process in cooperative learning and confirms its social and democratic nature. It can be thought of along several dimensions: our learning is public when it is known to others and ourselves; it is blind when it is known to others but not ourselves; it is hidden when it

is known to ourselves but not to others; and it is unconscious when it is not known to ourselves or to others (p. 16).

McConnell's hypotheses are explained graphically in the following figure:

Making learning public

Behaviour known to others ↓ Unknown to others	Behaviour known to self → Behaviour unknown to self	
	Public	Blind
	Hidden	Unconscious

Figure 6.1   **The public–private/conscious–unconscious dimensions of cooperative learning**
(after McConnell, 1994: 16)

Quote 6.18 J.S. Gould on the learner's innate resources:

[collaboration allows the learner] to marshal and exploit resources he or she already has available, but over which he or she does not yet have explicit and conscious control (Karmiloff-Smith, 1979). What all collaborative talk has in common is that one of the participants has a goal that he or she would like to achieve and the other participant engages in talk that helps the first to achieve that goal (Wells and Chang-Wells, 1992).

Gould (1996: 97)

However, McConnell (1994) also points out that cooperative or collaborative learning depends largely upon a *willingness* to work in this way: 'if the group does not address its own learning and come to some initial, and over time ongoing, agreement about itself then it is likely to fragment and the members will essentially end up learning in isolation' (p. 17). Essentially, this means that learners may completely disengage from the task and not learn at all and/or may pursue Johnson and Johnson's (1990) individualistic or competitive goals (see Section 6.1.3).

Wegerif and Dawes (1998) offer a related perspective on the significance of exploratory talk, suggesting that cooperation alone is not the essential ingredient to achievement but rather that it depends on accommodating disagreement and exploring hypotheses.

Without using the term, Wegerif and Dawes (1998) describe a process essential to constructivist learning: negotiation of meaning (see Section 5.7). Negotiation of meaning differentiates collaboration from more cooperative situations in which a group of learners simply are expected to complete a set of narrowly defined tasks with resources to which they have been directed.

> **Quote 6.19** R. Wegerif and L. Dawes on effective learning at the computer:
>
> group work around the computer is not always an effective vehicle for learning. The educational benefits of children working together depend on how they interact and particularly on the way in which they talk together. Underwood (1994) supports this point and offers a case study illustrating what he puts forward as 'the type of discussion to be fostered if a successful collaboration is to be seen in the computer classroom'. This type of discussion is characterized by a constructive relationship in which disagreement is accepted and leads to hypotheses being explored together.
>
> Wegerif and Dawes (1998: 14)

> **Quote 6.20** R. Wegerif and L. Dawes outline what they see as productive discussion, noting the place of cooperation and conflict:
>
> In characterizing his ideal type of productive discussion Underwood draws attention to the work of Kruger (1993). Kruger recorded and coded the talk of pairs on socio-moral problems and found that the quality of the outcome was related to the quality of the dialogue, particularly the amount of 'transactive reasoning' described as 'criticisms, explanations, justifications, clarifications and elaborations of ideas'. Kruger argues that it is neither conflict nor cooperation that is important in collaborative learning but a combination of the two in a form of interaction which encourages critical challenges within a cooperative search for the best solution.
>
> Wegerif and Dawes (1998: 14)

Essentially, Wegerif and Dawes's (1998) argument is that collaboration cannot take place if learners are not willing to apply critical thinking skills in a social context.

6.7 Collaboration, CALL and SLA

There are many benefits to collaboration including the above-mentioned socialization of learners. However, a concern of CALL is how collaboration promotes language learning through exposure to new language and opportunities to use it through negotiation of meaning with peers. Ellis (1997) notes that classroom settings are likely to be poor places for learners to acquire language compared to the world outside the classroom, in part because teachers dominate the conversation with display questions meant to elicit set responses. But Ellis's (1997) criticism is largely answered by collaboration, whether within or outside of a classroom context in which learners are able and encouraged to engage in discourse freely.

Quote 6.21 D. Barnes on the transformational aspect of language use in a collaborative environment:

Here lies the importance of pupil participation. It is when the pupil is required to use language to grapple with new experience in a new way that he is most likely to find it necessary to use language differently. And this will be very different from taking over someone else's language in external imitation of its forms: on the contrary, it is the first step towards new patterns of thinking and feeling, new ways of representing reality to himself.

Barnes (1969: 61)

In terms of the types of discourse in which learners engage in the classroom, Barnes (1969) suggests that teacher modelling should not be the sole method. Rather, it is only when learners ' "try it out" in reciprocal exchanges so that they modify the way they use language to organize reality that they are able to find new functions for language in thinking and feeling' (p. 62).

In particular, this points to the need for learners to personalize their language to suit their own needs and environment beyond the classroom. On the simplest level, this means learners being involved in adapting what they have learned to the type of discourse required to converse with peers, not just teachers.

Accommodating opportunities for personalizing discourse is among the best ways in which learners improve their language skills with computers. It is done through an aspect of CALL which is not usually designed into software packages: collaborative learning activities which implicitly or explicitly encourage various types of discourse. In discussing computers in the classroom, Nunan and Lamb (1996a) found that

> Some of the more exciting programs are those that were not specifically designed to teach language. These programs include simulations, design programs, and word-processing packages. Such packages can stimulate a great deal of interactive discussion if students are given the opportunity of working on the programs in pairs or small groups rather than individually (p. 195).

However, understanding the utility of group discussion at the computer requires that the discourse be examined to determine what conditions and features mark it as collaborative and supportive of negotiation of meaning, scaffolded instruction and SLA. This chapter now turns to a consideration of how collaboration is evidenced by discourse.

6.8   Collaboration at the computer as evidenced by discourse

The study of discourse dates back to ancient Greek times with the philosopher's division of grammar from rhetoric, 'the former being concerned with the rules of language as an isolated object, the latter with how to do things with words to achieve effects, and communicate successfully with people in particular contexts' (Cook, 1989: 12). In modern times, concerns with discourse analysis arose from the work of anthropologists and linguists. J.R. Firth, in 1935, urged the study of conversation as a way to find the key to better understanding of what language is and how it works.

Many took up Firth's call (although, curiously, not Firth himself; he continued to focus on phonology as well as other topics such as semantics) and research proceeded in different directions. Some researchers were more concerned with the context of utterances, arguing that any simple phrase could have different meanings depending on the situation and identity of the interlocutors. Sinclair and Coulthard (1975) were early advocates of the use of discourse analysis to examine teacher talk in the classroom but it was soon realized that it was also useful in examining a wide range of discourses of learners as well as teachers.

The discourse of learners and their interactions with the computer need to be investigated with an emphasis on the intentions of the learners to undertake different strategies. Grice (1975) suggests that four maxims of *quality*, *quantity*, *relevance* and *manner* govern the general cooperative intention in conversation. Cook (1989) summarizes these as: be true (the maxim of quality); be brief (the maxim of quantity); be relevant (the maxim of relevance); be clear (the maxim of manner) (p. 29).

These maxims are flouted by speakers who, for example, use conversational strategies to exaggerate, to express sarcasm, to obfuscate and so on. Together, the maxims, and even the flouting of the maxims, help to express certain social needs. These social needs include (but are not limited by): the need to be thought of as an expert at the expense of the truth; the need to hold the conversation and control the technology at the expense of brevity; the need to entertain or display irrelevant knowledge at the expense of relevance and the need to prevaricate when one does not know the facts at the expense of clarity.

Moreover, these social needs are evident in both verbal and non-verbal behaviours. Non-verbal, paralinguistic aspects of collaboration are visible and can be easily documented empirically. For example, learners at the computer may silently gesture to offer each other views of the screen or surrender control of the mouse pointer device or silently offer a collaborator the keyboard. Similarly, one partner in a collaborative process may simply give another a quizzical look and keep silent, allowing the other partner to offer new ideas or respond to existing ones.

6.8.1   Non-verbal discourse strategies

Non-verbal behaviours such as silent reading may not easily divulge the learners' progress and intentions. This is because, although it is possible to observe and electronically track what learners are looking at when at the computer and for how long, it is not a totally reliable measure of what learner processes are at work. For example, learners may be deeply engaged in the task or may be daydreaming, browsing or thinking of other tasks or problems when staring at or scrolling through a page.

In some cases, learners engage in inaudible reading in which they read in a mumbled voice. This may be to indicate to the other person that they want to hold space in the conversation until they are finished reading or that they do not want to be interrupted; new information should not be put forward until they are ready. The learner may be reading in detail but, alternatively, he or she may simply be taking a long time to skim and scan.

Wegerif and Dawes (1998) observed three non-collaborative strategies that also may not require discourse or whose underlying motivations be easily interpretable: unilateral action by the child with the mouse; accepting the choice of the most dominant child without supporting reasons; drifting together to one or other choice without debating any of the alternatives.

The importance to learning of paralinguistic strategies such as pointing at a common screen are often overlooked, especially in a CALL context where, for example, computers have been situated in carrels similar to those used for testing and privacy in listening labs. However, if one accepts that students use computers for collaboration and that such collaboration involves paralinguistic interaction, opportunities for such interaction can be defeated by a poor room design and layout of computers (see Example 6.1).

6.8.2   Verbal discourse strategies

The majority of collaborative and non-collaborative interactions are evidenced by verbal discourse and are easily documented. There are many ways of classifying social interactions at the computer. Murillo (1991) found that responses could be divided into the following four categories (paraphrased):

Example 6.1   Organizing the CALL classroom

There are many ways to organize a CALL classroom depending on funds available, the number of computers available (from one at the back of the

U-shaped classroom facing out

U-shaped classroom facing in

classroom to a class set), the shape of the room and so on. Three common examples include:

A traditional lecture classroom in which the focus is on teacher-led discussion at the front of the room.

A U-shaped classroom facing in so the learners face the teacher, but also have a good view of each other. However, the arrangement requires cabling (power, Internet) problems that may mean a false floor.

A U-shaped classroom facing out allows learners to turn their chairs for presentations or sit around a table for discussions. It is easier in this type of classroom for the teacher to see, at a glance, what each student is doing.

Lecture classroom

- Copying: repeating what was just read or said
- Repeating: repeating language from the screen
- Managing: dealing with the computer, the program and discussing progress made
- Conferring: offering or discussing solutions or a paths to solutions; disagreeing, agreeing, suggesting, explaining, or thinking aloud; spelling; correcting themselves or each other and asking questions

In many cases, Murillo's four categories simply define types of collaboration without examining their quality or the opportunities for SLA.

Examples provided by Tsui (see Quote 6.22) (requesting and accepting/declining requests, challenging other people's point of view) build on those

Quote 6.22 A.B.M. Tsui notes the opportunities for language learning through group work interactions

Group work provides the opportunity to practise a much wider range of speech functions. In lockstep teaching the predominant pattern of interaction is the teacher asking display questions rather than referential questions, students answering questions to display knowledge, and the teacher giving feedback on the answer. There is little opportunity for students to perform other speech functions that are frequently found in genuine communication, for example, requesting and accepting/declining requests, challenging other people's point of view, and so on. As a result, students have little opportunity to develop the kind of conversational skill that is needed outside the classroom. Group work enables students to engage in genuine communication, where the message is more important than the form. As Long and Porter (1985) point out, group work enables learners to develop discourse competence rather than just linguistic competence at the sentence level.

Tsui (1995: 95–6)

Quote 6.23 J.S. Gould on peripheral benefits of peer collaboration, specifically the use of scaffolded instruction:

In most cases, the participants in collaborative talk are of approximately equal status, each able to take the role of either facilitator or student and to benefit accordingly. Typically, the purposes of the peer interaction are achieved when the task is completed, or at least when the student is able to continue with the next step. However, the benefits of collaborative talk need not be limited to the function of facilitating the achievement of the task. Where one of the participants has greater expertise than the other, he or she can engage in interaction with the learner about the task with the deliberate intention of enabling the learner to acquire some procedure, knowledge, or skill that will be useful in other situations beyond that in which he or she is currently engaged.

Gould (1996: 97)

put forward by Murillo (1991) by adding a perspective of critical thinking to group work.

The next section identifies challenges to collaboration. General challenges are explored before going on to discuss specific challenges to collaboration in a CALL context.

6.9 Challenges to collaboration

This chapter's review of the literature points mostly to the benefits of collaboration. With few exceptions, the authors and researchers cited so far are almost uniformly in favour of collaboration or cooperation as a method of learning and offer no criticisms. What is lacking is an objective assessment of the challenges of collaboration. These challenges can be classified into two types: the general problems of collaboration in a language learning setting and the challenges to collaboration when learners work collaboratively at a task at the computer. In some cases, these challenges are not disadvantages of collaboration itself, but rather constraints on the potential of the teacher to foster collaboration in certain cultural contexts or with certain types of learners. However, the consequent effect of discouraging learning is generally the same.

6.9.1 General problems of collaboration in a language learning setting

Some researchers offer perspectives on the negative aspects of collaboration. Kinsella and Sherak (1998), discussing learners who have moved to a new country and are learning a new language say that they may be insecure about collaborative situations for the simple reason that they have performed well in competitive-orientated classrooms where collaboration has not been the norm.

Other perceived problems with collaboration include:

- the lack of input from some collaborative group members
- the inability of some teachers or learners to facilitate properly collaborative instruction to ensure the group remains on task
- the fact that collaborative learning may not (in the view of some teachers) seem an economical use of time
- teacher insecurity over unpredictable outcomes

This last point is a concern among some new teachers as well as a culturally specific concern of other teachers. While teaching at the Canada China Language Center in Beijing (1989–92) I noted the reluctance of experienced Chinese colleagues to use small group and open-ended activities. Their privately stated concern was that such activities produce questions the teacher might be unable to answer; the teacher would be embarrassed and 'lose face' with the students. Clearly skills training in collaborative approaches needs to encompass teachers as well as learners if everyone is to benefit from the opportunities that are presented in learning together.

Quote 6.24 D. Johnson and R. Johnson on skills that need to be taught to cooperative learners:

1. Forming: the bottom-line skills needed to establish a functioning cooperative group.
2. Functioning: The skills needed to manage to accomplish a group task and maintain effective work relationships.
3. Formulating: the skills needed to build deeper level understanding of the material studied; to stimulate reasoning strategies and to maximize mastery of the material.
4. Fermenting: The skills needed to stimulate reconceptualization of the material covered, search for new information and to communicate the rationale behind one's conclusions.

Johnson and Johnson (1984: 45)

Johnson and Johnson (1984) suggest that learners need to be taught cooperative skills. However, some learners will come by skills naturally or through prior experiences, and collaborative group members may induct others into collaborative skills. In some cases, the teacher may need to intervene if the learners are clearly not able to progress and accomplish the tasks and goals, but the process of acquiring such social skills may also provide valuable opportunities for negotiation of meaning. As Breen (1998) notes: 'The very salience of social trouble in the discourse will alert learners' attention to it while possibly involving the teacher and learners in exactly the kind of resolution work that may be directly beneficial to language learning' (p. 129). In other words, simply being involved in the challenges associated with collaboration may provide learners with opportunities to improve their language.

6.10   Challenges to collaboration in a CALL context

Challenges to collaboration in a CALL context are problems that arise when the aim of the teacher (although not necessarily of the learner) is to promote language learning at the computer. The learner need not be aware of the teacher's objectives to still benefit from the activity. For example, the learner may perceive the objective to play and win a game, when the teacher sees the objective of getting the learners to use language associated with the game's context, e.g. learning about money when playing the board game *Monopoly*.

It has already been mentioned that a wide range of cognitive strategies is used in collaborative learning discussions. For example, Sharan and Shachar (1988) offer the following (paraphrased):

1. Explain with evidence
2. Generalize
3. Offer a concrete example
4. Offer an unstructured idea
5. Organize ideas
6. Present a hypothesis or idea
7. Repeat
8. Repeat with expansion
9. Take a stand (pp. 60–4)

However, each of the above nine points presents only positive and productive aspects of discourse when, in fact, much discourse is not productive at all; participants in a collaborative discussion engage in many negative behaviours that are either counter-productive or peripheral to a collaborative task. This is partly because their individual goals do not always match the goals of the task or the goals of the teacher or the collaborative method by which they are expected to pursue it.

> **Quote 6.25** M. Breen on learner objectives in discourse:
>
> Learners selectively work through the discourse of the classroom not only as discursive practitioners within the immediate lesson but also on the basis of how they judge which social practices are appropriate in the particular classroom group. Their selective participation and the judgments on which they base it are derived from their definition of the particular teaching–learning situation and from their experience with other realms of discourse beyond the classroom. Learners therefore navigate the discourse in two constantly interweaving ways: for learning purposes and for social purposes. Differential outcomes from lessons may reflect the fact that learners will differ in their abilities to balance these two priorities and, crucially, in their relative allocation of attention to them.
>
> Breen (1998: 128)

Several factors which impact on the opportunities for collaboration include:

- learner characteristics may make the collaborating learners incompatible
- the goals/objectives of the program may discourage collaboration
- the pedagogical model may be overly behaviourist

- the methods of navigating the information (related to the structure and format) may be too obscure or difficult
- the content, or knowledge base, of the learning materials may discourage collaboration if it is too far above or too far beneath the level of the majority of the learners

Each of the above can be considered challenges to collaboration. In terms of the first point above, McConnell (1994) (see Section 6.6) has already noted a need for *willingness* to make cooperation work; a lack of willingness constitutes one challenge to collaboration in a CALL context and many other positive variables can be inverted to explain challenges in a collaborative situation.

Quote 6.26 R. Wegerif and L. Dawes on challenges to collaborative learning:

- One person appointed themselves [*sic*] leader, sitting centrally to the keyboard, and reading from the screen. They called out instantaneous responses to questions, and keyed them in. Other members of the group would agree, or start a futile 'Yes it is'/'No it isn't' exchange
- Children with home computers would become impatient with others who had no keyboard skills, and would again dominate both the keyboard and the decision taking. Alternatively, a quiet but literate child would work as secretary to a dictator.
- Less confident children would watch, agree, or withdraw, contributing little. If things subsequently seemed to go wrong, they were castigated for 'not helping'.
- Friends at work together simply agreed with one another. Other children always disagreed with whatever was suggested, but offered no alternatives.
- The content of the talk was observed to be directed towards a reestablishment of the children's friendship groups, or otherwise
- The most heated discussions were to do with who was seated where, who pressed the next key, and so on. Children spent a lot of time talking about how to make the task of actually operating the computer 'fair', an impossibility, but of great importance to them
- Talk became general and relaxed if the computer was sited out of the teachers' natural range. This was possibly because children realized that concentrating on the work would mean that their long-awaited turn at the computer would be over sooner and so they chatted about other things
- Children competed within the group, using the computer program as a game of some sort. Useless disputes ensued without a constructive outcome

Wegerif and Dawes (1998: 11)

Wegerif and Dawes (1998) summarize eight challenges to learning in groups based on a study conducted with primary school children. The first four of these points are generally applicable to learners of all ages, but the last four points are likely to be a focus of primary school classrooms only. However, some negative behaviours associated with primary school students unfortunately do not change in some individuals as they grow older.

> **Quote 6.27** J.C. Richards and R.W. Schmidt on turn-taking:
>
> Conversation by definition involves two or more people. But the distribution of talking among the participants is not merely random. It is governed by turn-taking norms, conventions which determine who talks, when, and for how long. A speaker with poor management of turn-taking rules is one who 'doesn't let you get a word in edgeways'. A speaker who doesn't contribute to a conversation arouses negative evaluations too, or may make the conversation terminate abruptly.
>
> Richards and Schmidt (1983: 141)

Turn-taking rules vary according to different situations and may be influenced by computer-based interruptions as new information appears on the screen; or inappropriate and unnecessary interruptions, such as flashing screens and senseless noises that disrupt both the collaboration and learning.

6.11 Discourse that evidences challenges to collaboration

Among the ways in which we examine classroom behaviour is through discourse analysis. Discourse analysis looks at classroom talk in linguistic terms through the study of transcripts which typically assign utterances to predetermined categories (after Nunan, 1992a: 3). In examining challenges to collaboration, it is necessary to see how they occur in terms of discourse. On the simplest level, one can try to determine when learners are using discourse to pursue Johnson and Johnson's (1990) *individual* and *competitive* goals instead of *cooperative* (or collaborative) goals.

As noted above (see Section 6.6), Wegerif and Dawes (1998) suggest that a mixture of cooperation and conflict is the best way to promote interaction and note that such discourse is likely to include criticism, explanation, justification, clarification and elaboration. Implicitly, these are all ways in which one learner acknowledges the ideas or presence of another learner.

However, criticisms may be hostile and without any attempt to offer another idea or support. Such criticism is negative in that it deters participation. Wegerif and Dawes's other categories (explanations, justifications, clarifications and elaborations), are basically ways of engaging in collaboration by following McConnell's (1994) hypothesis (see Section 6.6) that collaborative learning serves to make public those parts of our learning which are blind, hidden and unconscious. Therefore, other challenges are built on an *unwillingness* to offer explanations, justifications, clarifications and elaborations.

Based on the ideas elaborated in this chapter, four general social challenges to collaboration can be summarized as:

1. an unwillingness to engage in the activity
2. an unwillingness to accept the collaborative nature of the activity (i.e. pursuing individual or competitive goals)
3. an unwillingness to offer suggestions or explanations
4. an unwillingness to offer or accept justifications, clarifications, elaborations, criticism (i.e. groupthink) with supporting evidence or alternatives

In addition to these social challenges, additional challenges based on the computer include:

5. the complexity of the program's content
6. the navigability of the program's interface
7. the difficulty of program's model of instruction (behaviourist or constructivist)

These last three challenges can be summarized as technical challenges to collaboration. These challenges may either encourage or discourage discourse and SLA as learners perceive them as challenges to be addressed or problems to be avoided. In the next section, these social and technical challenges are expanded upon in terms of verbal and paralinguistic utterances and exchanges that can be coded and analysed.

6.11.1 Analysing discourse

Discourse analysis is a way of looking at records of spoken or written text to see if they suggest that the surface utterances are representative of underlying thinking and learning processes.

Analysing discourse involves transcription notations – writing out the utterances and describing the paralinguistic acts – and interpretive notations, deciding the motivations behind the utterances. Examples of transcription notations are noted below (Figure 6.2), and are followed by a framework of strategies learners use to engage in collaboration, strategies learners use to avoid collaboration and ambiguous strategies which may work either way, depending on the context or the respective attitudes of the learners.

There are many ways to examine discourse, for example, both quantitatively (counting the occurrence of certain phrases) and qualitatively (examining types of expressions). Discourse analysis is flexible and, depending on what the researcher is looking for, a framework of investigation can be newly created or adapted from existing research.

6.11.1.1   Transcription notations

Transcription conventions are important to establish exactly what the researcher is looking for when conducting research. Although there are many systems already in place, a researcher may have to adapt one or more systems to ensure that the conventions cover the aspects of language he or she is interested in. For example, for the same piece of discourse, one researcher might be interested in the significance of emphasis while another might simply be interested in circumlocutions. The goal of any transcription system, or set of conventions, is to ensure an accurate portrayal of the language being used to the extent that another researcher using the same conventions and looking at the same data would reach the same conclusions.

Symbol	Explanation
,	A normal pause as one would expect in speech.
...	A short pause of hesitation.
((pause))	A pause of longer duration than a hesitation but within the same utterance.
[ ]	Overlapping utterances, usually signalling an interruption
(( ))	Descriptions of paralinguistic and non-verbal behaviours such as ((pointing)) and ((laughing)).
((reading))	Reading aloud from the screen.
((inaudible))	An unintelligible utterance in which the subjects may be speaking to themselves and/or holding space in the conversation.
A P R I L	All caps with spaces indicate spelling a word aloud, either for himself/herself or for other learners.
I think he meant	Sentences lacking a comma, final ellipsis, full stop or question mark indicates an utterance interrupted by the speaker himself/herself.

Figure 6.2   **Sample transcription notations for scoring discourse**

In examining a text in terms of collaboration, it is necessary to identify those utterances and exchanges that exhibit characteristics of different strategies. These include strategies learners use to engage in collaboration, strategies learners use to avoid collaboration and ambiguous strategies which may be used either to engage in, or to avoid, collaboration.

Ambiguous strategies are the most problematical in terms of strategy identification as both their intentions and effects may differ in any situation. For example, a learner might employ humour to dispel tension, but his or her interlocutor might perceive it either as an attempt to avoid the task or to engage in lateral thinking. The reverse might as easily be true.

The following is a coding system for these various strategies developed after consideration of one by Kumpulainen and Wray (1999):

6.11.1.2   A framework for coding discourse strategies

The following framework is used to define the strategies used by subjects to collaborate and to avoid collaboration as well as those strategies which are ambiguous.

Strategies used in collaboration

- *Determine participants' expertise* (DE): determining expertise is classified as a collaborative strategy because it helps to clarify what each partner knows or does not know about a task. Learners who start off by determining expertise are better able to collaborate because they are better positioned to evaluate what they and the other person knows. If a partner indicates that he or she does not know or understand some part of the text or process, it leaves both partners more open to explore the text or process together.

- *Explain the text/task/ideas* (ET): explaining the text, the task and the ideas in a collaborative situation helps provide opportunities for negotiation of meaning and create a common understanding. If learners in a collaborative situation do not arrive at a common understanding of the text, the task and the ideas behind what they are studying, they are likely to work at cross-purposes.

- *Offer suggestions* (OS): offering suggestions is often marked by the phrase *I think*. A suggestion differs from a judgement in that the former offers a qualification and invites comment, while a judgement is presented as a final word on a subject.

- *Direct attention* (DX): directing attention to text or images on the computer screen or to something else such as the keyboard or mouse is classified as a collaborative strategy because it is a strategy which tries to involve one's partner in some aspect of the program.

- *Solicit suggestions/support* (SS): soliciting suggestions and support are collaborative actions because they directly ask one's partner's involvement.
- *Solicit clarification* (SC): soliciting clarification occurs when one learner asks the other for more information on a statement. It is a collaborative strategy essential to negotiation of meaning.
- *Signal interest in/show support of another's ideas* (SI): signalling interest or showing support of another's ideas are collaborative strategies that allow the learners to indicate a common direction in what they are doing or discussing.
- *Solicit support for or suggest actions* (SA): soliciting support for or suggesting actions most often occur when one learner is navigating or about to navigate in the program. Soliciting support is typically marked by phrases such as, *should we . . ., shall I . . .* and so on and is collaborative because it gives the partner a chance to discuss the working process.

Social strategies learners use to avoid collaboration

- *Ignore the test/task* (IT): ignoring the test or a task is strategy used to avoid collaboration because it often marks a learner's preference for pursuing individualistic or competitive goals. In some cases, the task may be too difficult for the learner, but not to even try to solicit suggestions signals a failure to take advantage of the collaborative partner's skills and makes ignoring the task a sign of avoiding collaboration.
- *Interrupt* (IR): interrupting is a strategy that avoids collaboration because it signals that one learner does not value what the other learner wants to say. In some cases, interrupting may be seen as a supportive strategy if, for example, one interrupts to supply information one is struggling to recall or formulate, but such interruptions are usually signalled by a pause in the speech by the other speaker. Such interruptions can be classified as offering suggestions (OS).
- *Ignore ideas* (II): ignoring ideas signals that one learner does not value what the other learner wants to say and does not care to discuss it. An idea might be a suggested answer or a suggested action, such as directing attention to something on-screen.
- *Offer judgements* (OJ): judgements are statements without qualifying phrases such as *I think. . . .* Sometimes a judgement is presented as a learner's simple statement of a fact, but it is often a strategy that avoids collaboration because judgements to not invite the collaborative partner to present opinions or negotiate meaning.

Ambiguous strategies in collaboration

- *Offer humour* (OH): in addition to the above methods of engaging in and avoiding collaboration are the sometimes negative and sometimes positive aspects of humour. Humour can be used negatively as an avoidance strategy or positively as a way of soliciting lateral thinking, smoothing social relations and dispelling tension. Humour may offer both negative and positive aspects depending on the attitudes of the participants towards the humour. A subject's laughter may be one form of humour in that it often serves to modify a serious statement, making it less so.

- *Read aloud* (RA): reading aloud may be a neutral strategy for holding space in the conversation while one learner reads what is on the screen or it may be a collaborative strategy for dictating or keeping the partner informed at each stage of learning. As it is difficult to assess the first learner's intention and the second learner's perception, reading aloud is classified as an ambiguous strategy.

A summary of the coding of discourse strategies

Strategies used in collaboration	
DE	• Determine participants' expertise
ET	• Explain the text/task/ideas
OS	• Offer suggestions
DX	• Direct attention
SS	• Solicit suggestions/support
SC	• Solicit clarification
SI	• Signal interest in/show support of another's ideas
SA	• Solicit support for or suggest actions
Social strategies learners use to avoid collaboration	
IT	• Ignore the text/task
IR	• Interrupt
II	• Ignore ideas
OJ	• Offer judgements
Ambiguous strategies in collaboration	
OH	• Offer humour
RA	• Read aloud

Figure 6.3   **Coding of the investigation's discourse strategies**

Summary

Defining collaboration is difficult because the term is used in different ways by different researchers, and is sometimes used in different ways by the same researchers. This chapter provided examples of collaborative issues including what several authors recommend to foster aims of promoting awareness and skill development, achieving pedagogical objectives, improving literacy and promoting language acquisition. The concept of collaboration was compared with other terms such as cooperation and teamwork. A workable definition of collaboration is put forward by Dillenbourgh *et al.* (1995), 'a coordinated, synchronous activity that is the result of a continued attempt to construct and maintain a shared conception of a problem' (p. 189). Although such a definition suggests a constructivist model of learning, it was pointed out that studies using a behaviourist model of learning often featured the use of the same collaborative approach.

Collaboration at the computer can be evidenced through discourse. Such discourse can show the strategies learners use to address and avoid a range of challenges to collaboration.

Further reading

Tsui, A.B.M. (1994) *English Conversation*. Oxford: Oxford University Press. – This book's title is somewhat deceptive; it deals with discourse analysis, presenting several approaches in a clear and logical fashion.

Chapter 7

Defining a model of CALL

This chapter explains the role of the computer and multimedia in language learning – more specifically, CALL – by examining a traditional model of the many factors which influence learning in the language classroom. This traditional model by Dunkin and Biddle (1974) is examined in terms of how it can and cannot accommodate CALL. Based on the differences, a new model for learning with CALL is offered. Collaboration is explored in terms of the challenges raised by learners themselves (social challenges) and challenges specific to the computer and CALL programs (technical challenges).

The principal concerns of this chapter can be summarized by the following three questions:

- What variables are traditionally involved in the educational process?
- How do these variables differ in CALL materials?
- How can CALL be portrayed in a model?

7.1 Defining model

The introduction of the computer into the classroom (in some cases, some places) has fostered changes to the practice of the teaching and learning of languages and related subjects, such as literature. Chapter 4 outlined new ways of looking at the study of literature taking into consideration the influence of emerging technologies, specifically the computer's provision of hypertext, hypermedia and multimedia. Of particular interest to CALL research is the ability of multimedia to increase comprehensible input and offer opportunities for comprehensible output thus fostering SLA, as outlined in Chapter 5. Chapter 6 outlined ideas to do with collaboration, a key construct in understanding opportunities for learning with CALL.

In order to elucidate the relationship between CALL and SLA, it is necessary to construct a model. A model is a pictorial representation of a metaphor; a way of looking at and understanding the world. A model can be used as a tool to examine processes and describe the ways in which teaching and learning may take place or may be improved upon.

New models arise over time as the factors within a process change or the understanding of the processes the model describes are themselves revised. Dunkin and Biddle (1974) note that there appears to be a never-ending supply of models but go on to suggest that there are good reasons for such being the case, 'teaching is a complex activity that reflects many factors. Most of these relationships have not been adequately studied, nor indeed do we always have an agreed-upon set of terms with which to express them' (p. 31). The idea of the model is further defined through examples over the course of this chapter.

This chapter first considers a model of a traditional view of what takes place in the classroom and examines how this model fits and does not fit CALL in general. But before considering a suitable model for the classroom, problems in creating CALL models are reviewed.

7.1.1   Problems in creating CALL models

There are problems inherent in any attempt to create a model for CALL in the classroom. One is the expansive scope of what is considered to be within the realm of CALL processes, especially considering the broad definition for CALL that takes into consideration its changing nature: *any process in which a learner uses a computer and, as a result, improves his or her language.* A model for CALL either has to accommodate this general definition or more narrowly define a set of significant aspects of CALL that might be considered. The model offered later in this chapter attempts to define CALL in terms of classroom practice rather than also deal with learners using CALL software in other contexts, such as at home or as an activity peripheral to another subject.

7.2   The need for a CALL model

The question of whether or not CALL is intrinsically different from traditional language teaching and learning has been addressed to a small degree in Chapter 2 through an examination of several historically innovative software programs. The fact that CALL is different from prior approaches and materials is also pointed out by Williams (1998) who argues that the potential for teaching and learning through CALL has not been tapped.

> **Quote 7.1** N. Williams on the need for reviews of the particular nature of CALL technology:
>
> Hypermedia allows everything to be linked to everything, just like human imagination. But teaching (as opposed to learning) requires rather narrower perspectives. Whilst the information within educational multimedia is extensive, attractive and complex, the interactions with and within that information, allowed by the authors of such systems, fail to realize the educational potential of the medium. We need more radical reviews of what learning might be through multimedia, combined with innovation in design (Stringer, 1997), to realize more fully the true potential for educational interaction in multimedia.
>
> Williams (1998: 170)

Creating a new model requires decisions on the range and types of variables that need to be considered. The first task in describing a new model for CALL is to identify a current model for teaching and learning and examine what variables might or might not need to be reassessed.

7.3   A model of current non-CALL language learning

Many authors have attempted to isolate the variables involved in learning and teaching language. Spolsky (1987), for example, lists 74 variables affecting learning. Such a high number of variables makes it difficult to isolate any one variable for careful consideration in, for example, an experimental examination of the variables influence on learning.

Further reading

Spolsky, B. (1987) *Conditions for second language learning: introduction to a general theory.* Oxford: Oxford University Press. – Although Spolsky does not focus on CALL, the book is important for delineating some of the factors that affect both teaching and learning. It should be a required text for educational software designers.

A general model that includes and adds to Breen's (1998) criteria (see Quote 7.2) is Dunkin and Biddle's (1974) model identifying aspects that might be studied in a language classroom.

Quote 7.2 M. Breen (1998) on variables affecting learning:

Any adequate theory of Second-language Acquisition (SLA) has to account for three key factors and, crucially, their interrelationship. These are: 1. what the learner brings or contributes to the process, from the innate predispositions, through the activation of certain psychological processes such as attention or memory, and through affective involvement in the process, to strategic behavior which may render the process more manageable and unthreatening; 2. the nature of the actual language learning process; and 3. the outcomes from the process in terms of linguistic or, more broadly, communicative competence in the target language.

Breen (1998: 116)

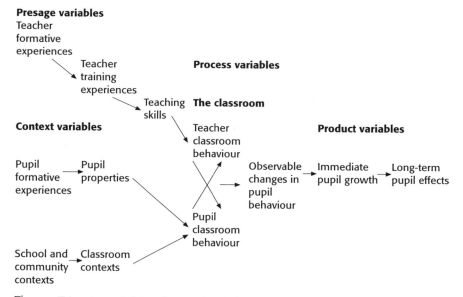

Figure 7.1   **A model for the study of classroom teaching**
(after Duncan and Biddle, 1974: 38)

The above model has been simplified by eliminating Dunkin and Biddle's examples: e.g. under *Teacher formative experiences*, they list *social class*, *age* and *sex* followed by an ellipsis. Dunkin and Biddle's model is a general one, in the sense that it covers all formal instruction, not just language teaching. The following sections examine Dunkin and Biddle's model in terms of its ability to accommodate CALL and outlines the differences that lead to a new model suitable for CALL.

7.4   Dunkin and Biddle's model in a CALL context

This section considers Dunkin and Biddle's model by reflecting how factors within the model change in a CALL context.

There are two ways of considering CALL: either as a supplementary learning material in which case CALL simply falls under the *Classroom contexts* heading in Dunkin and Biddle's model, or as an autonomous process: a kind of virtual teacher. (I do not ask whether a machine can, independent of any human teacher intervention, teach language; there is so far no empirical evidence of a learner completely acquiring a second language through CALL alone, although is an interesting area for a study; the task would be to create or assemble a comprehensive CALL software program(s) for a language unknown to the teacher, the learner and the community, such as Swahili in rural Saskatchewan.) Instead, it is assumed that the role of CALL is to help foster language learning by creating conditions that make some aspects of language learning easier.

However, it is also necessary to accept that the computer sometimes assumes functions beyond traditional materials and accept that its interactivity mirrors at least some of the functions of the teacher, especially when it is used autonomously, even though it cannot pretend to duplicate the teacher's range. It is with this view of CALL that Dunkin and Biddle's model is examined.

In Dunkin and Biddle's model, there are aspects that are broadly fixed in both non-CALL environments and CALL environments:

- School, community and classroom contexts
- Product variables of immediate pupil growth and long-term pupil effects.

School, community and classroom contexts are likely to change only in the sense that some learners presumably encounter computers and computer software well ahead of their introduction into the classroom; or through the adoption of a virtual classroom model; the idea of the virtual classroom is expanded upon in section 7.4.2 below. This view, as already mentioned, needs to assume that CALL materials are more than just a classroom context. Through exposure to computers and computer software, learners are prepared for the ensuing classroom variables; in some cases, they are given insight into what Dunkin and Biddle consider the *Presage variables*, discussed below.

The other factor unlikely to undergo significant change is Dunkin and Biddle's *Product variables* of *Immediate pupil growth* and *Long-term pupil effects*, although the ways of measuring such changes, both by the teacher and the learner, are likely to evolve, for example, through computer-adaptive testing programs in which the computer evaluates a learner's early performance in subtests and builds fuller tests, as well as scoring and tracking progress through learning programs.

The factors that are more likely to change are discussed and illustrated in a revised model based on that by Dunkin and Biddle.

Further reading

Rudner, L.M. (1998) *An On-line, Interactive, Computer Adaptive Testing Tutorial.* ERIC Clearinghouse on Assessment and Evaluation *http://ericae.net/scripts/cat* – This interactive tutorial explains the ideas and practicalities of computer-adaptive testing (CAT).

7.4.1 Presage variables

Presage variables include *Teacher formative experiences, Teacher training experiences* and *Teaching skills*. Earlier discussion considered whether or not software programs take the place of the teacher. It has already been pointed out (see Sections 4.9 and 5.4) that software programs might in some cases, with different emphasis, function as a virtual teacher, a teacher's helper, a teaching tool and a learning tool. Sloane (1990) as well as Boyd and Mitchell (1992) take a discourse approach and consider CALL a conversational activity shared among the learner, the machine tutor (i.e. computer program) and the educator/developer. But in many CALL programs, Dunkin and Biddle's teacher attributes are generally subsumed under the consideration of the program taking the place of the teacher. This being the case, the following shifts can be assumed:

Presage variables	Presage variables in a CALL context
Teacher formative experiences	Materials developers' collective experiences
Teacher training experiences	Ideas of models of instruction
Teacher properties	Technical affordances of the program

Figure 7.2 **Shifts in presage variables**
(Dunkin and Biddle, 1974)

In examining these shifts, we can see that Dunkin and Biddle (1974) assume that an individual teacher comes to the classroom with a wide range of experiences and skills. *Teacher formative experiences* include factors such as those experienced because of social class and sex. They also list age, race and physical appearance to illustrate the fact that *everything* about a teacher is inclined to be involved in how the teacher is 'likely to be treated differently both within and without the school' (p. 39). In terms of a CALL context, the formative experiences are likely to be homogenized into the collective experiences of the materials developers as many software developers, marketing executives are likely to be involved in any decisions in the creation of a CALL program.

Teacher training experiences refers to the formal education that a teacher receives from both academic institutions (i.e. teacher colleges, universities) and training in school placements. Dunkin and Biddle (1974) note that these include 'courses taken, the attitudes of instructors, experiences during practice teaching and in-service postgraduate education, if any' (p. 39). In the CALL context, again because of the collective nature of the creation of CALL materials, these experiences are likely to be homogenized into particular ideas of models of instruction. That is, the software developers and other personnel involved in the process will agree on a set way of organizing the approach to learning based on their perception of what is an appropriate model.

Teacher properties refers to psychological traits, motives, abilities and attitudes and rely on what Dunkin and Biddle (1974) note as 'the common view that teaching is largely a matter of personal relationships and personality, that such effects as teachers have are functions of their personalities (Nuthall, 1972, personal communication)' (p. 40). How a CALL context might have a 'personality' is difficult to assess, although Microsoft *Windows* and Apple *Macintosh* interfaces are often characterized as each having a different 'feel' and there are many aspects of an interface which can be measured in degrees of user-friendliness.

In a CALL environment, the feel or user-friendliness of the program is often determined by the affordances of the program (i.e. what the program is or appears to be capable of doing in terms of both intended and unintended functions) and how easy or difficult it is to understand these affordances. In general, the trend in CALL has been always to make interfaces and the information within them as easy to understand as possible. However, it may be that this does not reflect good teaching practice or real-life situations in which teachers and other interlocutors are likely to present information in obscure or veiled ways to encourage thinking on the part of the learner.

A CALL program is likely implicitly to state 'I have the answers to your questions; just click here.' A teacher is more likely to say, 'What do *you* think the answer might be?' or 'Why do you ask *this* question?' As already mentioned, it is difficult for computers to deal with ambiguous learner input, but this is an area of research that needs to be further investigated.

7.4.2   Context variables

Dunkin and Biddle's context variables of *Pupil formative experiences* and *Pupil properties* are different in a CALL environment because many learners are likely at least to come into contact with computers, if not CALL, before coming to school. In this way, they are pre-socialized into the idea and methods of learning with computers and develop their own competencies and learning strategies. Learners who bring computer and CALL formative experiences and properties to the classroom assist in defining the variables of a new model of learning because they see using the computer as something that is distinctly different from traditional classroom instruction.

This is in contrast to the experience of older learners, as explained by Dillenbourg (1992).

Quote 7.3   P. Dillenbourg on factors in a learning context:

The context of a learning activity is defined by various factors. Replacing the blackboard by a keyboard modifies one of these factors. Replacing the teacher by a computer and suppressing the other learners constitute more important changes. But on the other hand, some factors do not change. The 'scholastic' label of the activity often remains. Many scholastic concepts contribute to make the two contexts closer: exercises, errors, scores, tests, definitions . . .

And finally, the distribution of educational roles is not modified: with most ECSs (Educational Computing Systems), there is still an ignorant agent that has to learn and a knowledgeable agent that has to 'communicate' (in Wenger's sense) its knowledge.

The similarities between learning in a classroom and learning with a computerized teacher (sometimes in a classroom) mean that there is some overlap between the learner's respective models of learning interaction. The extent of this overlap determines the transfer process. For instance, device-dependent features of behavior will probably not be transferred: most learners know for instance that they cannot communicate with a computer by using the same language as they use with a teacher. But they may transfer more device-independent pieces of knowledge such as the necessity of systematic practice to reinforce newly acquired skills. Such transferable rules are more related to how knowledge is acquired, i.e. to the student's model of learning.

Dillenbourg (1992: 188)

Such transfer – or lack of transfer – may limit the variables of a new model because the learner may be unable or unwilling to accept new learning ideas and practices. This has certainly been the case with a generation of people who have pronounced themselves computer-phobic; but such a phobia is generally unknown among young children who have grown up with computers and take them for granted. Young learners are more willing to accept new models of learning because they are not conditioned into regarding the existing model (as described by Dunkin and Biddle, 1974) as a so-called 'right' or 'normal' way of doing things.

7.4.3   Process variables

It is within the area of *Process variables* that the sharpest differences between Dunkin and Biddle's model and a CALL model are apparent. To explore these differences, we need to consider various views of CALL and how they fit into Dunkin and Biddle's *Teacher classroom behaviour* and *Pupil classroom behaviour.*

7.5   Various views of CALL

As noted earlier, it is difficult to come to concise definition of CALL which does not lapse into generalities. Even the use of terms can be confusing: Computer-assisted Learning (CAL), Computer-based Learning (CBL), Computer-aided Instruction (CAI) and so on. Blease (1986) uses the term CAL and divides it into the following categories: by subject; by mode of presentation (relations between the teacher, learner and computer); by internal technique (models, simulations, chance and probability, information retrieval); by educational paradigm (instructional, revelatory, conjectural, emancipatory [in this last mode, there is a differentiation between what can be called authentic and inauthentic labour – the tasks which are related directly to learning or not at all]); by psychological theory and by clarity of structure (interface).

But depending on one's vantage point, these factors can shift. Morariu (1988) (see Quote 7.4) suggests four other factors from the point of view of the design of the learning environment that are not explicit in Dunkin and Biddle's model.

Morariu (1988) suggests that CALL materials' developers should decide where in Bloom's (1956) taxonomy of questions learners should be operating. When learners take in information, they use various strategies to make sense of it. These strategies may correspond to levels of questions or thinking outlined by Bloom (1956) in his *Taxonomy of Questions*. These questions range from low level knowledge and factual levels to higher levels of analysis and evaluation. Strategies, such as skimming and scanning allow learners to answer lower level questions while higher level strategies, such as reading for attitude, allow learners to answer higher level questions and, generally, to think in greater depth about a text.

Quote 7.4   **J. Morariu on the design of learning environments:**

- Goals/Objectives. Stated in behavioral terms, a full breakdown of the context and measurable outcomes for the entire instructional environment.
- Navigation. The user interface design that defines how the learner can move through the system (e.g. Are pre-determined 'tours' provided? How does the learner know where he/she is? Can the path be retraced easily? Are graphic icons used for browsing/selecting information or do users need to type key words?)
- Structure. The overall organization of the information (e.g. hierarchical with topics and sub-topics, associative with word/icon links).
- Format. Media for presenting the content/data (e.g. text, graphics, animation, audio, still images, motion video).

Morariu (1988: 18–19)

Concept 7.1   **H. Bloom's Taxonomy of questions**

Bloom believed that 95 per cent of all classroom questions were at the low level of checking for learner memorization of knowledge. He considered that questions could be classified in terms of complexity from the low recall level of knowledge to the advanced level of evaluation.

- **Knowledge**
  - remembering
  - memorizing
  - recognizing
  - recalling identification and
  - recall of information
    - Who, what, when, where, how . . . ?
    - Describe
- **Comprehension**
  - interpreting
  - translating from one medium to another
  - describing in one's own words
  - organization and selection of facts and ideas
    - Retell . . .

- **Application**
  - problem solving
  - applying information to produce some result
  - use of facts, rules and principles
    - How is . . . an example of . . . ?
    - How is . . . related to . . . ?
    - Why is . . . significant?
- **Analysis**
  - subdividing something to show how it is put together
  - finding the underlying structure of a communication
  - identifying motives
  - separation of a whole into component parts
    - What are the parts or features of . . . ?
    - Classify . . . according to . . .
    - Outline/diagram . . .
    - How does . . . compare/contrast with . . . ?
    - What evidence can you list for . . . ?
- **Synthesis**
  - creating a unique, original product that may be in verbal form or may be a physical object
  - combination of ideas to form a new whole
    - What would you predict/infer from . . . ?
    - What ideas can you add to . . . ?
    - How would you create/design a new . . . ?
    - What might happen if you combined . . . ?
    - What solutions would you suggest for . . . ?
- **Evaluation**
  - making value decisions about issues
  - resolving controversies or differences of opinion
  - development of opinions, judgements or decisions
    - Do you agree . . . ?
    - What do you think about . . . ?
    - What is the most important . . . ?
    - Place the following in order of priority . . .
    - How would you decide about . . . ?
    - What criteria would you use to assess . . . ?

Bloom (1956)

In a CALL program, it is important to have information structured on a series of levels encouraging readers operating at various levels, at any point, to delve deeper into explanations of the content. It is also important that programs challenge students to perform at higher levels within Bloom's (1956) taxonomy. For example, a program presenting vocabulary for shopping might allow learners to follow hyperlinks to delve deeper into more complex expressions and vocabulary. Such a program might also ask learners to recall information but also to apply what they have learned to new situations and generate their own rules about the grammatical rules that are involved.

7.6 Teacher and pupil classroom behaviour: activities used in CALL

Computers inherently allow for a greater autonomy because, unlike a teacher, they are available beyond the time and space confines of the classroom; a learner who wishes to revisit and extend his or her learning at any time or place (that is, any place with a computer) has potentially rich resource with which to do so. CALL resources are extremely limited when compared to a well-qualified teacher but, as already discussed in Chapter 4, in many cases they far exceed what is available from a textbook. Dunkin and Biddle's *Teacher behaviour* is likely to be considered *Program Interface* which also serves to govern learner behaviour to the extent that a CALL interface provides different kinds of tasks and encourages learner behaviours such as strategies and role identification.

The range of tasks and exercises available in CALL can be organized into various taxonomies based on the stated focus of the software (e.g. grammar, vocabulary, fluency), targeted language skills (e.g. reading, writing, speaking and/or listening), Bloom's (1956) levels of questions and learner characteristics based on age, gender and level (e.g. beginner, intermediate, advanced). But a more general way of envisaging what goes on at the computer can be based on the degree of involvement with which learners access information. This measure can be seen within a continuum of locus of control.

7.6.1 Locus of control

Locus of control refers to the continuum between the program's and the learner's responsibility for decisions about the outcomes, sequence of learning, learner interactions and even the content. Jonnassen, Wilson, Wang and Grabinger (1993) see the distal ends of the continuum as representing objectivist and constructivist orientations towards learning. Another view is found in Chandler's (1984) model (Figure 7.3 below) in which *Tutorial* (and in some cases, *Games*) represents a behaviourist model of instruction in which collaboration and negotiation of meaning are not encouraged. Instead, emphasis rests on individualistic and competitive goals. *Simulation games* and *Experimental simulations* are more likely to fall into a constructivist model of instruction that acknowledges that learning best takes place when learners struggle with information while trying to fit it into a meaningful schema.

Chandler's categories of content-free tools and programming languages may be seen as neutral in terms of a model, although they are likely to be combined with tasks and used in a classroom in a constructivist approach to learning.

Chandler (1984) arranges types of CAI/CALL activities into the following table:

Locus of control

Program ←——→ User

Tutorial	Games	Simulation games	Experimental simulations	Content-free tools	Programming languages
Programmed instruction Drill and practice	Computer as player or referee	Computer as game-world: e.g. Empire-style games and the adventure genre	Mathematically based models of processes such as scientific experiments	Word-processors sound and graphics manipulators databases scientific instruments control technology	Logo BASIC Smalltalk
Hospital model: User as patient	**Funfair model:** User as emulator	**Drama model:** User as role-player	**Laboratory model:** User as tester	**Resource centre model:** User as artist or researcher	**Workshop model:** User as inventor

Figure 7.3 **The locus of control in CAI**
(Chandler, 1984: 8)

Perhaps too late for Chandler's model and Hannafin's observations is the increasingly popular use of the Internet for various forms of learning and discourse, summarized by Turkle (1995) and Seaton (1993). Also not specified in Chandler's model is the extent to which various programs can be used to foster language learning. That is, software programs in which learners develop their language as an activity peripheral to the completion of other tasks such as the study of literature, science, mathematics and other more specialized topics.

7.6.2   Observable changes in pupil behaviour

Changes in learner behaviour are likely, in many cases, to remain constant but what differs between Dunkin and Biddle's model and a CALL model is *what* is measured and *how* it is measured. CALL essentially presents different kinds of language learning opportunities from those available in a traditional classroom. There are also more opportunities for learners using the same CALL program to study different things or study the same things in different ways.

Traditional measurement of language learning depends on teacher observations and tests. But CALL programs present many opportunities for different kinds of measurement. For example, a learner's links can be tracked to see the extent of a program a learner explores and the time he or she spends in each section. More importantly, many CALL programs allow for a learner to obtain immediate feedback on progress, that is, an opportunity to observe their own changes in behaviour. This differs from a traditional classroom teacher's random spot-check of learners' comprehension or a final test.

7.7   A virtual classroom

A new context that differs from Dunkin and Biddle's model and incorporates the idea that new technology builds on the already mentioned idea of a virtual teacher to suggest a *virtual classroom*. If the assumption is made that a CALL program can act in some ways as a virtual teacher, instead of simply a supplementary classroom teaching material, CALL in general can be seen to shift many related assumptions about how classroom teaching may be held, including the creation of virtual classrooms where a teacher is not present.

Concept 7.2   **Virtual classroom**

Derycke, Smith and Hemery (1995) credit Roxanne Hiltz as coining the term virtual classroom and explain its qualities:

> The electronic classroom becomes virtual because it can relax the spatial constraints (users at different locations no matter how far apart) and the temporal constraints (users interacting over time via asynchronous communications). In fact the classroom is a virtual place where the learner can find not only pedagogical resources but also human (social) resources to support him/her in the distance learning process (p. 182).

Wesley and Franks (1994) suggest the virtual classroom class is 'an electronic classroom which can be expandable in time, space and content. Its informational territory can grow indefinitely as new knowledge and resources are acquired and as the capabilities of new members are added' (p. 3). They also suggest that the virtual classroom has continuity through time in that it is not limited to conventional academic time segments (semesters, school years, etc.). As successive groups of learners are added, previous learners need not leave, but can remain to continue their learning and to support the learning of the new students: 'Any member of a Virtual Classroom can be in contact with any member of any other connected classroom, whether virtual or physical, so that information and problem-solving capabilities can be mutually shared and reinforced through collaborative interconnection' (p. 9).

Most of these thoughts focus on a distance-learning model using email and the WWW for computer-mediated communication (CMC). However, most CALL materials work in similar ways.

7.8   Aspects of a CALL model

As already mentioned, a model for CALL is difficult to describe in absolute terms, partly because of the many variables involved, partly because of the ever-changing nature of the technology, and also because of the wide variety of applications that are considered as CALL programs. If some CALL programs can be considered to take the place of the teacher, offering many of the functions of the teacher outside of the traditional classroom, then the following adaptation of Dunkin and Biddle's model might better describe what goes on in a CALL environment.

A model for the study of multimedia learning materials

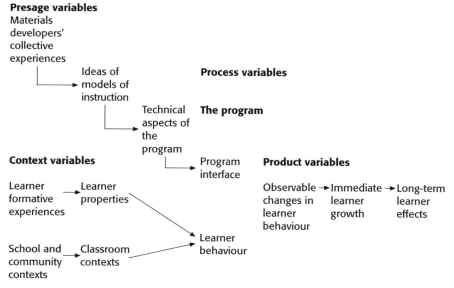

Figure 7.4   **A model for the study of classroom teaching**
(after Duncan and Biddle, 1974: 38)

However, even an adaptation of Dunkin and Biddle's model, simply taking into consideration the differences in a CALL context does not show all the variables mentioned above by Collins (1991) and Derycke, Smith and Hemery (1995).

Although Dunkin and Biddle (1974) refer to challenges among teacher proprieties such as authoritarianism and anxiety, the above adaptation to a CALL context does not address all the challenges in the learning process but serves as a starting point to examine what goes on in CALL contexts. Chapter 8 builds on the model and focuses on some of these challenges.

Summary

This chapter has tried to build on what was illustrated about the special nature of multimedia presented in Chapter 3 to define the idea and constituent parts of a model for CALL. The chapter began by defining the idea of a model, suggesting that it can provide a description of a process that can then be compared to what actually goes on in the classroom.

This chapter also noted that the creation of CALL materials suffers from peripheral problems, including a lack of funds, a lack of expertise and a lack of suitable tools in the form of authoring programs that in turn create problems with defining a suitable model. It was argued that these practical considerations often impede good pedagogy from being included in CALL materials. However, this only strengthens the need for a CALL model that can help to guide materials developers and those who assess CALL materials.

Dunkin and Biddle's (1974) model provides a picture of the scope of the variables currently involved in learning and teaching. However, in a CALL context, presage variables, context variables and process variables all differ. To understand these, various views of CALL were presented along with a summary of activities used in CALL and an overview offered in terms of a model of locus of control at the computer. This model suggests that activities in CALL can range from little or no control on the part of the learner to complete control. It was suggested that the former signals a behaviourist approach while the latter falls into a constructivist approach.

From this discussion the idea of the virtual classroom was introduced followed by a model based on that by Dunkin and Biddle (1974) which accommodates CALL as a kind of virtual teacher. However, while an adaptation of Dunkin and Biddle's model provides a sense of what may change in a CALL context, it does not highlight all the variables in consideration in CALL.

Chapter 8

Theoretical and pedagogical concerns

Computers and multimedia are not seen solely as positive agents of change in the classroom; they also face criticism. In the already mentioned example of young and second-language learners lacking dictionary and library search skills, a multimedia resource may prove to be too seductive an information source. The result is a delay in their learning of traditional and useful information-search skills just as a reliance on electronic calculators has discouraged some learners' basic numeracy skills.

The concerns of this chapter can be expressed in the following two questions:

- What are the problems with computers in general and CALL in particular?
- What solutions are there for these problems?

8.1　Concerns for software development

As already mentioned, traditional materials tend to follow a set scope and sequence that lay down the paths and principles of learning and this is the general route followed by most computer-based learning materials that are, in some cases, adaptations of existing textbooks. However, a strength – and a weakness – of some computer-based materials is their lack of a clearly determined scope and sequence. Instead, they allow individual learners to pursue links which they perceive as being both useful and interesting. This ability to choose a path of learning means that different learners are not all constrained to learn the same materials in the same way but may instead find new answers and solutions to questions and problems.

A now common example of this method of learning is a teacher-assigned task that asks learners to use resources on the WWW. The ever-growing

WWW now consists of billions of individual pages that learners can enter using search engines and links. But learners using the WWW who lack clear direction can often become muddled, distracted and lost in the enormous sea of information.

Quote 8.1 J. Conklin on getting lost:

Along with the power to organize information much more complexly comes the problem of having to know 1. where you are in the network and 2. how to get to some other place that you know (or think) exists in the network. I call this *the disorientation problem*. Of course, one also has a disorientation problem in traditional linear text documents, but in a linear text, the reader has only two options: He can search for the desired text earlier in the text or later in the text. Hypertext offers more degrees of freedom, more dimensions in which one can move, and hence greater potential for the user to become lost or disoriented. In a network of 1000 nodes, information can easily become lost or even forgotten.

Conklin (1987: 38–41)

The same potential for being lost and opportunities for disorientation are found in some computer-based constructivist learning materials that present a wide range of resources and learning materials. For such resources and materials to work, learners may need more guidance in the form of on-screen help that appears not just when asked, but also whenever the learner appears to be stalled or engaging in what are perceived to be unproductive strategies.

A form of this (quite irritating to those more confident in their writing skills) was included in Microsoft *Word 2000* (since discontinued in later versions) and other programs in the form of a so-called 'office assistant'. When one types words that suggest a certain kind of document such as a letter or a memo, the office assistant is automatically prompted and offers advice. A similar tool in the form of a helpful teacher would be useful in many computer-based learning programs to direct learners in need of help.

Another problem is with CALL affordances and misaffordances (see Concept 3.1). Affordances should be made clear: what a program can do and can offer a learner should be made clear to that learner through such devices as maps of the resources, clear menus of options, help buttons and easy navigation options. All affordances should be considered in order to minimize those misaffordances that simply distract the learner.

Example 8.1   Making software more responsive:

Learners often seem unaware of, or unconcerned with, some of the resources that would help them complete a task. Better software programs could perhaps be more active in advertising their resources through timed prompts (i.e. prompts that appear after a certain time of keyboard and mouse inactivity) modelled after the practice of a good teacher such as, *Click here to go to a resource that might help you answer this/find out more about this topic.*

In collaborative situations at the computer, a good interface would be one that prompted learners to share control. This is often done in game software and some web applications that require two or more users to register their names. These names can be used as prompts for computer-directed actions and turn-taking. In an educational program, having learners register would present opportunities for personalized prompts as simple as: *(X student) has given this answer, (insert answer). (Y student) do you agree?*

More sophisticated prompts could use Eliza-based questioning (see Chapter 3) to challenge answers: *Well (X student and Y student), your answer to (insert the question) is (insert the answer). You've worked on it for (insert elapsed time since beginning the task) and still have (insert the time available to complete the task) so you might want to take a little time to think about it now and consider (insert key points about the question, secondary questions, resources within the program). You might also want to check your (inset grammar if problems with the grammar are perceived; insert and/or spelling if problems with spelling are perceived).*

The above pedagogical implications for software development mostly concern perceptions of the technology, but the other aspects could also be addressed in similar Eliza-like fashion by including prompts that ask students about themselves, how they intend to approach the problems before them and what priorities they decide upon.

Quote 8.2   D. Nunan on expectations:

It has been suggested that one reason for the mismatches which occur at the level of program implementation is that program planners and teachers have one set of expectations while learners have others. This seems to be confirmed by studies into learner expectations and preferences as well as by classroom research.

Nunan (1986: 183)

If a computer-based learning environment were to make use of the points outlined above, in particular the use of questions and prompts, a high degree of learner centredness would be possible while, at the same time, guiding learners into good collaborative learning practices. If nothing else, these suggestions warrant further research.

This chapter now turns to the pedagogical implications that occur for classroom practice.

8.2 Pedagogical concerns for classroom practice

This section considers the role of the computer as a kind of virtual teacher, or at least taking the place of the teacher for some functions at some times as learners increasingly engage in autonomous learning. The metaphor of a computer program as a teacher has been criticized (see Williams, 1998). However, it is necessary to assess the role of computers and computer software within the current model of classroom practice. Different software programs have been variously promoted as a virtual teacher, a teacher's helper, a guide, an instrument, a teaching tool and a learning tool.

Quote 8.3 N. Williams criticizes even the metaphor of the computer as a teacher:

there may be learning drawbacks through the use of limited metaphors of computer interaction, and that learners may develop false notions by virtue of the interactions they engage in with computers, because of the reinforcing message of these metaphors. In particular, they may get false ideas of

- what computers are
- information systems and how they might work
- other forms of interaction, such as interaction with other people

Williams (1998: 162–3)

Although it is easy to see where a computer program might assume some of a teacher's functions, there are clearly limits to the ways in which software is able to take the place of a teacher.

Several of these teaching functions outlined by Richards (1997) (see Quote 8.4) are now assumed by software learning packages. The degree to which they are effective depends upon the environment at the computer, the model of instruction for the software, learning and working styles of the participants and other factors.

> **Quote 8.4** J.C. Richards suggests that teaching typically involves the following:
>
> selecting learning activities, preparing students for new learning, presenting learning activities, asking questions, conducting drills, checking students' understanding, providing opportunities for practice of new items, monitoring students' learning, giving feedback on student learning and reviewing and re-teaching when necessary.
>
> Richards (1997: 196)

However, Fox (1991) considers one aspect of the teacher's role, providing feedback, and emphasizes the limitations of the computer:

> **Quote 8.5** J. Fox on computer feedback:
>
> While most computers at present in use for CALL are used for comparatively simple operations, teachers, on the other hand, continually perform operations of amazing, yet somehow invisible, complexity. Tripp (1993) makes this point in relation to the question of teacher professionalism. In the case of L2 learning, one has only to reflect on the decisions teachers have to take when handling errors in the classroom. Do they ignore them? Do they repeat the wrong form with, perhaps, a questioning intonation? Do they model the right form? Do they write examples on the blackboard? The decisions involved in the ongoing process of classroom instruction are extremely complex, though generally unnoticed.
>
> Fox (1991: 222)

Bailin (1995), writing on ICALL, criticizes several aspects of the effort and investment noting the limited effectiveness so far documented and suggesting that teachers do a far better job anyway. He also notes that ICALL has not (to his knowledge) led to fewer teaching hours. However, it may simply be that, in this case, Bailin is too narrow in his definition of the computer as a mechanical servant of the teacher, ignoring its role as a learner's tool for the general enhancement of learning and increased comprehensible input.

As already mentioned in relation to ICALL (see Section 3.2), it is difficult to know whether or not some of the above issues will be addressed in future computer and software developments. But at least an awareness of such issues helps to set the agenda for future research and development of CALL learning materials.

8.2.1   Software objectives

There are still questions whether a behaviourist or a constructivist inter-face better facilitates collaboration at the computer, negotiation of mean-ing and opportunities for SLA. Atkins (1993) suggests, 'The empirical record supports the inductive approach of constructivist design but sug-gests that provision of suitable metacognitive frameworks is problematic. The issue of user control versus program control also remains unresolved' (p. 251). An effective CALL environment perhaps needs to offer different interfaces or combinations of interfaces to accommodate different learning styles as appropriate to different skills.

Explaining what skills each software package attempts to improve is an important task for teachers and learners. Dunkel (1991) asks teachers to consider which kinds of CALL lessons augment development of particular L2 skills such as reading and listening comprehension, oral proficiency and knowledge of grammar.

One way to do this on a more individual level is for teachers to brain-storm with learners what they think they need to learn in terms of language. This serves as a starting point for deciding the categories and sub-categories in which they may wish to have CALL interaction and can be used to make decisions on what kinds of CALL software programs to include in a classroom as well as to create learner contracts for learning. An initial level of categories includes basic skills of reading, writing, speak-ing and listening as well as the more general category of computer literacy. Sub-categories might include micro-skills and vocabulary related to local and individual needs.

Language teachers generally aim to increase learner-centredness, or locus of control toward the user, in activities in which, as Nunan (1984) suggests, learners can be more closely involved in the decision-making process of what is taught and how it is taught. Posting a schema or mental map of a learners' needs along with notes on the software packages which match each need is a good way to allow learners to organize their own learning. Such a chart should also include an overview of the curricular objectives to indicate how learners should progress through levels of language learning. This can involve learners in the process and make them much more responsible for their learning and, in doing so, also increase intrinsic motivation.

8.2.2   Making better use of existing materials

In order for learners to learn, they need to reflect upon their learning in discussion with teachers and peers, in diaries and in reports. In this way, learners begin to examine learning materials and their strategies for approaching them thus benefiting even when a CALL program does not meet their learning needs. When a CALL program is not suitable, learners and teachers might need to examine ways in which it can be adapted. In some cases, this might involve a learner drawing up a set of questions that will guide another user on how to use the program. The creation of such customized user manuals is beneficial to future learners as it is more likely to focus on the essentials necessary to use the program, and is beneficial to the manual's author because, as Hutchings and Hall *et al.* (1992) suggest, 'those who prepare the course material may learn much more than those who receive it'.

The same is true of another possible activity, adding layers of tasks to materials to make them more challenging or more appropriate to the user. For example, learners might create a treasure hunt for key words and concepts within an encyclopedia software program (for similar ideas, see Keobke, 2000).

8.2.3 Establishing an environment where CALL may take place

For collaboration at the computer to be successful, a supportive environment needs to be established. It was noted in Chapter 1 that learners often collaborate at the computer, even though it is not the expectation of the setting that they do so. That is, the environment of traditional schools is not usually or ideally suited to the delivery of CALL or other types of computer-aided learning in a collaborative context (for more on this see Logan, 1995).

What is necessary for collaboration at the computer to take place is an environment which matches the social and interactive nature of CALL activities. A learning environment built on the traditional library model, with individual carrels isolating each computer and each user with signs urging learners to be quiet, is unlikely to promote collaborative learning based on learners discussing tasks. Similarly, if computer access is restricted, either in terms of time (e.g. 15 minutes at the end of a class) or space (e.g. please find the teacher with the key) then CALL will be discouraged.

The problem faced in most classrooms is how to isolate, or provide privacy, for an individual student while allowing a group of students the collaborative opportunity to excitedly discuss and negotiate. For example, a large-screen computer projection system allows for group discussion of a common screen while a networked program such as *Lotus Notes* has the advantage of allowing several people to work on the same document at the same time. However, the cost and difficulty of learning such programs need to be balanced against the ease and expense of traditional activities, for example, using a large sheet of paper on a table.

One of the challenges to collaboration is the need to determine the working process. If this is subverted by an environment unwelcoming to collaboration, it becomes more difficult for learners to learn.

8.3   Evaluating software

Learners are seldom aware of the model of instruction nor would the names *behaviourist* and *constructivist* make sense to them. However, from the point of view of the classroom teacher, knowing the model of instruction can help moderate his or her own and the learners' expectations of the type and organization of a software program's tasks.

The model of learning featured in a particular CALL software package is seldom stated, and software packages sold as so-called learning games are often simply highly behaviourist tutorials. If CALL software packages are to be properly evaluated and matched with learning needs, they need to be classified by teachers. One way for teachers to do so is by collecting reviews of software from professional publications such as *CAELL Journal*.

Another, more personalized, way to classify materials is through the creation of in-house reviews, similar to book reviews, which outline key aspects of the program. For example, one might evaluate where a program fits into Chandler's locus of control (see Section 7.6.1) and suggest how and why a learner might use a particular software program. In a school setting, these reviews might include the reviewer's name so that users might gauge the reviewer's opinion. In a classroom or self-access learning centre, these reviews could be posted or otherwise made easily available. In these tasks, the teacher should take the role of the editor, having learners engage in critical thinking about the learning materials they are using.

This is a particularly important process to undertake when evaluating materials which claim to offer collaborative opportunities but which simply offer shallow cooperative activities in which learners do not need to negotiate meaning, the task or the process of finding answers.

Further reading

Software Evaluation Guide *http://www.owlnet.rice.edu/~ling417/guide.html* – This online guide is based on the Hubbard chapter below.

Hubbard, P. (1992) A methodological framework for CALL courseware development. In Pennington, M. and Stevens, V. (eds), *Computers in applied linguistics*. Clevedon: Multilingual Matters.

8.4   Learning and working styles

Although many statistical instruments exist for this purpose (see Renzulli and Smith, 1978), defining learners' learning styles can be difficult, time consuming and non-transferable across disciplines. For example, a learner who excels in the rote memorization of baseball statistics may not transfer such skills to mathematics or learning vocabulary. Nor may the skills be appropriate to all subjects and situations such as the learning of creative writing or emergency procedures.

There is also the question of whether a learner's preferred learning style is the most appropriate for learning. Some learners may say they prefer learning passively through a lecture, but may actually learn better through a simulation. One way in which teachers (and the advertising community) unconsciously define learning styles is through publication of review phrases such as *if you enjoyed this, you may like this*. Learners should examine how they prefer to learn, but they should also consider on an on-going basis whether their current learning style(s) is efficient and, if not, where it is in need of some improvement. Learners need to develop multiple learning styles.

There are numerous challenges in completing tasks and acquiring knowledge in what is supposedly a collaborative environment. In their attempts to succeed at tasks, learners adopt strategies and sometimes articulate and negotiate those strategies. In the absence of teacher and wider class interaction, there is a great need for these strategies to be appropriate to the task and for learners to interact in a way that shows an appreciation of personal and group dynamics. With increased use of computers in the classroom, teachers need to be aware of their roles in fostering better habits, collaborative strategies and interpersonal relationships.

8.5   Evolving technology

The cost of technology can be a barrier both to getting involved in CALL and maintaining the latest technology. Materials created only a few years ago on the Microsoft Windows 3.1 operating system may not function properly or at all on the latest versions of Windows. Other problems centre around developing new CALL programs, including a lack of funds, expertise and authoring programs.

8.5.1   Lack of funds

The previously mentioned ALLP (see Section 2.3.3) project was singular in attracting funding in excess of US$70 million. Few commercial organizations spend even a fraction of this amount in software development and non-commercial programs are written on far smaller budgets or, more commonly, on no budget at all. Instead, many teachers create software with their own time and resources. In such cases, authors may act conservatively as they are wary of not achieving a return on their investment of time and money.

However, in the time since the ALLP was set up, many of the costs of producing quality multimedia have been dramatically reduced. For example, computers have become exponentially more powerful while costs have continued to drop. Now authoring tools and related programs for the creation of graphics, animation and video, which were previously developed from scratch, are now commercially available at reasonable prices. However, in an endless cycle, a parallel consumer (e.g. learner) demand for greater sophistication in learning materials usually follows each new capability of these authoring programs so underfunded developers may find it difficult to interest learners.

8.5.2   Lack of expertise

Those creating CALL software programs are often experts in computer programming, design or pedagogy, but are seldom experts in all three fields; while one aspect in a finished program may shine, others may be problematical. Authoring professional software is a labor-intensive enterprise employing the skills of many different people including materials writers, content editors, graphic designers, sound designers, musicians, voice actors, marketers, animators, videographers and so on. A single teacher or group of learners may be disappointed with their efforts when compared with professional products.

One solution in a school context is to assemble a team of experts (or at least people skilled in one or more areas), but even within academic institutions this is not always practical and requires both resolution and organizational skills. This problem is particularly severe in the case of individuals trying to create a small program to solve a local task. A second solution is liaison with commercial publishers, who might help edit and develop locally relevant software packages – as long as doing so does not shift the focus and defeat the purpose of developing learning materials for the local market.

Example

Online collaborative projects: Creating 'Call for Participation' projects

Unless you plan to do the project on your own, you'll need some partners. Before you ask people to join your project, you need to do some planning. First, create a 'Call for Participation' that provides potential participants an overview of your project. Second, develop the materials that you and your participants will need for the project such as lesson plans and project guidelines.

Call for Participation

A 'Call for Participation' should have the following elements:

- Topic/Title:
- Content/Curriculum areas:
- Outcomes/Standards:
- Overview/Summary:
- Target audience, Ages of participants:
- Timeline or Schedule (begin/end):
- Registration information & dates:
- Participant requirements (location):
- Type/Level of interaction:
- Technology needed:
  (hardware, computer/student ratio, software, time needed online)
- Format used:
  (email, chat, video conferencing, forum, web, traditional mail)
- Procedure (project description and assessment):
- How to participate:
- Contact person:

Project materials

A project should also have the following project materials:

- Project materials
- Projects guidelines
- Lesson plans
- Activities (Observation, Discussion/Analysis, Creation/Synthesis, Exchange, Evaluation)
- Classroom management ideas
- Student materials (such as worksheets, guidelines)
- List of participants
- Assessments

8.5.3 Lack of suitable authoring programs

Many authoring programs are limited in the question types and information collection systems that they offer. Authoring programs for CALL and other subjects most commonly include low-level question types such as true/false and multiple-choice questions as opposed to higher-level synthetic, analytical and evaluative tasks. Developers tend to use what is available and lack either the skills or the inclination to develop new authoring tools. Conversely, new software features are often included regardless of whether or not they are pedagogically appropriate. This latter problem is less easy to address, but new software is slowly being developed that is based on competition and consumer demand for improved interactivity, intuitiveness and other features.

Example 8.2 Macromedia *Authorware*

Like many software authoring programs, *Authorware* offers a Wizard to automate the process of creating a software program. The Wizard helps determine the look of the program through various templates then presents different question types to be included. Any decisions made during the Wizard phase can be modified later.

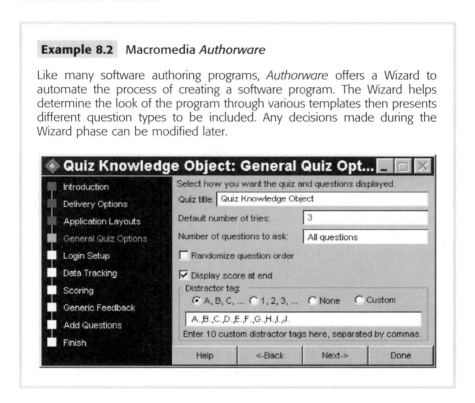

A list of authoring programs is found in Section IV (with WWW addresses) with details, examples and costs.

8.6 Commercial software

Computer-based learning materials have largely been taken out of the hands of educators. Instead, the cost involved in the creation of interactive educational software means that it is often designed on the basis of what engineers decide is possible and what marketing executives decide can be sold. Of course, this is often also the case with textbooks.

Currently, software programmers, engineers and marketing executives, rather than educational academics and teachers, make many of the critical decisions on the creation of popular educational software. Moody (1995) provides an extended example in his documentation of a year-long creation of the children's multimedia encyclopedia *Explorapedia* at Microsoft Corporation. In 301 pages describing the process, there is only one mention of a person with a background in education being consulted. It may be assumed that, for the major developers of commercial software, what is technically possible and what is commercially viable are more important than what is pedagogically appropriate.

Concept 8.1   **Adapting materials**

Software developers often focus on transferring existing materials to a computer-based medium. They sometimes assume that the educational thinking appropriate for print is also suitable for the computer and fail to see the pedagogical implications of the different processes involved. A common example of this is found in teachers who place their lecture notes on the WWW without bothering to link those notes to further resources or develop them in a way that takes advantage of the computer's ability to offer images, animation, sound, video or interaction.

Quote 8.6   A. Bailin on the need for classroom teachers to develop software:

Computers are slowly but surely being applied to every aspect of human activity, from cooking to driving cars to space travel. They are already used in teaching language, and unless we see a dramatic reversal in social trends, their use will be ever increasing. We can either develop language-learning software ourselves or watch others do it. If we take the latter road, we must be prepared to have software that suits the needs of other cultures but may not suit our own. In a world where language skills are increasingly important, this is a rather risky proposition.

Bailin (1995: 328)

Computers are an increasing fact of life in the classroom. But if teachers and schools are to have an influence on the creation of materials they purchase and use these materials effectively, it is necessary to study the issues in creating and using them.

8.7   Making better use of existing materials

Ravitch (1987) reviews the history of technology in the school, including film, radio and television with some pessimism, suggesting that factors peripheral to the technology itself (organization, cost, schedules) have resulted in repeated failures. She also wonders whether new learning materials 'will devalue printed materials and wonders whether technology's instant gratification will dampen learners' abilities to analyze materials' arguing that in 'literature, for example, certain genres were meant to be read, not performed. Novels, short stories, essays and poems were meant to be read' (p. 32).

However, the idea that literary forms should only be appreciated in their original medium is not generally shared. For example, few have heard Homer's *Iliad* sung aloud as the author 'intended' and the plays of Shakespeare have been not only staged, but also widely read and reinterpreted in art, opera and movies. Multimedia can be used simply as a new tool for examining old forms as well as for creating new ones, such as hypertext novels. It is important for learners to be involved in using computers as tools to activate their knowledge by transforming their learning into new media.

Concept 8.2   **Writing the hypertext novel**

Although they have not had wide commercial appeal, many authors are now working in non-linear hypertext novels in which the story changes depending on which links one chooses to follow. A pioneer in this field is Michael Joyce. Examples of his work are found at: *http://www.eastgate.com/ people/Joyce.html*

8.7.1   Determining expertise, motivation and roles

When making use of a CALL program, learners need to determine what they know and what they do not know. Learners who take the time to determine what they know about a task and the way of approaching the task, if only to acknowledge that they know nothing, are better positioned to engage in an investigation than learners who do not bother to determine their expertise or, in a collaborative situation, misrepresent their expertise to the other learner.

Of course, misrepresenting one's expertise can be an innocent error and one's collaborative partner might also mistakenly bestow one with expertise, but the failure to clear up, or take responsibility for, any such misunderstanding amounts to the same problem.

Example 8.3 Beatty (2001) from a study of students collaborating on tasks in a new computer program:

Demonstrations of expertise are seen as learners try to show their mastery over the computer, the interface, and even the contents of the program (which none of the subjects had previously seen). In the example of this session, as the hour set aside for the task progresses, Debby's assertions over her prior knowledge (having seen the movie and having strong opinions of how to navigate the interface on the basis of her experience on the computer) diminish Jesse's participation as an equal collaborator. Rather than work to establish and define her own role, Jesse withdraws and participates less (p. 234).

Debby: ((reading)) was a child... Taylor... came to visit her father... part of the poem... how and why.... So we should read that first. I think that ... where's this thing... ((inaudible)) Full stop. ((shakes her head)) ((reads the summary of Rime of the Ancient Mariner)) One of every three people to tell his story. He stops a young man going to a wedding and tells how killing an albatross led to tragedy for him and the rest of the crew. ((reading)) his first part, the Ancient... ((incorrectly rephrasing)) Ancient stop by the old man going to. Remember about the story that, um, when when when the film begin um and this one should be, uh, Victor Frankenstein, the scientist who invents the Frankenstein

Jesse: [Mm.]

Debby: [and] then come up to the screen and then sat down and said to one of the sailor, this is the crew of sailors who is lost and they go to an island and then suddenly Victor come out and say 'Don't, I am going to tell you a story somehow and this is the story and then he stop.' Uh, it's very similar. I don't know how to say it.

Jesse: You can type it in.

Debby: Yes, I suppose so. You want to see this part? ((reading)) ((inaudible)) Let's try maybe. ((looking at her watch and whispering)) Almost finished.

Jesse: ((laughs))

Debby: Yo!

Jesse: ((laughs)) Yeah. ((pause)) Go on. Go on Question four.

Debby: I I also get some com... uh some words and that that I I can't forget... I can't [remember.]

Jesse: [((laughs)) Can't forget.]

Debby: I can't remember.

Jesse: Okay, then go to the answer. Here, click.

Similarly, it helps for learners to determine their motivation for completing a task. Good learners develop intrinsic motivation for learning; poor learners decline responsibility for learning and depend more on extrinsic rewards or ignore intrinsic and extrinsic rewards altogether.

Associated with motivation in collaborative situations is the determining of roles for the participants.

A range of different roles is available to learners in a collaborative situation: for example, a leader, a teacher, a follower, a facilitator, a devil's advocate and so on. It is not always necessary for learners to articulate these roles openly and, in fact, the roles of each learner may change over the course of a few turns of conversation. However, when one learner takes a role that excludes the other from collaborative participation, problems may develop in motivation and participation. Even for learners working on their own on a CALL program, if the program assumes certain roles through the design of its interface, opportunities for participation can be denied the learner.

8.7.2 Determining the working process

Many learners have difficulty in determining the working process. In an intensive study of twenty learners using a new software program (Beatty, 2001), many simply entered into the tasks without any discussion whatsoever. They failed to consider how they might go about examining the tasks, how they might find information to enable them to answer the questions/tasks and, finally how they might best answer the questions/tasks.

To a certain extent, a failure to engage in critical thinking and, when confronted with partial knowledge, not to engage in scaffolded learning is related to the inability of the learners to determine a working process. The net effect is to reduce collaboration. On the other hand, those who spend time determining the working process, present themselves with more opportunities to progress intelligently through the materials as well as to reduce the social friction that might emerge from misunderstandings that might otherwise arise.

Of course, there are times in a collaborative situation when the task, resources and answers are all so obvious that they do not require any conscious elaboration or determination of the working process. But if this is indicative of the entire task, it would suggest that the task is not truly collaborative, rather only requiring cooperation, if that (see Section 6.1.3).

A challenge to CALL is to create materials which encourage learners to shape their roles and working process. In CALL materials using behaviourist models of learning, this is predetermined, but in more constructivist CALL materials, where learners must make decisions about what to do and how and when to do it, there could be some prodding on the part of the program.

8.7.3 Determining goals and priorities

Determining goals and priorities is a central concern of CALL because computer-based multimedia present a new pedagogical problem: too many materials. In traditional learning materials, there is a strong emphasis on limiting scope and sequence. As suggested by the terms themselves, all learners usually proceed through the scope and sequence of traditional materials in much the same linear way.

Both the non-linear organization of many CALL learning materials and the tendency to include extensive background materials presents learner with the problem of defining their own scope and sequence. Essentially, learners must balance task completion with exploration. This balance is sometimes dictated by the constraints of the learning situation: learners faced with an important time-limited close-ended test question might be expected to minimize exploration while learners working on an open-ended project question for which they have a lot of time might tend to explore much more.

Decisions on how much to explore should be balanced against the need to address the tasks and questions, but learners may be unable to manage their time properly.

Learners who collaborate well are likely to discuss time management thus allowing them to address the tasks and answer the questions better.

8.7.4   Perceptions of the technology

Because technology (i.e. the computer and its accessories) is the most significant variation from traditional classroom learning, it is no surprise that perceptions of the technology have an influence on collaboration at the computer.

For some learners, a new CALL program can present an interesting challenge to be addressed through exploration. To others, it can appear as an impenetrable and frustrating barrier that discourages exploration. Within CALL interfaces there are often many affordances and misaffordances. If learners address their problems with the interface, affordances and misaffordances, they can create opportunities for negotiation of meaning, both with the computer and with other learners.

8.8   Copyright and plagiarism

All computer-based information, whether text, graphics, music or software programs, is essentially digital in nature. Digital means that the core data can be broken down into strings of binary numbers: ones and zeros. The practical side of this is that much of what we see on the computer can be copied and manipulated. This is especially true of text and images found on the WWW. Student projects often feature text and images borrowed from existing websites. In many countries, a *fair use* provision within copyright law allows for learners to use some materials for in-class projects. However, it does not give learners the right to repost images and text onto the WWW. Plagiarism using materials from the WWW is also common but tools such as those found at *www.plagiarism.org* can be of some help to teachers who suspect their students of failing to acknowledge what they have borrowed.

Example 8.4 Dealing with plagiarism

The WWW presents unparalleled opportunities for plagiarizing materials but it also presents some defence. The simplest tool a teacher has to check for plagiarism is to type a string of suspect text into a search engine and see whether it leads to one or more websites from which the suspect text may have been taken.

Plagiarism.org *http://www.plagiarism.org/* – This website essentially automates the above process but rates the likelihood of plagiarism on a phrase and section level. The website also includes examples of a plagiarized document.

Web Tools Newsletter

http://wwwtools.cityu.edu.hk/news/newslett/plagiarismrevisited.htm – This issue of the Web Tools Newsletter focuses on plagiarism and draws together several references and resources. An index points to many other interesting and useful topics.

Further reading

Negroponte, N. (1996) *Being Digital.* New York: Vintage Books – Negroponte is co-founder and director of the MIT Media Laboratory. The Media Lab is currently supported by nearly 170 corporations worldwide, and has led in the development of now-familiar areas such as digital video and multimedia. *Being Digital* expands on the importance of bytes over bits; that is, computer-based digital information (bytes) rather than its physical counterpart (bits), especially in publishing.

8.9 Viruses

Viruses are distributed through the WWW and email and can destroy files. There are currently about 50,000 viruses in circulation with approximately 250 being added each week. Some viruses end up costing computer users millions of dollars simply by slowing performance of computers.

Others destroy data. It is difficult and sometimes expensive to maintain anti-virus software to handle the latest versions of viruses which, almost by definition, are designed to thwart existing anti-virus programs.

A virus is a program and, in most cases, must be activated by the user to make it work. Typically, viruses carry an .exe file name, that is, *executable* files, but they may have various other endings. A common way to receive such files is through unsolicited email. Once a virus enters your computer, it will often spread itself by taking advantage of the address list in your email program, sending a copy of itself with an email to each name on your address list.

A certain amount of what is called 'social engineering' is used to make such viruses successful. For example, with the popular I love you virus, the subject of the message is: *I LOVEYOU*. The body of the message is: *kindly check the attached LOVELETTER coming from me*. Attached to the message is the file *LOVE-LETTER-FOR-YOU.TXT.vbs*. Many people are variously flattered, surprised and confused about receiving such a message and open the attachment out of curiosity (see *http://www.symantec.com/avcenter/venc/ data/vbs.loveletter.a.html* for more information about the *Loveletter* virus). Sometimes, such messages purport to be anti-virus messages and their attachments are similarly opened.

Concept 8.3   **Anti-virus rules**

Teachers need to educate themselves and their students about how to deal with viruses. The following are six anti-virus rules that offer protection from most viruses.

1. Purchase good commercial anti-virus software.

2. Update the Virus Definitions frequently (at least once a week).

3. Scan each new program with anti-virus software, especially an email attachment, regardless of who the file is from.

4. Turn on Macro Virus Protection in Microsoft Word. Beware of all *Word* Macros, especially if you don't know what they are.

5. Run Windows Update at least once a month.

6. If someone unexpectedly sends you an .exe (executable) file or .vbs (*Visual Basic* script) file, delete it.

These rules are adapted from *The Top 6 Anti-Virus Rules* (*http://linz1.net/wdev/antivirus.html*) which also offers detailed explanations for each rule.

8.9.1 Thought viruses

Misinformation is one of the greatest challenges on the WWW and in many ways constitutes a form of thought virus in which erroneous information is passed on from one host reader to another, often through redistribution of email messages. Many such hoaxes have racist overtones, such as the oft-repeated story of someone seeing Santa Claus nailed to a crucifix in Japan, that seem attractive as a cultural misunderstanding but which never actually occurred. Instead, such urban legends are often a way of denigrating the intelligence and sensitivity of another culture. As a piece of humour, it is questionable but far more insidious to send hate websites which purport to confide suppressed truths while promoting lies. Part of the problem is in learners' inability to distinguish between legitimate sites, for example about the history of the Second World War and neo-Nazi anti-Jewish websites.

Fortunately, people learn not to believe everything they read, but various types of misinformation and hoaxes continue in wide circulation. Of these, some hoaxes are simply urban legends, or stories meant to appeal to our sense of the bizarre. Sociologists believe that modern urban legends serve to allow us to confront our fears and frustrations with modern life in (often) humorous ways. But some of these urban legends are a waste of time, such as the Craig Shergold hoax and its many variations. In this hoax or one of its many variations, people are told a sad story about a little boy and asked to send letters or continue a chain letter. The problem with this sort of hoax is that it misdirects people's goodwill and serves to make people cynical and less likely to support true good causes. There are many urban myths and hoaxes on the WWW as well as places that discredit them.

Example 8.5   Urban Legends Reference Pages

The Urban Legends Reference Pages is an excellent resource for discrediting urban legends and hoaxes on the WWW as well as a useful site for teachers to glean general information about customs and beliefs (not limited to mistaken ones).

The legends and stories on each page are preceded by coloured bullet points:

• green for true statements
• red for false statements
• yellow for statements of undetermined or ambiguous veracity
• white for legends of indeterminate origin

Urban Legends Reference Page *http://www.snopes2.com/*

8.10   Safety online

A popular cartoon shows a dog sitting at a keyboard with the caption 'In cyberspace, no one knows you're a dog'. The cartoon reflects the fact that people often assume new personae and different genders online. A sad consequence of this is that, on unmoderated chatlines, learners may encounter paedophiles posing as children or even older learners asking inappropriate questions and using inappropriate language. In my own experience, some of my students were using a popular ESL chatline and were taught swear words and asked detailed questions about their sex lives. Newspapers frequently carry stories of young people who have been seduced into meeting someone they have met on a chatline. The best defence is to raise learners' awareness of such problems.

Example 8.6   Computer safety rules

Kids' rules for online safety

1. I will not give out personal information such as my address, telephone number, parents' work address/telephone number, or the name and location of my school without my parents' permission

2. I will tell my parents right away if I come across any information that makes me feel uncomfortable.

3. I will never agree to get together with someone I 'meet' online without first checking with my parents. If my parents agree to the meeting, I will be sure that it is in a public place and bring my mother or father along.

4. I will never send a person my picture or anything else without first checking with my parents.

5. I will not respond to any messages that are mean or in any way make me feel uncomfortable. It is not my fault if I get a message like that. If I do I will tell my parents right away so that they can contact the service provider.

6. I will talk with my parents so that we can set up rules for going online. We will decide upon the time of day that I can be online, the length of time I can be online, and appropriate areas for me to visit. I will not access other areas or break these rules without their permission

7. I will not give out my Internet password to anyone (even my best friends) other than my parents

8. I will be a good online citizen and not do anything that hurts other people or is against the law. *http://www.safekids.com/kidsrules.htm*

8.10.1   Censorship

Governments have used censorship to control some of the negative aspects of the WWW, for example by shutting down Internet Service Providers (ISP) who carry negative content or content they do not like. However, it is often difficult for an ISP to know about and be responsible for every page and every message being sent on their services. A preferable though imperfect option are *net* nannies. Products such as *CYBERsitter* are aimed at children while other products such as *Hate Filter* are aimed at helping adult audiences. However, such programs also have their drawbacks. For example, they may object to the words sex and Nazis respectively, but these choices would block informative sites on biology and world history unless otherwise specified.

Example 8.7   CYBERsitter

Promotional information for *CYBERsitter 2001* explains that it can be used to block the WWW, newsgroups, chatlines, email and messaging programs and provide information on users who attempt to access forbidden functions through activity reports sent to parent or administrator by email. Internet access can be controlled by day and time (for example, turning it off when a parent is using the computer).

While for some, such programs will have an aura of Big Brother watching, they can be useful in assuring parents and teachers that young learners are not being subjected to questionable websites.

http://www.cybersitter.com/

8.10.2   Pornography

Pornography is usually defined as depictions of sexual violence, especially against women and children. The Internet is a common place for pornography because it can be distributed in both picture and video formats and accessed internationally.

Children are often exposed to pornography unwittingly. Despite claims that one must be of a certain age to access websites, they often feature deceptive web addresses or are forwarded from common misspellings of more famous web addresses. Another tactic is to co-opt recently abandoned web addresses in hopes of attracting viewers following links from legitimate websites. For example, recently the national airline of Cambodia went out of business and its website address was snapped up by a pornographic website. Anyone looking for information on the airline is automatically forwarded to the pornography website.

8.11   Technological have-nots

Quote 8.7   S. Berger on the Digital Divide:

The term 'Digital Divide' has been coined to refer to the gap that is being created between the 'haves' and the 'have-nots' in our rapidly developing computer culture. A recent report by the Gartner Group revealed 35 per cent of adults in the lower-socioeconomic-status bracket have Internet access, compared to 53 per cent in the lower-middle bracket, 79 per cent in the upper-middle bracket, and 83 per cent in the top bracket.

Berger (2000)

Although computers are used widely in industrialized countries around the world, access is far more limited in the developing world and, even in industrialized countries, access is restricted along socioeconomic lines. This is changing as computers fall in price and a sense of need for them as educational tools rather than technological playthings rises. However, it is too often the case that a school willing to spend lavishly on the setting up of a classroom set of computers will not set aside appropriately matching funds for software, training and upkeep. This means, in some cases,

Quote 8.8   M. Rao on multilingual publishing on the Internet:

There are five key drivers of multilingual publishing on the Internet: a need for localization, online news publishing, government concern, education and electronic commerce.

Though the original and key push for the Internet market comes from the US, the percentage of US Internet users as a percentage of worldwide users is dropping: from 65 per cent in 1994 to 55 per cent in 1997, and further down to 40 per cent in 2000. What this means is that the proportion of non-US, non-English-speaking Internet users is growing rapidly.

Hence many US companies are realizing the need to publish Web content in languages other than English – Intel and Federal Express being two good examples. Others include Cisco (with online content in 14 languages for 49 countries) and Netscape (with over 10 languages). Governments from Japan and Singapore to New Zealand and Andhra Pradesh are venturing into multilingual Web publishing, with varying degrees of success (n.p). *http://www.isoc.org/oti/articles/0798/rao.html*

Rao (1998)

computers remain idle. In other cases, it is the teachers themselves who deny access to their students, locking the computers away when not in use for classroom assignments.

There are many non-profit organizations which donate computers to those who need them. While this is admirable, sometimes such programs end up shipping defective computers which are of no longer of any use, or for which no suitable software has been supplied.

Another area for concern is the number of websites published exclusively in English. The shift in statistics seem to be encouraging with more and more websites publishing in other languages and, of course, the availability of translation engines (see Further reading, below) able to give the gist of some web pages.

Summary

There are many challenges facing CALL, some of which suggest directions for research projects. For many of the problems facing children using the WWW, proper education as to the nature of problems and what to do about them is the best defence.

Further reading

Murray, D.E. (1999) Access to information technology: Considerations for language educators. *Prospect* 14: 4–12. – This paper summarizes some of the CALL-related issues of computer have-nots.

Wresch, W.C. (1996) *Disconnected: Haves and Have Nots in the Information Age.* New Brunswick NJ, Rutgers University Press – This book deals more generally with access to technology and does not focus on language teaching and learning.

Falling Through the Net, an American clearinghouse on issues related to the Digital Divide: *http://www.digitaldivide.gov/*

A parallel privately operated site, *www.digitaldividenetwork.org*, is organized by high-tech firms, including Microsoft and America Online, and non-profit groups, such as the National Urban League, the Benton Foundation and Ford Foundation.

Magid, L.J. (1998) *Child Safety on the Information Highway.* National Center for Missing and Exploited Children *http://www.safekids.com/child_safety.htm*

The following are two websites that feature free translation software:

Altavista Translation Service *http://babelfish.altavista.digital.com/cgi-bin/translate*

The Translator's Home Companion *http://www.rahul.net/lai/companion.html*

Section

III Researching CALL

Chapter 9

Current research interests

This section begins with an examination of the current research interests in CALL. As is common in many other fields, research interests in CALL have tended to follow trends; for example, the focus of many early studies was on a quantitative justification of CALL. In these studies, the computer was usually pitted against the classroom teacher and measured for effectiveness in teaching a discrete set of knowledge. For example, measuring student learning of grammar at a computer with a teacher-led class serving as a control group. Such studies are still undertaken, but they are not as frequent, or perhaps not even as necessary since CALL is now perceived as something that is inherently different and/or complementary to classroom teaching.

To assist in an examination of the current research interests, this section reviews and categorizes 145 publications in the field to try to define current areas of interest. Brief summaries of several of the articles are given and a range of issues is highlighted.

9.1   A new field: reporting CALL research

The discipline of CALL is relatively new and differs from other fields of study within Applied Linguistics for the basic reason that the rate of change of the technological aspects deeply influences theory, practice and research. For example, in the past twenty years, the technology has improved:

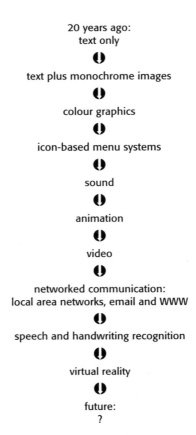

Figure 9.1   **Progression in computer presentation technology**

Twenty-year-old research providing findings critical of text-only modes of representation is largely irrelevant and obsolete, other than from a historical perspective. And one may assume that this trend of perpetual obsolescence will continue as computer interfaces become more powerful, more transparent and easier for learner interactions and teacher programming.

Older programs are not even able to run on current computer platforms, let alone appeal to learners with their austere presentation and limited range of functions. This is especially true as twenty-five years ago the personal computer did not exist, yet is now becoming as common as other household appliances and completely familiar to the current generation of learners in those schools where computers are used. Such students commonly view computers not as scientific and educational tools, but as sources

---

Concept 9.1   **Edutainment and the transfer of skills**

Edutainment is a combination of *education* and *entertainment*. It refers to educational applications which are packaged as games. In most cases, the learning objectives are thinly disguised under game objectives. The use of toys, games and other materials which are intended for other purposes may be incorporated into CALL.

The first computers were strictly for scientific and military research but among computers' most popular uses today are as platforms for arcade-style computer games. While such entertainment applications have certainly increased general computer literacy and served to make computers more familiar and less threatening to the average young person, a question that needs to be addressed is *How do learners transfer their computer skills and enthusiasm to disciplines such as CALL?* It may be that learners' familiarity with the possibility of what computers are capable of makes them less tolerant of educational applications that do not match the average computer game's exciting presentation of information. There are also questions about what computer games teach young learners and do to develop cognitive processes.

---

of entertainment; the need to meet such expectations has given rise to a field of courseware known as *edutainment*.

9.2   Approaches to research in CALL

The pace of change in computer technology and the usual delay in conducting, reporting, publishing and disseminating research also serves to differentiate CALL from other areas in Applied Linguistics. This delay means that even in the case of reporting research through a non-paper medium such as on the WWW or by email, a great deal of research may be out of date before it reaches its intended audience. The nature of this delay has led not just to an extensive duplication of effort, but also to a lack of recognition of leadership in CALL research as the usual incremental debates and advances are labelled irrelevant if the software on which they are based has been superseded by newer versions which address some of the earlier shortcomings.

Duplication of effort is also common because of the distributed nature of personal computers. The early years of research in computers required access to mainframe facilities at key universities but, with the advent of small, inexpensive and powerful computers, research need not take place in universities and trickle down. Instead, it has become increasingly common for trained teachers to conduct and report research based on data gathered in their own classrooms.

9.3   The computer as a tool of research

The computer is not only a subject of research, it is now a universally important tool in conducting research. On the simplest level, computers are used to save time previously spent compiling and presenting statistical data. On more advanced levels, the computer is used to collect data. For example, computers can collect information about the users' actions at the keyboard, such as by recording each single keystroke in real time. These can be played back by the researcher to see, for example, successive drafts in the writing process and use (and abuse) of tools such as spelling and grammar checkers and templates.

Data stored on a user's hard drive can provide a rich source of data for corpora. For example, letters and memos, copies of emails and other documents. Surveys are easily conducted and tabulated.

9.4   The role of commercial publishers

A further difference between CALL and other areas of Applied Linguistics is that the commercial software industry, not university academics, is the major instigator/creator of the most commonly used learning materials. Although it can be argued that the same is true for traditional publishing, the relationship between educators and print publishers is more of a symbiotic nature, particularly as governments, schools and universities tend to have syllabi to which publishers' materials must conform. The same is seldom true for CALL materials for the simple reason that there are not enough CALL materials to choose from and the market is not yet as competitive or adaptable to local needs, especially considering the high costs of producing a CD-ROM, a process more akin to producing a movie than publishing a textbook. Overall, changes in CALL tend to be governed more by the above-mentioned advances in technology than by pedagogical insights.

9.5 Reviewing current studies: a survey

As mentioned in Section I, the areas of research emphasized in CALL are in a constant state of change. More than in most other fields, such changes are influenced by key questions being answered by empirical research or by concerns being made redundant by the introduction of new technology. For example, a principal concern in CALL during the mid-1980s to early 1990s was disorientation as a learner navigates hypertext and hypermedia links within an information space (see Conklin, 1987; Liu, 1992; Marchionini, 1988). However, concerns about hypertext and hypermedia have since been largely replaced by concerns about *multi*media. Although navigation and disorientation are still concerns, a combination of better and standardized interface designs (e.g. see Howlett, 1996), as well as increased computer literacy among both teachers and learners (see Chapelle and Jamieson, 1991, Deegan and Sutherland, 1990) have made many related issues irrelevant.

For this section, an attempt is made to give a rough overview of current research interests in CALL. Defining the parameters of such an overview presents several challenges although it is easy to imagine what the perfect solution might be: one would survey everyone doing every kind of research in CALL in all languages in every country worldwide. However, even identifying all the members of such a group would be an impossible task as would be the job of soliciting and assessing their contributions.

Levy (1997) narrowed the task and contacted what he labels *key practitioners* in 24 countries. This was done through a process of first identifying prominent contributors to CALL literature and asking each key practitioner to recommend one or two others. In this way, 213 individuals were identified and sent detailed questionnaires with 104 individuals from 18 countries eventually returning usable questionnaires. Problems with this approach include those inherent in questionnaire design, such as possible author bias on, and wording of, the questions asked and areas of research that might be covered. This method is also time-consuming and reliant upon the goodwill of the participants although, in the case of Levy's study, the response rate – almost 49 per cent (all percentages have been rounded off) – was excellent. A further problem is that those who are established in the field of CALL may have established their reputations and research focus on technologies that are no longer on the cutting edge. For example, for a question on what CALL encompasses, traditional gap-filling tasks rank second highest in importance among Levy's respondents, yet in the review undertaken in this book, it was reported in only one of 145 studies (Coniam, 1997) and, even then, only as a drawback of traditional CALL software. One reason for this discrepancy might be the very reason for writing this present book; the topics emphasized in CALL research have changed since Levy's survey which, while not published until 1997, was actually completed in March 1991.

A slightly less daunting task would be to survey for a short time period all publications likely to contain articles related to CALL, including journals, conference proceedings, dissertation abstracts (at both the MA and PhD levels) and recent books. And although this methodology would be marginally more workable, it would also present problems. For example, issues tangential to CALL research often appear in a broad range of journals (e.g. software engineering) that may have little or no other focus on computers and language learning; simply identifying the journals to examine would be problematical, let alone the task of obtaining, examining and assessing them.

In the case of the thousands of conferences held each year, a single important presentation on CALL might be lost among other topics. Reviewing current dissertation abstracts is also problematical as such abstracts may represent research begun as long as ten years earlier and, in keeping with the nature of higher level academic research, are more likely to focus on a specialized topics. A similar problem faces attempts to review all pertinent books; although published research in the quickly changing field of CALL is likely to yield useful principles, some information may be quickly outdated. Books also tend to focus on a broader range of concerns and are less easily classifiable.

Based on these concerns, an expedient method of obtaining an overview is to review a large database of recent journal articles (including newsletters). Journal articles generally present a broader and more representative range of issues than books or dissertations and have the advantage of a relatively shorter lag-time between research and publication. Also, authors of books and dissertations often put their principal concerns into journal articles, so the ideas important in their main publications are still likely to be represented.

In reviewing journals, the most convenient method was to conduct a search of a journal abstract database. Several databases were searched for the keywords *computer + assisted + language + learning*. These keywords may seen a bit narrow in focus, excluding as they do a range of related acronyms such as CAI, CAL and CMC, but, even in studies on CAI, CAL and CMC that do not mention CALL, keyword summaries often include the phrase *computer-assisted language learning*.

Of the various databases reviewed in December 1999 for the keywords *computer + assisted + language + learning* over the dates 1997 to 1999, Educational Research International Clearinghouse (ERIC) provided the most responses: 153. Of these 153 entries, seven were discarded because they referred to collections of articles in books, reports or conference proceedings. An eighth was discarded because it was description of a draft curriculum with only passing mention of CALL. The remaining 145 are examined below.

Note: Replicating the survey methodology

One of the reasons for creating the methodology used in this survey is that it can be easily replicated by anyone interested in the latest developments in the field. Choose keywords, perhaps narrowing the focus by adding languages (e.g. Hindi, Tagalog) or technologies (e.g. speech synthesis). Search a database such as ERIC and download the complete abstracts of all the results. Read and discard the inappropriate ones and use a search and replace function to take out unnecessary phrases, such as the guide words in the headings. The resulting document, or corpora, can be searched for key-words by using search and replace with an asterisk (*) for the replace item. This will give you the number of each occurrence. Simply 'undo' after each search and the document will return to its original state. For a more sophistic-ated approach, use corpus analysis software to examine your results.

9.5.1   Languages

To a certain extent, the languages found in the survey reflect the English language and American biases of ERIC, an American government service. Despite the fact that Eric invites submissions worldwide, only 31 of the 145 articles (21 per cent) are published outside of the USA and only one of these (Ganderton, 1996) is written in another language: French. Of course, local databases from different countries would be likely to reflect similar biases, emphasizing, for example, Japanese in Japan. However, seven other languages are mentioned, sometimes in combination, in many of the 145 articles. These include German 14, French 12, Spanish 12, Japanese nine, Korean two and Chinese and Italian with one each.

One of the studies (de Graaff, 1997) uses a modified form of *Esperanto*, which the author labels *eXperanto*. An artificial language can be a useful tool in examining language processes. In this study, de Graaff's use of a modified form of *Esperanto* to examine two subjects' acquisition of four second-language structures based on the interaction between the presence or absence of explicit instruction and the variables complexity and morphology/syntax. The CALL aspect of the study is in the computer-controlled post-tests, which de Graaff claims confirm the hypothesis that explicit instruction facilitates the acquisition of L2 grammar.

As de Graaff's study only used two subjects, its conclusions may be con-sidered limited. Nunan (1987) expresses concerns about the extrapolation of data from small sample sizes but notes that Brown's (1973) seminal study of discourse only had three subjects.

9.5.2   Skills

The emphasis of the four key skills in language learning reflects to some extent the relative ease (and difficulty) that computers have with dealing with learner input and output: reading: 15 articles out of 145 (10 per cent); writing: 24 articles (17 per cent); speaking: 11 articles (8 per cent) and listening: 7 articles (5 per cent). Writing is the easiest way for a learner to input ideas and information on a computer. It is currently far easier than speaking which requires the use of special software (e.g. Dragon Systems *Naturally Speaking*) and extensive 'training' of the computer for each user of the system. In many software programs (e.g. *Triple Play Plus* language programs) a subroutine asks learners to repeat key words and sentences and digitally measures the sound waves against model pronunciation in a graphic way visible to the learner.

Although it is easy to input writing to a computer and it is also becoming easier to input speech, it is extremely difficult for a computer to evaluate meaning in such writing and speaking. In terms of reading and listening, it is easy for computers to present stimulating input for the learner and to provide layers of help and testing that measure comprehension.

Another way in which computers promote interaction through at least some of the four skills is by providing a platform for collaboration and cooperation. The three studies in this area contained in the survey provide three different approaches with different levels of sophistication. Van Handle and Corl (1998) used email to create a pen pal situation between students studying German at two American universities. As already mentioned, email is an asynchronous communication technology in which messages are sent like letters and replies received at an undetermined later time. It has many advantages such as allowing interlocutors to take their time in composing and replying to messages but it lacks the spontaneity or the demands of real conversation.

Chan (1997) makes use of a synchronous communication technology: WWW-based chat line software that allows learners to communicate in real time or, rather, as fast as they can type. Chan's paper describes the use of collaborative writing software and simultaneous electronic chats. One of the advantages of such computer-mediated communication (CMC) is that transcripts of such sessions can be made available to the teacher/researcher for analysis. But in Chan's session, besides using the transcripts for evaluating the performance of individuals and groups in terms of topic, fluency, accuracy and logic, the transcripts of the chat sessions are also used by the students for reference material for developing composition ideas.

Beyond email and chat lines is text-based virtual reality. Turner (1998) uses this approach with a group of adult learners to create imaginary characters and have them interact in an imaginary town. This approach and the use of Multi-User Domains (MUD) or Multi-user domains, Object Oriented (MOO) spaces (mentioned in two studies) (see Section 4.5.3) on the computer are slowly shifting from text-based virtual reality into a situation where visual representations are much stronger. As with any new technology, however, there are concerns about the cognitive overhead required to learn about the technology balanced against the learning benefits. Specifically, one questions whether participating in a virtual community compares favourably with participating in a real community with the accompanying richness of facial expressions, body language as well as social interactions.

As with email, it is sometimes difficult to separate skills from technology (dealt with below). Other basic skills besides reading, writing, speaking and listening include grammar, which comprises 19 of 145 entries (13 per cent), vocabulary with 19 entries (12 per cent), translation with six entries (4 per cent) and one entry for phonetics in which Hwu (1997) created a program to teach Spanish phonetics to college level students.

Grammar is often mentioned in CALL in connection with grammar checkers. Early studies generally focused on the workability of such programs. They generally concluded that such programs are either inadequate because of the nonsensical suggestions that they are likely to make (e.g. blanket rejection of the passive voice and long sentences) or that they simply need to be used like any other tool in the classroom, with thoughtful supervision (adjusting the parameters and lexical items which might be considered by the grammar program). Several of the current studies in this review still focus on evaluation, but the evaluation is of complete grammar programs (in which learners follow a course of grammar exercises) rather than simple grammar checkers (which check grammar as a side-function of a word-processing program), but several others focus on the difficulty of creating such programs.

Vocabulary is similarly dealt with in terms of evaluating and creating such programs, but there is also a focus on second language acquisition, as measured through vocabulary. For example, Duquette, Renie and Laurier (1998) examined and compared vocabulary acquisition by two groups of learners of French-as-a-Second-Language using multimedia and video support respectively. The extent of vocabulary acquisition was considered along with another variable, personality trait, by Grace (1998).

Translation in CALL often features computer-based or so-called machine translation (MT) programs but only one of the articles (Lewis, 1997) deals with the topic in a review of computer systems attempting automatic natural language translation and of how one system can be used in CALL at the college level. Some of the other articles that mention translation focus on translation as a learning strategy. For example, Nagata (1997) examines the effectiveness of computer-assisted metalinguistic instruction for teaching complex grammatical structures such as Japanese particles and finds that learners tend to use two strategies to assign a particle in a sentence: they either follow a specific rule or rely on an English translation.

Other articles review low-level programs that provide translation of key words or phrases. For example, Berleant et al. (1997) describes a system that processes English unrestricted text by translating selected English words in it into foreign words before presenting the text to the student.

The problem with current translation programs is that they are often inadequate to the task of dealing with natural language and their translations, particularly when faced with eloquent or imperfect L1 input, are often poor.

Example 9.1   Free online translation

Many websites offer low-quality but free translations. An example is found at *http://world.altavista.com/* which offers translations of up to 150 words between various languages, including languages with non-Roman character sets such as Arabic, Chinese and Korean.

9.5.3   Processes

The processes involved in many of the articles give an idea of the general interests of researchers. Developing learning materials is a major focus featuring in 49 of the 145 studies (34 per cent) and is even higher if the term *creating* (12 or 8 per cent) is considered along with the keyword *develop*. This is followed by *designing* (40 or 28 per cent) and *evaluating* (27 or 19 per cent). The term *research* is mentioned in 20 (14 per cent) of the studies but a careful review suggests that most studies labelled research are simply literature reviews with little or no actual research being conducted. This is a concern as such reviews purporting to be research may refer to studies of older technologies and techniques rather than investigating newer technologies and techniques in the field. The term *reviewing* mentioned in several of the studies (14 or 10 per cent) would be a more accurate term.

Missing from the list is the term *predicting*. There are no entries for predicting the future of CALL; many now shy away from committing themselves (see Concept 2.6) to the future of CALL as it has been so difficult to predict in the past.

9.5.4   Technologies

New technical possibilities (for example, see Section 4.8) always offer opportunities for new ways of offering CALL and video, a technology which is becoming more accessible on faster computers, is mentioned in 19 of the 145 studies (13 per cent). These papers usually deal with video in an interactive context; that is, the video in the software reacts to the learner's progress through the CALL program. CD-ROMs are mentioned in seven out of the 145 articles (5 per cent) with one (Wright, 1997) focusing on the CD-ROM and its projected obsolescence due to Digital Video Disc DVD technology.

Although it is not primarily thought of as a storage medium, the Internet can serve as one. Through linked pages, storage is virtually limitless, although downloading speeds make high-quality video impractical for most systems. The Internet features in 23 or 16 per cent of the studies, a number that doubles when one considers the World Wide Web (16 or 11 per cent) and email (7 or 5 per cent). The Internet is mentioned in relationship to the already described MOOs and MUDs and often overlaps with WWW. Both the Internet and the WWW present opportunities for a wide range of activities and resources. For example, Cahill and Catanzaro (1997) outline a method for teaching a college-level introductory second-language course entirely online, using a distance-learning approach that incorporates electronic messaging, multimedia, World Wide Web, and Internet assignments. Distance education accounts for eight of the 145 articles (6 per cent). King, Tolzman and Staczek (1998) typify the foci of many such courses which not only conduct classes on the WWW, but use the WWW as a resource, in their case, business-based research on the WWW and online instruction in business-English classes for international students.

Related to distance learning is an article by Fox (1997) who is concerned with how a distance second-language learning program can reconcile the respective advantages of autonomous distance study and traditional face-to-face classes. Autonomy and independent study was the focus of nine articles (6 per cent). Moeller (1997) emphasizes the importance of having pedagogical control over the use of technology rather than technology control pedagogy.

Creating online courses is often a challenge and, in some articles, authors introduce web-authoring programs, including ones particularly suitable for language teaching. Chen and Zhao (1997) for example, introduces two web-authoring programs *EWeb* and *Home Page maker* and Siekmann (1998) talks about *WebCT* (Web Course Tools). WebCT is a particularly flexible tool with an easy to use interface offering many types of activities, such as email, bulletin board, chat rooms and quizzes, as well as places for tutorial and lecture notes.

Concept 9.2   **WebCT**

WebCT (Web Course Tools) is an integrated set of educational tools for developing and delivering courses or course components over the WWW. It was developed at the University of British Columbia and is now used at universities and colleges all over the world. There are many advantages, the greatest being standardization. Students who learn WebCT in one course can transfer that learning to another course. The teacher can track student's progress through and participation in the online material – including the number of minutes spent using the course materials. Online quizzes can be timed for release at a specific time for a specific duration then graded for quick student feedback.

The program also has several features for managing class activities, such as a calendar, email and bulletin boards. Learners can also use features to create their own web pages within WebCT. Unlike the use of the WWW in general, WebCT provides password protection so that only the students enrolled on a course at the time of the course have access to the materials and each other's writing. Such an arrangement also means that, once a learner is immersed in the WebCT environment, she/he is more likely to focus on communication with classmates and the teacher, as opposed to the world at large.

Example 9.2   WebCT

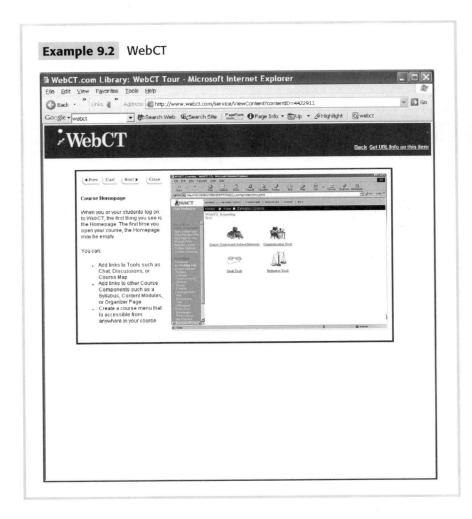

Authoring programs, used to develop software applications and web pages for teaching and learning, are also mentioned in five other articles in relation to hypermedia (Tillman, 1997) and HyperCard (Laidlaw and McCall, 1997) (7 or 5 per cent), a commercial product from Apple Computer. Hypermedia (11 or 8 per cent) and Hypertext (7 or 5 per cent) are also mentioned, sometimes together. But as mentioned at the beginning of this section, hypertext and hypermedia are giving way to multimedia, which is discussed in 26 of the 145 articles (18 per cent). Levy (1997) discusses multimedia as a form of nonlinear text, as compared with the linear nature of books and Liou (1997) examines online help in multimedia instructional materials among 20 native Chinese-speaking English language learners. But most of the studies take multimedia for granted and consider it simply as a mode of presentation (see Example 8.2).

Several varieties of CALL have already been outlined (see Concept 1.2). In this survey, Intelligent Computer-Assisted Language Learning (ICALL) features in seven articles (5 per cent) but none would actually qualify as ICALL as defined in Section I. Instead, ICALL is closer to artificial intelligence as discussed in one article by Dodigovic (1998) but, only then, as an aside about research as an important but unnoticed part of the development process.

Educational technology features in 30 of the 145 articles (21 per cent) but most often as a label, including four articles (3 per cent) on language labs. Gaer (1998) provides a useful type of an article, a question and answer (Q&A) session, in which she asks and answers the following questions related to conducting software evaluations:

1. What types of software are available?
2. What kind of software is appropriate for adult ESL classrooms?
3. How do I select software for the classroom?
4. What kind of technical expertise do I need?
5. What do the students need to know about computers?
6. How do I coordinate the software with the curriculum?
7. How can I integrate the software into instruction?
8. How can I follow up the software with activities?
9. How do I prepare my students to use the specific software?

Such articles are perhaps more typical of CALL than other fields in Applied Linguistics as the ever-changing nature of software and hardware means teachers need to learn new technologies quickly. Such articles also have the function of gently addressing computer phobias.

In early writings on computers from the 1950s through the 1970s, there was often emphasis on hardware, the computers that ran the software programs. In the 1980s and 1990s in particular, there were debates over the superiority of Macintosh versus Windows-based interface. Because these debates tended to drop to levels of personal attack, CALL bulletin board services (BBS) often exclude such postings. However, with the rise of cross-platform software (software which works on both Macintosh and Windows-based computers) and the rise of Windows as a more common platform, emphasis has shifted from hardware (4 articles or 3 per cent) to software (42 articles or 29 per cent). Some aspects of CALL, however, are mixtures of hardware and software, such as speech synthesis and voice recognition which require sound cards, speakers and microphones, all of which are becoming standard features on computers. An example of research investigating the potential for speech synthesis is by Shilling (1997) who examines the written and oral discourse of kindergarten children. Shilling suggests speech-synthesized feedback may be most supportive when children exhibit metalinguistic awareness or cognitive clarity.

9.5.5   Concerns

The 145 papers in this survey voice a number of concerns to do with CALL. For example, promoting various aspects of CALL such as learning strategies (28 or 19 per cent) and teacher and learner attitudes toward CALL (15 or 10 per cent). Attitudes are generally to do with learner and teacher impressions of working with CALL such as a study by McMeniman and Evans (1998) at Australia's Griffith University which indicates that, with appropriate support, CALL has a significant positive effect on teaching and learning and creates minimal disruption.

In helping to shape the role of CALL, *principles* are a concern of six articles (4 per cent). Collentine (1998), for example, outlines principles of cognitive processes that can be used in the design of CALL programs. Similarly, *models* are part of 11 or 8 per cent of the articles. For example, Fucaloro and Russikoff (1998) construct a model to examine the effects of an online French civilization course on teaching and learning, noting opportunities for faculty–student contact, speed and type of feedback, time on task and concerns with learning styles.

Models, in turn, support a consideration of paradigms, but only one article, by Chapelle (1997), addresses this topic in a discussion of approaches to CALL research, borrowing from methodologies adopted by other disciplines. Several researchers distinguish new approaches to learning as requiring a fundamental shift in the ways in which we structure basic learning.

Among the most problematical of the above paradigm shifts (see Quote 9.1) is the move to individualized learning. In this, the classroom has the opportunity to become truly learner-centred as learners explores those resources in which they are most interested and of which they are in most in need.

> **Quote 9.1** A. Collins on shifts in computer-based learning:
>
> - a shift from whole class to small-group instruction
> - a shift from lecture and recitation to coaching
> - a shift from working with better students to working with weaker ones
> - a shift toward more engaged students
> - a shift from assessment based on test performance to assessment based on products, progress, and effort
> - a shift from a competitive to a co-operative work structure
> - a shift from all students learning the same things to different students learning different things
> - a shift from the primacy of verbal thinking to the integration of visual and verbal thinking
>
> Collins (1991: 28)

Four of the articles (2 per cent) deal with problem solving. For example, Sinyor (1997) describes several sources of errors made by students of Italian and their problem-solving behaviours. Offering tips and resources (10 or 7 per cent) is a common theme in many CALL articles as old resources become less useful and new ones are introduced. An example of such an article is provided by Kitao (1997) who describes a directory of resources for the WWW. Similarly, DiBella (1997) gives suggestions for developing Web-based lessons for German-language classrooms.

Such tips and resources overlap with methods (38 or 26 per cent) and include articles on dictation, multiple-choice, cloze exercises, simulations, games and so on. Testing is mentioned in 15 (10 per cent) articles but none of these features computer-adaptive testing (CAT), the process of presenting a learner with increasingly difficult questions based on his or her ability to answer each preceding question successfully.

Special needs accounts for only one of the 145 articles. In this article, Schery and O'Connor (1997) reviewed three other studies exploring the effectiveness of computers and parent volunteers for remedial language-skills training in young children with Down's Syndrome and severe language, learning and behavioural disabilities. The article suggests that computer-based intervention is useful.

9.5.6   Subjects

The subjects of the articles included in this survey tend to be at the university level with only ten of the 145 studies (7 per cent) featuring children.

There are perhaps several reasons for this disparity. More research is done at the university level and university students are more accustomed to being used as experimental subjects. University lecturers may also have better understanding and access to academic publishing and are more likely to share their results in published forums than are teachers of young children for the simple reason that university researchers are compelled to do research as part of their academic work.

9.6 Conducting research

Research is concerned with looking at problems, asking questions and finding answers or solutions. There are many ways of looking at the research process and Brown (1988), for example, divides it into *primary*, where the researcher relies on first-hand data, and *secondary* where the researcher examines second-hand data, such as by summarizing studies by other researchers. Primary research is further divided into *case study approaches* and *statistical approaches*. Case study approaches, often ethnographic in nature, are dealt with separately below. Statistical approaches are divided into *survey approaches* and *experimental approaches*.

> **Quote 9.2** C. Crook challenges computer versus traditional teaching
>
> If we do wish to conduct evaluations of what is learned in computer-based contexts, we must go beyond the input–output designs that characterize much research in the area. . . . Computers are unlikely to function as magic bullets – effortlessly releasing their therapeutic effects at points identified by teachers. The unfamiliarity and wizardry that surrounds them may cultivate such notions, but the real impact of learning through this technology may need to be measured with attention to how it is assimilated into the surrounding frame of educational activity.
>
> Crook (1994: 9)

Traditionally, much research on CALL has focused on whether or not students learn better with a computer. But, as mentioned earlier, the question is no longer *whether* or not computers should be used in the classroom. Questions now include *how* computers should be used and *for what purpose.* One of the ways for classroom teachers and other researchers to approach these questions is through Action Research, an approach ideally suited to the increasing involvement of teachers as researchers.

9.7   Action Research

Action Research asks the question *Is there a better way?* and usually includes three stages of *planning, acting* and *reflecting*. In planning, the classroom researcher tries to imagine a teaching/learning problem and think of ways in which intervention might solve it. Consultation is encouraged, both with teaching colleagues and the learners or subjects of the action. Although planning a timeline is encouraged, action researchers should also be open to adapting their plans and actions, depending on the feedback and results they receive along the way.

The acting stage involves putting some kind of change into place. During this stage, the researcher should look for measurements of change and the success of those changes. These measurements can take the form of questionnaire results, learner logs, notes from informal discussions with colleagues and so on. In this stage, they should be shared in discussions with colleagues, posting or publishing of results and meetings with concerned parties.

The reflecting stage involves assessing not just how an intervention has solved the problem set out in the planning stage, but also how the researcher's own biases and priorities may influence the interpretation of the results. A certain openness to unexpected results is also encouraged in Action Research.

A key feature of Action Research is that it encourages the researcher constantly to revisit each stage in what is usually termed and/or diagrammed as a spiral fashion. Also, Benson (2001) contrasts Action Research to experimental research, suggesting that it: 'does not necessarily require the "subjects" of the research to be kept in the dark about the researchers' purposes' (p. 183).

An Action Learning model (after McLean, 1995) features the following: *conceptualization, implementation* and *interpretation*, which can be defined as is detailed below.

Conceptualization
Delineate teaching/learning process
Identify inputs
Identify outcomes

Implementation
Measure outcomes
Identify comparison
Analyse comparison

Interpretation
Judge effectiveness

Judge cost benefit
Determine action

In a typical CALL Action Research project, a teacher/researcher might go through the above stages in this way:

Conceptualization

Delineate teaching/learning process: the teacher defines a specific problem concerning the effectiveness of CALL then presents it to a group of learners (let's say, a class of 14 year-olds from several language groups learning English) using the school CALL lab. After discussion with colleagues and the learners themselves concludes that a solution might be peer-teaching approach, pairing the stronger and weaker students and having them share a computer.

Identify inputs: the teacher defines the inputs as the assignment of pairs and the change in seating patterns. Other factors that might also influence teaching and learning also need to be identified and accounted for.

Identify outcomes: The teacher expects to see a speedier move along the CALL learning curve and increased participation. As the students' common language is English, the teacher also hopes to see a much greater use of English.

Implementation

Measure outcomes: the teacher collects data by informally asking learners about how they like the new arrangement and what problems they might be having. With appropriate permissions, unobtrusive video might be taken and data collected from the computer from tasks, records of emails and chatline discussions and even keystroke records (through a program such as Lotus *Screencam*) on some assignments. Some adjustments are made, based on the data.

Identify comparison: as hoped, computer use and use of English both increase. As an unexpected outcome, learners now ask for access to the computer lab outside of class hours. However, not all the pairings are successful and some learners want to pair with peers from their own language group which the teacher fears may simply lead to the students using their first language and ignoring English.

Analyse comparison: the teacher analyses the benefits and drawbacks of the changes. The experiment is changed to allow learners to choose their own partners, but the teacher introduces an English-only policy in the CALL lab. Other teachers are invited to watch the class and comment. At the end of the semester, students write their reflections on the changes and preferred working styles. The teacher notices that the partners who were selected as the more-abled peers had a lower degree of satisfaction than the less-abled peers.

Interpretation

Judge effectiveness: at the end of the semester, the teacher finds that many students publicly state that they prefer to work on their own, but this seems contradicted by their eagerness in their pair-work participation. She/he has also noticed that attendance has improved.

Judge cost benefit: the teacher tries to assess the extra time involved in managing the change and finds that it is inconsequential compared to the improved language use and participation.

Determine action: for the next semester, the teacher decides to repeat the experiment, but allow learners a choice of selecting their own partners or working alone. She also decides to improve the 'marketing' of the ideas and advantages behind peer work, emphasizing that the more-abled peer is likely to improve as he is forced to think about how to explain new concepts. Before then, the teacher writes up her findings with one of her colleagues and presents them at a local conference.

Quote 9.3 C. Crook (1994) on the evaluation of outcomes

It may not be enough to expose a pupil to some software and, some time later, do an outcome test of understanding. The reason this is inadequate is because any such computer experience is more or less situated in some broader framework of teaching activity. In short, there is a risk of casting this educational technology in terms that suggest a medical model of how it works.

Crook (1994: 9)

Summary

As mentioned in Chapter 1, the distinction between the classroom teacher and the researcher is disappearing. Also, learners are becoming more involved in the research process, contributing perspectives and commenting on findings. This chapter has presented several different kinds of research as well as a general methodology, Action Research, that the teacher can make use of in the classroom.

Further reading

There are many resources available both in print and on the WWW, although Action Research is not confined to education; it is very popular within management disciplines. To begin with, three bibliographic sites that give WWW references as well as book references are:

- The Action Research Collaborative of St Louis: *http://www.csd.org/arc.html*
- University of Minnesota Extension Services Action Research Resources: *http://www3.extension.umn.edu/people/fhoefer/educdsgn/actresrc.htm*
- *http://www.scu.edu.au/schools/gcm/ar/arp/arphome.html*

Beatty, K. and Bremner, S. *An Investigation of the Computer-Based Writing Strategies of Business Students. http://www.cityu.edu.hk/ls/letters/* – This website provides an example of the application of a commercial product, Lotus *ScreenCam*, to the study of student writing at the computer. The program unobtrusively captures the successive keystrokes and plays them back in a format similar to a video and, as a research tool, is well-suited to examining process writing in which the researcher is curious about how a learner edits her work and accepts or refuses automated computer corrections.

Levy, M. (1997) *Computer-assisted language learning: context and conceptualization*. Oxford, Oxford University Press. – This book presents a general overview of CALL and includes the results of an extensive 1991 survey on the subject.

Corbel, C. (2000) Beyond burn rate: Sustainability online. In *Lens on Literacy*. Proceedings of the Australian Council for Adult Literacy Conference, 21–23 September. Perth, Western Australia: ACAL. *http://cleo.murdoch.edu.au/confs/acal/procs/corbel.html* – In this paper, Chris Corbel talks about some of the challenges of making distance education work.

Burns, A. (1999) *Collaborative Action Research for English Language Teachers*. Cambridge: Cambridge University Press. – This book recommends collaboration between teachers, using their individual experience as the basis for their collaborative Action Research.

Chapter 10

Research

The nature of CALL is changing because of improvements in computer literacy among learners and advances in computer hardware and software. However, creating a better fit between good pedagogy and technology continues to be a major challenge. Nowhere is this clearer than in a survey of Leech and Candlin's (1986) collection of papers from a conference on the use of computers in English language teaching and research. The conference, which took place in Lancaster, England in 1984, raised many concerns and research issues in computing that are still valid today. For example, what Davies (1986) has to say about authoring packages is often true today:

> The disadvantage of authoring packages is that they can be restrictive and result in rather unimaginative courseware. The user is saddled with the framework set up by the creator of the authoring package, and although the tutorial material itself can be infinitely varied, the form of presentation tends to become monotonous (p.15).

Similarly, Knowles (1986) asks the simple question, 'Why use computers?' He suggests that the computer should be able to do something the teacher cannot and give learners a richer learning experience.

Quote 10.1 Williams suggests the need for researchers to consider the particular nature of CALL technology:

We need more radical reviews of what learning might be through multimedia, combined with innovation in design (Stringer, 1997), to realize more fully the true potential for educational interaction in multimedia.

Williams (1998: 170)

Research in CALL is no longer restricted to laboratories or university researchers. Instead, teachers, software developers and the learners themselves are all involved in participating in research in classrooms and anywhere else where computers are used to improve language teaching and learning.

Several methodological approaches are discussed below with examples. Each begins with a research context followed by a sample research project. Each research project includes a description of aims, a suggested step-by-step procedure, an evaluation and further reading, outlining one or more related studies to which the researcher can refer to learn more about the topic or to adapt a research methodology. Researchers are also encouraged to refer to texts on research methods by Chapelle (1997, 2001), Grotjahn (1987) and Nunan (1992b), cited below.

Further reading

Chapelle, C. (2001) *Computer Applications in Second Language Acquisition.* Cambridge: Cambridge University Press. – This book focuses on three related areas: computer-assisted second language learning, computer-assisted second language assessment, and computer-assisted second language research. The book also discusses software evaluations and issues in teaching and learning at the computer.

Chapelle, C. (1997) CALL in the year 2000: still in search of research paradigms. *Language Learning and Technology* 1(1): 19–38. – This paper reviews the ways in which research is done in CALL and arrives at the conclusion that in some cases, quantitative approaches are ill-suited to the study of CALL.

Grotjahn, R. (1987) On the methodological basis of introspective methods. In Faerch, C. and Kasper, G. (eds), *Introspection in Second Language Research.* Clevedon: Multilingual Matters. – This paper gives a good overview of different approaches to research.

Nunan, D. (1992b) *Research Methods in Language Learning.* Cambridge: Cambridge University Press. – Although not orientated to CALL, this book offers a wealth of insights on conducting research, including a useful chapter of common problems faced by researchers and possible solutions.

Holliday, A. (2002) *Doing and writing qualitative research.* London. Sage.

A basic and general research methodology in CALL should include a question to be answered, a clear idea of the subjects and situation, a method for collecting data, a timeline for collecting data, an idea of how to interpret the data and an intention to share.

- *a question to be answered* is likely to arise out of problems in teaching and learning, teacher curiosity or challenges to published research. The question can be as broad as 'What is there to know about spelling checkers?' or as specific as, 'How can I help my students improve their spelling with a computer?'

- *a clear idea of the subjects and situation* is important for purposes of documentation and comparison. You may find published accounts of contrary research findings to your own experience but the reason may be attributable to factors to do with differences in the subjects or the research or the context.

- *a method for collecting data* is necessary to ensure that the research can be consistently repeated.

- *a timeline for collecting data* is important to ensure that the researcher has limits to a research project, or limits to this phase so that the other phases can proceed.

- *an idea of how to interpret the data* is not always necessary at the outset – for example, a case study might not anticipate some of the data, but in other cases, it is useful to direct the research.

- *an intention to share* is important to get feedback on the research. Sharing can be through a talk with the subjects (the learners), a posting to the WWW with contact information for those interested in discussing the problems, a presentation to other teachers (informally or at a conference), publication in a newsletter or journal, and/or a letter to the developer whose materials you used and critiqued. This last possibility – contacting the hardware or software developer – is often overlooked in academia, but it should be a necessary step if researchers/ teachers/ learners are to have a greater impact on commercial CALL materials.

10.1   Research context 1: The literature review

Most often, a literature review is an early part of an experiment, providing a background to understand whether or not a question has already been answered or a hypothesis already proven. A literature review can also provide data by summarizing several studies that, individually, may not statistically support any one point of view. As mentioned earlier, for example, Chapelle and Jamieson (1991) summarize ten studies from 1971 to 1986 and suggest that they do not provide strong empirical evidence for the superiority of CALL over classroom instruction (p. 37). However, a more recent review by Meich, Nave and Mosteller (1996) in an examination of 22 empirical CALL studies conducted between 1989 and 1994 concluded the opposite: CALL can 'substantially improve achievement as compared with traditional instruction' (p. 1).

The conclusion is not that one group of researchers were wrong and the other group was right, but rather that factors may have changed. In this case, it may be that programs are better, platforms are more standardized, learners are more computer-literate and so on. But each of these conjectures is only the kernel of a hypothesis that would have to be explored through further research.

10.1.1   Research project 1: A literature review on learners' search for information at the computer

Aims

- To understand a variety of perspectives on a single issue.
- To determine where there is a lack of research on an issue.

Procedure

1. Begin with a question or a general area of concern. In conducting a literature review, it helps to have an open mind about what the research might offer – for example, both the productive and less than productive ways in which learners search for information at the computer. At the same time, it might be necessary to narrow the search, for example focusing on the WWW and ignoring searching for information using email, chatlines and computer help pop-up boxes within software applications.
2. Define the area and try to think about as many related terms as possible, for example, *World Wide Web*, *Internet*. Use a thesaurus.
3. Narrow the research in a sensible way. For example, if there are too many articles, you might only consider research done in the past five years or research of university-level learners rather than younger learners.
4. Collect and review the resources, summarizing them and working them into a framework based on important features.
5. Make the literature review available to others and continue to maintain it, perhaps by inviting others to help you maintain it on a dedicated web page with a submission form prompting other researchers to answers the same questions you asked when reviewing other work.

Quote 10.2 In her book, *Secrets of the Super Net Searchers*, R. Basch suggests researchers ask seven basic questions:

What information are you looking for?
What do you plan to do with the information?
How much information do you need?
Where are you likely to find the information?
Where is the best place to start?
How much time should you spend looking?
How will you know when to stop?

Basch (1996: xx)

Evaluation

A literature review is best measured by its extent, its annotations and how current it is. In fact, all literature reviews should be considered as works in progress.

Concept 10.1   **Bibliographic software**

Endnote (*http://www.isiresearchsoft.com/en/enhome.htm*) is one of several programs used for compiling bibliographic references, with notes. A related program, *Endlink*, can search online databases and download both the references and, in some cases, full papers.

Further reading

Peterson, Mark (1997) Language teaching and networking. *System* 25 (1) (March): 29–37. – This literature review looks at the impact of computer networking on foreign language teaching. The paper includes a description of how Internet-based activities operate in the classroom. This last part provides context to the literature review.

10.2   Research context 2: A pilot study

A pilot study is a precursor for further, fuller research. In a pilot study, all the research considerations such as hypotheses, subjects, procedures and analysis methodologies are in place; it is only that the data are not considered substantial enough to support firm conclusions.

Pilot studies are typically done with small groups of subjects and serve to test the methodology as well as a hypothesis or hypotheses. An inherent suggestion in all pilot studies is that a further – usually larger or longer – study will be held. However, in practice, this is not always the case. Sometimes the results from the pilot study suggest further study is unwarranted, sometimes the researcher intends that others might follow up the pilot study and sometimes the researcher simply moves on to other areas of interest. When evaluating a pilot study, one should consider whether any follow-up has been done and, if not, why not. The answer may point to problems in the research topic or methodology. If there has been no follow-up study where one should have been done, it may present an excellent opportunity for research as much of the preparatory work has already been done.

In CALL, many pilot studies may falter because of inadequate technology. It is a worthwhile avenue of research to revisit historical issues in CALL that have failed to progress past the pilot study stage to see whether they might be better addressed with today's technology. For example, questions twenty years ago about the influence of graphics on student performance are likely to be dramatically different today, as the computer's presentation of graphics has become much more sophisticated. The basic questions remain, but the answers and the ways of finding the answers have changed a great deal.

10.2.1   Research project 2: A pilot study examining automatic correction systems

Aims

- To understand the role of automatic correction systems in common word-processing software.
- To determine whether such systems influence learners to abandon responsibility for correcting the errors themselves.

Concept 10.2   **Examining the role of affordances and misaffordances**

Affordances (i.e. what the program is or appears to be capable of doing in terms of both intended and unintended functions) and its opposite, misaffordances, differ from software program to program but some are becoming generalized as they are adopted by popular programs such as office software commonly pre-installed on a computer. For example, the ideas of FAQs, windows, trash, grammar and spelling checkers are all invented affordances that now have wide application to learning programs. However, their roles in encouraging and discouraging learning need to be more closely considered.

Procedure

1. Begin with a thesis or statement, for example, *A computer program's automatic corrections, for example, the imposition of default American spellings and capitalization of initial letters at the start of a sentence, discourages learners from taking responsibility for such actions themselves.*
2. Consider ways in which the statement could be operationalized into an experiment to measure the truth of the thesis. In this case, you might create a task in which twenty students complete an assignment (e.g.

writing a letter for a job application) using a common word-processing software program with the automatic dictionary and capitalization functions suppressed (the test group) while another twenty students use the same program with the features not suppressed (this is the control group).

3. Select a group of learners. Find a way of randomly assigning them to one of the two groups. Make sure you leave the learners unaware of what is being measured.

4. Have the learners complete the task and compare the results between the two groups.

5. Determine if there is a difference and consider whether it is likely to be a result of the key factor being considered or something else. For example, was one group in a different room, using different computers, at different times? Was the makeup of the two classes somehow different? Was the test group aware of the problem and compensated?

6. Determine whether the differences are likely to be statistically significant.

7. Share the results to solicit further feedback and decide whether a full-scale study is possible and/or desirable.

Evaluation

The success of a pilot study depends on the isolation of the key variables being tested. If, in retrospect, the results of a pilot study cannot be attributed to the factors under consideration, it must be re-done with a more reliable methodology. If a clearer idea of a problem is revealed in a pilot study, a researcher may shift the focus of the research to solving the problem, perhaps through the creation of a new piece of software or a change to teaching and learning methods. On the other hand, a pilot study that does not reveal any difference is not a failure; such a finding adds to one's understanding.

Further reading

Fox, M. (1997) Beyond the technocentric – developing and evaluating content-driven, Internet-based language acquisition courses. *Computer Assisted Language Learning* 10 (5): 443–53 – This paper presents a review of an ongoing project in which the author is involved. This reflective approach is common although it may be threatened by a lack of objectivity. Among the conclusions of the paper is that there is room for a sub-discipline of CALL, which the author labels *pragmatic* (practical/common sense) *CALL*.

10.3   Research context 3: Corpus linguistics

As discussed in Chapter 4, corpus linguistics is concerned with looking at a collection of texts and trying to find meaningful patterns of vocabulary and grammar within them. A teacher may look for patterns in his or her own writing or speech, those of colleagues or those of learners. The patterns may then lead to change, perhaps in the form of new teaching and learning materials.

Alternatively, a teacher may use a concordancing program in the classroom, teaching learners how to use it and setting them to work on their own explorations and discoveries of language use and patterns. This approach is particularly suitable for language learners at a higher level who are already producing extended writing samples; oral samples carry with them the challenges of transcription.

10.3.1   Research project 3: Investigating online language

Aims

- To understand the constituents of online language used in emails and chatlines.
- To create learning materials based on the vocabulary and grammar of online language.

Procedure

1. As with most projects, begin by creating a profile of the subjects of the study. This means describing them to give a clear picture of their age, socio-economic background, interests, first language(s) background, target language level and so on.

2. Partner with the learners. Engage them in the research as co-investigators and imbue them with a sense of the importance of the research.

3. Explain that you want to create a corpus of online messages. Ask the learners to collect emails and/or chatline messages for you. Explain that the purpose will be revealed at a later date so as not to influence the content of the messages.

4. Once you have a sufficient number of messages saved, explain the purpose of the research: to understand how learners use online language differently than the written and spoken norms of the target language.

5. Divide the learners into two or more groups. Make the first group responsible for examining the corpus for occurrences of unusual language use, such as *U* for *you*, *4* for *for* and listing each item's frequency. A simple word processor's spelling checker will help to find some of the

odder examples. Make the second group responsible for looking into odd grammatical constructions; a grammar checker might be useful for this. Other groups may look for other information/examples, such as the use of non-target language words in exchanges.

6. Have the learners compile their findings into a dictionary and grammar text, perhaps with reference to frequency and appropriateness.

7. Use the findings to help learners who inappropriately use casual online language in their everyday speaking and writing.

Evaluation

Getting the learners involved as co-researchers in a project helps to increase their enthusiasm to participate and, at the same time, makes them curious about the language they may be taking for granted. The above research project might be used as a pilot project, for example, for a larger project investigating the influence of online language on student writing.

Further reading

Jones, R. (2001) *Beyond the Screen: a participatory study of computer-mediated communication among Hong Kong youth.* A paper presented at the Annual Meeting of the American Anthropological Association 28 November – 2 December 2001. *http://personal.cityu.edu.hk/~enrodney/Research/ICQPaper.doc* – This paper focuses on the use of ICQ or chatlines in a situation where the subjects kept records of their interactions. Video-taped interviews and mind maps were used to interpret the issues further.

Murray, D. (2000) Protean communication – the language of computer-mediated communication. *TESOL Quarterly* 34(3): 397–422. – This paper provides an overview of many of the issues in online language and includes extensive references that will be useful for directing further research.

Turnbull, J. and Burston, J. (1998) Towards independent concordance work for students: lessons from a case study. *On-Call* (12) (2): 10–21 – This paper describes a longitudinal (over an extended time) case study of concordancing strategies used by two postgraduate students who were not native speakers of English. In the study, a software program was used to correct the students' English written expressions. These texts were then used in a corpus for the students' concordance work. As is common with case studies, this project had few subjects or participants – only two. In some instances, a researcher may begin with more subjects but, for various reasons, have them drop out of the research study.

10.4   Research context 4: Error analysis

Error analysis focuses on interpreting the errors made by learners and interpreting them as patterns related to processes or problems in learning.

When dealing with errors at the computer, such as errors in writing, error analysis is simplified by the computer's ability to collect information unobtrusively from the learner. For example, programs such as Lotus *ScreenCam* can replay in a movie-like format all individual keystrokes, mouse pointer-device moves and successive portions of a program viewed by the learner.

Quote 10.3 T. Chanier, M. Pengelly, M.B. Twidale and J.A. Self on the history of error analysis:

Error Analysis has a long tradition. Until the late 1960s, it consisted mainly in building large collections of 'common' errors and their linguistic classification. The goals were pedagogic: errors provided information for teaching and for designing remedial lessons. No theoretical framework existed for explaining the role played by the errors. In accordance with Behaviorist learning theory, the prevention of errors was more important than the identification of errors. Most people considered errors as a faulty version of the foreign language. The Contrastive Analysis Hypothesis (errors are the result of differences between the learner's first language and the foreign language) reinforced this view with the notion of 'interference': existing habits prevent correct utterances from becoming established; errors are signs of learning failure and thus are not tolerable.

At the beginning of the 1970s new studies changed the approach to the Error Analysis problem. Following the new Mentalist theory of language learning, these theorists asserted that the second language learners could be viewed as actively constructing rules from the data they encounter and gradually adapting these rules in the direction of the target-language system. This means that learners' errors need not be seen as signs of failure. On the contrary, they give some evidence for the learner's development systems. Today theories of language learning are increasingly learner-oriented. Error Analysis is still of interest since errors which represent the product of learning, can be used to get hints about the underlying process of learning and particularly the learner's strategies.

Chanier, Pengelly, Twidale and Self (1991: n.p.)

Further reading

James, C. (1998) *Errors in language learning and use*. Harlow: Addison Wesley Longman. – Although this book does not focus on computer applications to error analysis, it is a worthwhile explanation of the issues involved.

10.4.1   Research project 4: Systematic learner writing errors

Aims

- To understand the nature of systematic errors influenced by a first language in learning a target language.
- To create materials to address such errors.

Procedure

1. Contrastive linguistics is a field that provides insights into typical errors expected from a speaker of one language learning another. This type of research often makes use of corpus linguistics, examining extensive examples of errors. In this project, the scope can be narrowed to errors made in learners' written work on the computer.

2. As you correct learners' errors (preferably all from a single first-language group) ask them to keep track of both the errors and the corrections made.

3. Code the errors for each learner and then compile all the errors into a common database and ask learners to help determine patterns. For example, a common error of Chinese speakers learning English is to add the word *colour* to the colours themselves, e.g. **My book is blue colour.* instead of *My book is blue.*

4. Ask learners to try to generate rules about the errors and, where possible, consider why they occur, e.g. unlike English, Chinese uses a separate particle (*se*) to mark colour words.

5. Organize the information into a guide, table or database for current and future students, perhaps on a web page.

6. Share the findings with others and encourage them to add to the guide on an ongoing basis.

7. Create learning materials, perhaps in the form of a software program, to address the errors.

Evaluation

A standard examination of the contrasts between two languages may simply repeat published materials so, rather than reinvent the wheel, the researcher should take time to do a literature review. An area of related research would be critical thinking in a computer-based environment: how a software program could offer intelligent computer-based intervention to encourage critical thinking about typical errors. This presumes, of course, that learners take such advice when it is offered; it would be of interest to know whether, when, how and why learners routinely ignore responsibility for editing details that are automated for them through computer-based grammar and spelling checkers. Also, do learner attitudes towards spelling and grammar at the computer transfer to their hand-written work?

Further reading

Dagneaux, E., Denness, S. and Granger, S. (1998) Computer-aided error analysis. *System*. 26 (2) (June): 163–74 – This paper talks about the use of computer-aided error analysis in which a computer-based editor tags seven major error categories in a corpus of English written by native speakers of French. These errors are then classified in terms of frequency and help to rate French learners of English.

Yang, J.C. and Akahori, K. Error analysis in Japanese writing and its implementation in a computer-assisted language-learning system on the World Wide Web. *Calico Journal* 15 (1–3): 47–66. – This paper reports on a web-based program developed by the authors which evaluates errors in written Japanese and gives feedback for correction. The authors collected 1,000+ sentences, analysed them and found that the program's corrections were correct about 84 per cent of the time. Presumably, the program's performance can be improved based on a consideration of where it last went wrong.

10.5 Research context 5: The experiment

An experiment is a way of finding out information by creating an artificial situation and changing the variables at play. If we wanted to find out if hyperlinked sound recordings of text improved reading skills, it would be easy to create a program to do so and test it on one group. But to make the experiment 'measurable', it would be necessary to have a baseline to compare the learners' progress.

Concept 10.3   **Ethics in experimental procedures**

Any experiment is bound by ethical guidelines. The researcher should not bring harm, mental or physical, to the subjects, regardless of the value of the research. For example, it would be unethical to investigate repetitive stress syndrome at the computer with a test group likely to hurt themselves physically. Similarly, it would be unethical to have students participate in an experiment in which their privacy might be compromised or their mental health affected by an artificial situation. One must pay particular attention to control groups; it can be unfair to deny some learners opportunities provided to an experimental group. For example, if in a test of the influence of computing skills, one group was given a set of computers while the other was denied access to computers for a year. Most institutions where research is conducted offer guidelines for ethical research and it is the researcher's duty to be familiar with them.

10.5.1   Research project 5: Investigating the influence of models of instruction on collaborative learning

Aims

To understand the influence of different models of instruction on collaborative learning with the learners working at the same computer.

Procedure

1. Create a database of information around a particular topic, for example, a single poem. The information would include various media such as hypertext annotations, commentaries, illustrations, sound and video deliveries of the poem.
2. Identify a rationale for the construction of questions/tasks.
3. Create a set of tasks/questions.
4. Create two interfaces for the database using different models of instruction: behaviourist (see Section 5.5) and constructivist (see Section 5.6). For example, the behaviourist interface might focus on a simple lock-step series of examples followed by questions. The constructivist interface might rewrite the same questions into more interesting tasks that direct the learner towards the answers.
5. Select learners to act as subjects for the investigation.
6. Divide the subjects randomly into two groups.
7. Allow subjects to work in pairs and use the learning materials in a controlled situation to complete a series of tasks.
8. Observe and record the extent and quality of interactions through video.
9. Transcribe the video interactions.
10. Examine the answers of the learners.
11. Examine the *Lotus ScreenCam* files of the mouse-moves and keystrokes.
12. Identify key interactions in which the subjects exhibit aspects of collaboration or a lack of collaboration.
13. Have an independent examination of the key interactions to ensure the accuracy of the transcriptions.
14. Examine the quality of the key interactions through discourse analysis.
15. Analyse and interpret the findings
16. Construct a model to explain the analysis and interpretations.
17. Explain the implications for learning.

Evaluation

The above experiment would be time-consuming and it might be difficult to extrapolate conclusively any findings to apply them to a larger population. CALL researchers should consider experiments that take advantage of the WWW to capture large numbers of subjects.

Further reading

Ford, N. and Ford, R. (1994) Toward user models for intelligent computer-assisted learning; an empirical study. *Journal of Education for Library and Information Science* 35 (Summer): 187–200. – In this study, Ford and Ford (1994) examine student expectations by using what was essentially a trick experiment. A group of university students was told that they were conversing with a new computer system equipped with natural language capabilities, that is, the computer could supposedly respond more or less intelligently to any queries presented to it. What the students trying the system did not know was that they were in fact electronically connected to two trained researchers who answered their questions. The study, therefore, is mainly about students' question types and other factors that impact on their success in learning. However, it also outlines ideas learners have about computer interface and might serve to point a direction towards how learners prefer to interact with computers.

Pask, G. and Scott, C.E. (1972) Learning strategies and individual competence. *Man–Machine Studies* 4: 217–53. – An interesting study with good formatting for the experiment. Suggests five methods of competence determination: Questioning and selecting during free learning (human administration); Questioning and selecting during free learning (machine administration); content analysis of essays; Tutorial (teachback) procedure (human administration) and Tutorial (teachback) procedure (machine administration).

10.6   Research context 6: A case study

Case studies are often fishing expeditions in which one hopes to clarify suspicions and uncover the unexpected. Case studies are more likely to make use of the collection and presentation of detailed information about a particular participant or small group rather than a large group representative of society as a whole. As such, a case study may not even have a clear research agenda other than attempting to document a subject, time and place as thoroughly as possible. Other case studies are likely to begin with a question. One of the advantages of case studies is that, while they may yield fewer definitive conclusions, they often present further directions for research.

In CALL, case studies are very common, particularly as Action Research projects (see Burns, 1999) or as reports on the implementation of programs of study or the effectiveness of hardware and software.

10.6.1   Research project 6: Evaluating software effectiveness

Aims

- To understand the effectiveness of a particular CALL software package with a group of particular students.
- To develop guidelines for the use of the software package.

Procedure

1. Review guidelines for software evaluation. This can be done by compiling guidelines used in various CALL journals (see Section IV) and by reading software reviews and noting categories and the points of interest. Mark Peterson offers a simple evaluation form for CALL programs:

   http://iteslj.org/Handouts/Peterson-CALLQuestionnaire.html that can serve as a starting point. A more detailed consideration is found in Bradin, C. (1999) CALL issues: instructional aspects of software evaluation. In Egbert, J. and Hanson-Smith, E., *CALL Environments: Research, Practice and Critical Issues*. Alexandria, VA, TESOL: 159–177.

2. Examine the stated objectives of the software package. What does it purport to do?

3. Think of ways to measure learner interaction with the program as well as the benefits in relation to the package's objectives. You might decide to create a questionnaire for the learners, interview them, ask them to use think-aloud protocols to discuss what they are thinking while using the programs and/or use a background keystroke capture program (e.g. Lotus ScreenCam) to review what parts of the package the learners have visited and what they have done.

4. Allow learners to use the software package.

5. Collect and review the data. Share the process with the learners to ensure that your interpretations match their perceptions and intentions.

6. Create guidelines for the effective use of the software package. For example, you might find that the package is only suitable for students of a certain language or computer-skills level, that it is best used as a game-like diversion or perhaps for a remedial purpose.

7. Share what you have found with learners and peers and, if possible and practical, engage in dialogue with the creator of the software. Giving feedback to the designers and producers of software may help to inspire

improved versions and better products. Publish your findings as a case study in a journal or as an extended review online or in an academic or commercial publication.

Evaluation

A case study methodology may serve to bring to light the unexpected and lead to further research. A case study might reveal that a software package, while living up to its claims, is heavily biased in terms of gender. The teacher might decide to do further research to determine whether this emphasis on gender influences learning.

Quote 10.4 A.B.M. Tsui on hyperlink design as a way of simulating and anticipating the way the human mind works:

In determining where a link should be put, the designer is trying to antici-pate the point at which the user may wish to find out more information, whether the information is necessary for the user to proceed, and what kind of information is likely to be needed by what kind of user, and try to cater for as wide a range of users as possible. This kind of design may be very useful for a user working on their own, it may or may not cause problems when more than one user is using the same interface because their minds work differently. One user may wish to click one link and another may wish to click another. If they verbalize their thinking and negotiate which link to click, then the effect is positive. More negotiation of meaning will take place. However, if, like your subjects, they do not verbalize it and one user simply clicks the links without consulting the other, it may be a frustrating exper-ience for him or her because he or she may not be able to follow his or her partner's thinking.

(Tsui, personal communication, 26 November 2000)

Another general area of interest is how the design of the interface influences learning, particularly when more than one learner works at the same computer. Much research has been done on interface design (see Edwards, Holland et al., 1994; Mardsjo, 1996; Williams, 1998) but as interfaces are always changing depending on what is technically possible, research continues. A case study might reveal that, while a program is fine for a learner working alone, problems arise when learners share a comput-ing space.

Further reading

Felix, U. (1998) *Virtual Language Learning: Finding the Gems Amongst the Pebbles.* Melbourne, Victoria: Language Australia. – This book profiles useful websites to enhance teaching and learning.

Richards, J.C. (ed.) (1998) *Teaching in Action: Case Studies from Second Language Classrooms.* Alexandria, VA. TESOL. – This book, although focused on language learning in general and not CALL, offers insights into the ways in which Action Research can be done in the language classroom. It also presents a good format with each entry critiqued by an experienced researcher.

Sokolik, M. (1997) *Review of Planet Arizona. http://www-writing.berkeley.edu/chorus/call/reviews/archives/escape.html* – In an excellent approach to reviewing software, Sokolik compares using EF Multimedia's *Planet Arizona* to the program's published claims.

Carliner, S. (2001) Modeling information for three-dimensional space: lessons learned from museum exhibit design *http://saulcarliner.home.att.net/id/museumsandwebdesign.htm* – This article examines the educational experience of going to a museum and considers how it should inform the interface of web pages.

10.7 Research context 7: The survey

In looking for information from a larger group, a researcher can use the computer to capture their responses. One of the easiest ways to do this is to create an online task that the test subjects can complete on their own. A survey does not need to be structured as a straightforward questionnaire; marketing companies routinely 'hide' their web-based questionnaires in games that ask users to fill in their preferences as part of the 'fun'. For example, a marketer studying phone colour preferences might have users register on the website (collecting socio-economic data) then offer a game where the user uses an online paint palette to colour a domestic scene that includes a telephone. If a high percentage of users pick cherry-red for the phone, the marketer would recommend that as a colour for the production of real phones.

10.7.1 Research project 7: A survey of learner preferences

Aims

- To understand the relationship between learners' abilities and their enthusiasm.
- To understand the relationship between the presentation of information and motivation.

Procedure

1. Begin with a question. How do young learners transfer their computer skills and enthusiasm to disciplines such as CALL? It may be that young learners' familiarity with the possibility of what computers are capable of makes them less tolerant of educational applications that do not match the average computer game's exciting presentation of information. At the same time, recollection of tasks might be influenced by multimedia presentations; learners may be overwhelmed by the exciting and interesting aspects of the presentation rather than remembering what they have learned.

2. Create a short lesson on a grammar point, for example, the use of the subjunctive.

3. Use the lesson as a starting point to make three web-based presentations of the information; one as a very simple unadorned explanation and task, a second web page, heavily illustrated and a third web page where the information is organized into an interactive game.

4. Include a registration page to keep track of learners' participation including the time they choose to spend on the task.

5. Randomly assign students to complete the tasks on one of the three websites. Once students have completed writing the page, measure their attitude by having them complete a Likert scale (in which learners indicate their agreement on a scale of one to five or one to seven degrees for each item).

6. After enough students have completed the assignment, give a test to measure both their retention of the learning they have undertaken as well as their attitudes toward the website they have used.

7. Examine the data, rating the learners, performance on the websites and correlating their attitudes to performance. Do students do worse or better on what they perceive to be a plainer, less exciting interface?

8. Draw conclusions about the study and examine whether there may have been factors which interfered with the data, for example, students telling each other about the tasks.

9. Share the information with the learners and see how their perceptions match the conclusions you have drawn.

Evaluation

This type of a study, although difficult to construct, may run by itself once it is in place and, if sufficiently automated, may attract subjects from all over the world for an extremely large sample. Associated issues to the ones outlined above include the roles of extrinsic and intrinsic motivation. Learners at the computer are usually faced with extrinsic motivation and manufacture intrinsic motivation when it suits them. It would be of interest to study what conditions support the manufacture of intrinsic motivation at the computer and whether intrinsically motivated learners perform better than extrinsically motivated learners.

Example 10.1

Among the most popular computer-based testing programs is Questionmark's *Perception* (*http://www.qmark.com/uk/home.htm*). The program works within some other programs, such as WebCT (see Concept 9.2) and offers a wide variety of ways of evaluating learner performance and the use of banks of items to help individualize tests over repeated attempts.

- **Drag-and-drop:** the learner answers by dragging and dropping up to ten graphics into position.
- **Essay question:** the learner answers by typing up to 30,000 characters of text. Correct and incorrect answers can be defined in advance by entering a list of acceptable answers. A logic feature can score based on the presence or absence of key words or key phrases and the text saved for later consideration by a teacher.
- **Fill-in-the-blank:** the learner is presented with a statement where one or more words are missing and completes the missing words; multiple words can be listed as acceptable including mis-spelled words.
- **Hotspot:** a learner clicks on a picture to indicate a choice.
- **Likert scale:** the learner selects one choice from choices such as 'strongly agree' through 'strongly disagree' that are weighted with numbers to aid analysis of the results.
- **Matching:** two lists of statements/words are presented and the learner must match items.
- **Multiple choice:** the learner selects one choice from up to 40 possible answers. There is no limit to the length of each answer.
- **Multiple response:** similar to multiple choice except the learner is not limited to choosing one response; he/she can select none, one or more of the choices offered.
- **Matrix:** this question type presents several multiple choice questions together where the learner selects one choice for each statement or question presented. This question type is used to cross-relate responses from a single item.

- **Numeric questions:** a learner is prompted to enter a number that is scored as an exact answer with another score if the response is within a range.
- **Pull-down list (selection question):** a series of statements are presented and the learner can match these statements to a pull-down list.
- **Ranking (rank in order):** a list of choices must be ranked numerically.
- **Select-a-blank:** the learner is presented with a statement where a word is missing and words can be selected from a pull-down list to indicate the answer.
- **True/False:** the learner selects 'true' or 'false' in response to a question.
- **Word response (text match):** the learner types in a single word, or a few words to indicate the answer.
- **Yes/No:** the learner selects 'Yes' or 'No' in response to the question.

(adapted from *http://www.qmark.com/uk/perception/index.htm*)

Further reading

Moore, Z., Morales, B. *et al.* (1998) Technology and teaching culture: results of a state survey of foreign language teachers. *CALICO Journal* 15(1–3): 109–28. – This paper presents the results of a survey of language teachers and offers ideas that could well be replicated elsewhere. However, the survey was done in paper format; an electronic format, such as a questionnaire on a web page, would do away with time-consuming data entry.

_____. Innovative Technology Use In Middle School Language Arts Programs *http://www.albany.edu/~cela/survey.html* – This is a simple example of an online survey collecting information on computers and technology. What is lacking from the format is contact information, information about how the data will be used, how one might find out the general results and the timeframe of the survey; often such surveys are 'forgotten' and left online collecting information long after a project is finished.

10.8   Research context 8: The ethnographic approach

An ethnographic approach is similar to a case study and may be a case study, but the focus is on a social group. This group may be learners or teachers or a combination of the two. The purpose of an ethnographic study is to observe and understand the behaviours of a group. The documentation of such a study can be used as a benchmark, for future comparison with the same subjects or comparison with other subjects.

10.8.1   Research project 8: The culture of a MOO

Aims

To understand the ways in which learners communicate with in a MOO (see Section 4.5.3) environment.

Procedure

1. Make use of an existing MOO or create a MOO; this could be done with the aid of advanced learners.
2. Create a set of activities for the learners to do inside the MOO to encourage participation and use of the target language. Such activities could include the investigation of places such as shops and things a tourist might normally visit in a country using the target language.
3. Observe the behaviours of the learners. Try to determine what they are doing and why.
4. Look for patterns in the behaviours. Determine how these behaviours help or hinder the subjects in their tasks.
5. Consult with the subjects.
6. Share the observations and conclusions.

Evaluation

An ethnographic investigation is useful in a project such as this as it may serve to provide valuable insights into how the MOO environment might be altered. The computer helps provide a certain detachment as the researcher can collect data unobtrusively as an observer of the MOO environment.

Concept 10.4   **Fidelity**

Fidelity refers to the degree of realism in a computer simulation. As computer-based presentations of information improve through the use of video and virtual reality, the fidelity (or authenticity) of learner materials is increasing. However, in CALL simulations would seem a promising area of research to correlate the fidelity of a program with opportunities for SLA. For example, it may be that if learners are forced to use a greater degree of imagination (and therefore more negotiation of meaning) in a program with less fidelity, they might engage in a greater degree of negotiation of meaning.

Further reading

Gruber-Miller, J. and Benton, C. (2001) How do you say 'MOO' in Latin? Assessing student learning and motivation in beginning Latin. *CALICO Journal* 18(2): 305–38. – This paper talks about the use of a MOO environment, *Vroma*, for teaching beginner Latin. The paper gives a good indication of what is possible for making the most of a MOO environment. The paper also refers to other language MOOs and offers a feedback questionnaire at the end which could be adapted by other researchers for other software.

Turkle, S. (1995) *Life on the Screen: identity in the age of the Internet*. New York: Simon & Schuster. – This book investigates a range of issues to do with computer-mediated communication (CMC), including the use of MOOs.

Conclusion

If for no other reason than science fiction-fuelled fantasies, one may consider what would be necessary for a computer to replace a human teacher (and learner peers) completely for the teaching of language. As mentioned in Section 7.4, the test of such a task would be to engage in research to create or assemble a comprehensive CALL software program or set of programs for a language unknown to the teacher, the learner and the community, such as Swahili in rural Saskatchewan.

If nothing else the attempt and a consideration of what might need to go into such a package might serve to enlighten what it is that teachers do best and what computers do best.

Quote 10.5 N. Stephenson on a young girl's first encounter with a stolen 'book' – in fact an extremely sophisticated computer – that bonds with her and begins to teach her, using a fairytale incorporating herself and those around her. Her question prompts the book to break off from the story and offer a multimedia lesson to teach her part of the alphabet.

'What's a raven?' Nell said.

The illustration was a colorful painting of the island seen from up in the sky. The island rotated downward and out of the picture becoming a view toward the ocean horizon. In the middle was a black dot. The picture zoomed in on the black dot, and it turned out to be a bird. Big letters appeared beneath.

'R A V E N,' the book said. 'Raven. Now, say it with me.'

'Raven.'

'Very good! Nell, you are a clever girl and you have much talent with words. Can you spell *raven*?'

Nell hesitated. She was still blushing from the praise. After a few seconds, the first of the letters began to blink. Nell prodded it.

The letter grew until it had pushed all the other letters and pictures off the edges of the page. The loop on top shrank and became a head, while the lines sticking out the bottom developed into legs and began to scissor. 'R is for Run,' the book said. The picture kept on changing until it was a picture of Nell. Then something fuzzy and red appeared beneath her feet. 'Nell Runs on a Red Rug,' the book said, and as it spoke, new words appeared.

'Why is she running?'

'Because an Angry Alligator Appeared,' the book said, and panned back quite some distance to show an alligator, waddling along ridiculously, no threat to the fleet Nell. The alligator became frustrated and curled itself into a circle which became a small letter. 'A is for Alligator. The Very Vast alligator Vainly Viewed Nell's Valiant Velocity.'

The little story went on to include an Excited Elf who was Nibbling Noisily on some Nuts. Then the picture of the Raven came back, with the letters beneath. 'Raven. Can you spell raven, Nell?' A hand materialized on the page and pointed to the first letter.

'R,' Nell said.

'Very good!' You are a clever girl, Nell, and good with letters,' the book said. 'What is this letter?' and it pointed to the second one. This one Nell had forgotten. But the book told her a story about an Ape named Albert.

Stephenson (1995: 85–6)

Section

IV Resources

This section provides specific tools for learning more about CALL and conducting research. These tools include a list of references both traditional and virtual, that help you conduct research. Links in the form of addresses and websites provide easy access to professional conferences, organizations and publications concerned with CALL.

Following this section is a Glossary of key terms with definitions for ideas used throughout the book. The References at the end of the book include all publications that are mentioned in the text as well as others for further reading.

Journals and newsletters

CALICO Journal
Duke University
014 Language Center, Box 90267
Durham, NC 27708-0267 USA
http://calico.org

Canadian Journal of Learning and Technology
(formerly Canadian Journal of Educational Communication)
c/o Richard F. Kenny
Distance Education and Technology, Continuing Studies
University of British Columbia, Vancouver Canada B.C. V6T 1Z4
rick.kenny@ubc.ca

Computer-Assisted English Language Learning Journal
1787 Agate Street
Eugene OR 97403 USA
iste@oregon.uoregon.edu

Computer-Assisted Language Learning
PO Box 825
2160 SZ Lisse
The Netherlands
k.c.cameron@exeter.ac.uk

Computers and Composition
Department of Humanities
Michigan Technological University
Houghton, MI 49931 USA
http://www.cwrl.utexas.edu/~ccjrnl/

On-CALL
Centre for Language Teaching and Research
The University of Queensland
Brisbane, Queensland 4072

Australia
On_CALL@CLTR.uq.oz.au
http://www.cltr.uq.oz.au:8000/oncall

System
Elsevier Science Ltd, The Boulevard
Langford Lane
Kidlington, Oxford OX5 1GB, UK

TESOL CALL Interest Section Newsletter
c/o TESOL
1600 Cameron Street, Suite 300
Alexandria VA 22314 USA
tesol@tesol.edu

Research guides

Immerse yourself in reading published research by identifying an area of interest and conducting a literature review. There are many aids in doing so, such as searching databases of journal abstracts, like the Educational Research International Clearinghouse (ERIC) and Modern Language Association (MLA) Database as well as catalogues and databases of local libraries. If you do not have access to these, you can still conduct a literature review by using your key terms in a search engine such as *www.google.com*

Nunan, D. (1992) *Research Methods in Language Learning*. Cambridge, Cambridge University Press. – Although this book does not focus on CALL, it still provides a good overview of the issues involved in planning, conducting and publishing research.

Conferences and workshops

Because CALL operates on the periphery of so many other disciplines in language teaching and learning and applied linguistics, one is likely to find at least one CALL presentation at a broad range of conferences. These include conferences dedicated to individual languages as well as conferences focused on anything from computer games through to voice recognition technology.

Conferences which cater specifically to CALL are periodically mounted around the world. Some of the larger annual international CALL conferences are *ED-MEDIA, E-Learn, Eurocall, FLEAT, ICCE, SITE* and *WorldCall*. Find out the latest information by typing in the name of the conference and the year you are interested in attending by using a search engine such as *www.google.com*

Professional associations

There are many international professional associations for CALL practitioners but you may wish to look for one locally as it will enable you to participate more frequently in presentations and workshops. If you cannot find one locally, you may consider starting a group to meet informally to discuss common CALL problems and consider research.

Some of the more popular associations and organizations promoting CALL, many of which have their own conferences, include:

Association for the Advancement of Computers in Education (AACE)
PO Box 296
Charlottesville, VA 22902 USA
aace@virginia.edu
http://www.aace.org/

Association for Educational Communications and Technology (AECT)
620 Union Drive, Room 143, North Indiana University–Purdue University
Indianapolis, IN 46202 USA
http://www.aect.org/

Chorus@CALL
http://www-writing.berkeley.edu/chorus/index.html

Computer-Assisted Language Instruction Consortium (CALICO)
Duke University
014 Language Center, Box 90267
Durham, NC 27708-0267 USA
http://calico.org

Computer-Assisted Language Learning Interest Section
317 Liberal Arts
Southwest Texas State University
San Marcos, TX 78666 USA
http://darkwing/uoregon.edu/~call/

Computers and Information Technology (C&IT)
University of Hull
Hull, HU6 7RX, UK
cti.lang@hull.ac.uk
http://www.lang.ltsn.ac.uk/cit/

Computer-using Educators (CUE)
1210 Marina Village Parkway, Suite 100
Almeda, CA 94501 USA
http://www.cue.org/

EuroCALL
(C&IT)
University of Hull
Hull, HU6 7RX, UK
http://www.eurocall.org/

International Society for Technology in Education (ISTE)
University of Oregon
1787 Agate Street
Eugene, OR 97403 USA
ISTE@oregon.uoregon.edu

Email lists

Email lists are writing spaces on the WWW for those interested in a particular subject to share views and questions. *Newbies* (those new to a list) are encouraged to read the frequently asked questions (FAQ) and spend some time observing the exchanges before participating.

EST-L (Teachers of English for Science & Technology)
listserv@asuvm.inre.asu.edu
(send message *subscribe est-l yourfirstname yourlastname*)

JALTCALL (Japan Association for Language Teaching CALL)
majordomo@clc.hyper.chubu.ac.jp
(send message *subscribe jaltcall*)

LLTI (Language Learning and Technology International)
listserv@dartmouth.edu
(send message *subscribe llti yourfirstname yourlastname*)

NETEACH-L (Using the Internet for teaching ESL)
listserv@thecity.sfsu.edu
(send message *subscribe neteach-l yourfirstname yourlastname*)

TESL-EJ
North America: *http://violet.berkeley.edu/~cwp/TESL-EJ/*
Asia: *http://www.kyoto-su.ac.jp/information/tesl-ej/*

TESL-L (Teachers of English as a Second Language)
TESLCA-L (Computer-Assisted sub-branch of TESL-L)
listserv@cunyvm.cuny.edu
(send message *subscribe tesl-l yourfirstname yourlastname*)

International Student E-Mail Discussion Lists
Nine lists for ESL/EFL college and university students
announce-sl@latrobe.edu.au
(for information send a blank email message)

Websites

General websites

Open University Language Studies' web directory
http://www.open.ac.uk/education-and-languages/links/languages.cfm

Agora Newsletter homepage
http://www.agoralang.com/

I Love Languages (formerly Human Language Resource Page)
http://www.ilovelanguages.com/

Language fonts

Microsoft Corp
http://www.microsoft.com/ie/download/

Accent Software
http://www.accentsoftware.com/

Globalink Inc
http://www.softwarecenter.com/library/p_171.htm

World Wide Fonts
http://wwfonts.com/index.html

Yamada Language Center
http://babel.uoregon.edu/yamada/guides.html

Language Translation

Altavista Translation Service
http://babelfish.altavista.digital.com/cgi-bin/translate

The Translator's Home Companion
http://www.rahul.net/lai/companion.html

Software mentioned in this book

The following is a list of software mentioned in this book. The web
addresses and the companies that own the software may change, but
looking for the name of the product in a search engine such as
www.google.com will generally lead you to the new website.

- Adobe *Atmosphere http://www.adobe.com/products/atmosphere*
- Apple *HyperCard http://www.apple.com/hypercard*

Questionmark Perception

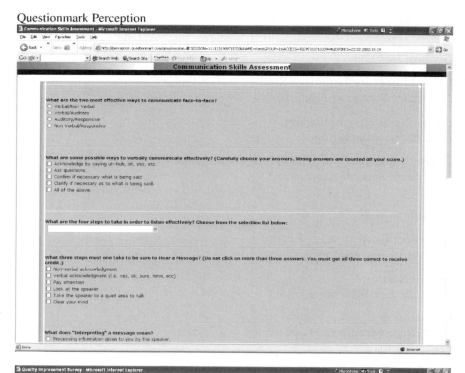

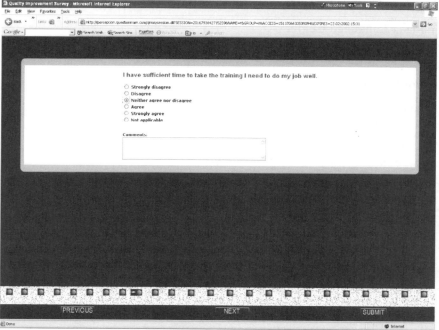

- Apple *Quicktime Authoring Studio* *www.apple.com/quicktime/qtvr/ authoringstudio/*
- Asymetrix *Toolbook* *http://www.asymetrix.com/en/toolbook*
- Cybersitter *Cybersitter 2001* *http://www.cybersitter.com/*
- Dragon Systems *Naturally Speaking* *http://www.lhsl.com/ naturallyspeaking/*
- Inspiration Software's *Inspiration* and a simpler version for young children *Kidspiration* *http://www.inspiration.com*
- ISI Researchsoft/Thomson Scientific *Endnote* *http://www.endnote.com/*
- Lotus *Notes for Workgroups* *http://www.lotus.com/home.nsf/ welcome/notes*
- Lotus *Screencam* *http://www.lotus.com/home.nsf/welcome/screencam*
- Macromedia *Authorware* *www.macromedia.com/software/authorware*
- Macromedia *Director* *http://www.macromedia.com/software/director*
- Macromedia *Dreamweaver* *http://www.macromedia.com/software/ dreamweaver*
- Microsoft *FrontPage* *http://www.microsoft.com/frontpage/*
- Microsoft *Office* (including Word and, in some versions, FrontPage) *http://www.microsoft.com/office/*
- Questionmark *Perception* *http://www.qmark.com/uk/home.htm*
- Softkey *Story Book Weaver Deluxe* *http://www.softkey.com/*
- Syracuse Language Systems *Triple Play Plus* *http://www.syrlang.com*

Bibliographies

The writing of a bibliography is a noble contribution to any discipline. Many CALL practitioners maintain bibliographies in the form of annotated links on their personal websites. You might consider adding to the body of knowledge by creating a CALL bibliography for a particular language or a particular area of interest. The following are some published and web-based bibliographies. And if you conduct research and publish, you might consider including your papers online.

- Paul Brett's bibliography on multimedia and second-language learning – with special emphasis to listening comprehension. *http://pers-www.wlv.ac.uk/~le1969/*
- John Higgins's bibliography on CALL features sections on background books, mainstream treatments of CALL, collections of articles, concordancing, uses of the Internet and journals. *http://www.marlodge.supanet.com/callbib.htm*

- Jim Duber's Chorus@CALL details software reviews, product announcements and demos of web technology. *http://www-writing.berkeley.edu/chorus/call*

Concordancing resources

The WWW is an ideal source of information about corpus linguistics and concordancing software as well as tools for conducting research. Some simple tools are available free of charge while more comprehensive and useful programs must be purchased. In most cases, a copy can simply be downloaded.

McEnry, T. and Wilson, A. (2001) *Corpus Linguistics.* Edinburgh: Edinburgh University Press. – This book has a dedicated website which includes supplemental material for the first four chapters of the book: *http://www.ling.lancs.ac.uk/monkey/ihe/linguistics/contents.htm*

Corpus Linguistics by Michael Barlow provides corpora on various languages and information on corpus linguistics: *http://www.ruf.rice.edu/~barlow/corpus.html*

The *Bergen Corpus of London Teenage Language (COLT)* provides limited online searches: *http://www.hd.uib.no/colt/*

The British National Corpus (BNC) features 100 million words. Limited searches are available online: *http://www.hcu.ox.ac.uk/BNC/getting/online.html*

The Michigan Corpus of Academic Spoken English (MICASE) offers general information and online searches: *http://www.lsa.umich.edu/eli/micase/micase.htm*

The Cobuild Corpus Sampler offers limited searches of 56 million words: *http://titania.cobuild.collins.co.uk/form.html*

University Centre for Computer Corpus Research on Language (UCREL) at Lancaster University: *http://www.comp.lancs.ac.uk/computing/research/ucrel/*

Tutorial: Concordances and Corpora by Catherine N. Ball, Georgetown University: *http://www.georgetown.edu/cball/corpora/tutorial.html*

Grammar Safari gives students ideas for looking for common and 'exotic' grammatical structures using the WWW as a corpus. The argument for this approach is that it provides real language in a natural context: *http://sun1.bham.ac.uk/johnstf/timconc.htm*

The WWW as a corpus for grammar exploration: *http://www.iei.uiuc.edu/resources/TESOL/Ann/grammarcorpus_index.html*

Concordancers

WordPilot 2000 is a commercial program which has a free 30-day download. *http://www.compulang.com/download.htm*

Wordsmith Tools developed by Mike Scott at Oxford University Press. Go to the page below and follow the instructions: *http://www.liv.ac.uk/~ms2928/wordsmith/screenshots/* or visit Mike Scott's homepage: *http://www.liv.ac.uk/~ms2928/index.htm*

J-BAT KWIC by Masatoshi Sugiura is a Java-applet concordancer: *http://oscar.lang.nagoya-u.ac.jp/program/*

Corpus Wizard, a shareware program, is available at: *http://www2d.biglobe.ne.jp/~htakashi/software/CWNE.HTM*

Monoconc, a commerical program available in Windows and Macintosh versions: *http://www.ruf.rice.edu/~barlow/mono.html*

Glossary of key terms

affordances are the visual clues that an object gives to its use as well as what the program is capable of doing in terms of both intended and unintended functions. A chair is for sitting on and the size of the seat suggests that it might be comfortable for that purpose, but the chair can also be stood upon or used as a weapon; these are other affordances. An object can have both affordances and *misaffordances*, things that distract from the object's intended use. Affordances can be both obvious and learned. A misaffordance for a chair would be design features that disguised its purpose or interfered with its principal purpose of being sat upon.

AI artificial intelligence refers to the ability of a computer to mimic human thinking processes.

AILA Association Internationale de Linguistique Appliquée.

ALLP the Athena Language Learning Project developed at Massachusetts Institute of Technology.

ALTE Association of Language Testers in Europe.

asynchronous refers to communication that takes place at different times, for example, through email in which a message is sent and may be read at leisure by the recipient.

avatar is an online personality that might resemble a person or almost anything else. Avatars are used in MOOs to represent a person and can be manipulated to move around an environment and interact with other participants' avatars.

CAI Computer-aided Instruction refers to learning at the computer, but not necessarily to do with language. Although not necessarily intended by all those who use the acronym, the term *instruction* suggests a teacher-centred approach.

CAL Computer-assisted Learning. Similarly to CAI, CAL may refer to the learning of any subject (including language learning) using a computer. But in contrast to CAI, CAL emphasizes the learner.

CALI Computer-assisted Language Instruction, a term commonly used in North America.

CALICO Computer-assisted Language Instruction Consortium.

CALL Computer-assisted Language Learning can be defined as learning language at the computer either as a direct activity through structured lessons or during an activity peripheral to the study of language but that, nonetheless, promotes language awareness and acquisition. In some cases, computer software that is used for teaching subjects other than language, such as mathematics, is included under the umbrella of CALL if the software's language has been simplified or otherwise adapted for use by non-native speakers. For the sake of brevity, in this book CALL is used as a collective term to include related terms except where a specific distinction needs to be made or in quotes from the literature where an author's original choice of term is preserved.

CALT Computer-assisted Language Testing.

CAT Computer-assisted Teaching (or Computer-adaptive Testing).

CBL Computer-based Learning.

CBT Computer-based Training tends to refer to programs used for corporate training with narrow and short-term instructional goals but may refer more generally to any kind of training. The term is not often used in the language-learning context except where it refers to the teaching of some discrete language learning skills, such as listening training.

CD-ROM Compact Disk-Read Only Memory is a disk storage format that can hold approximately 600 megabytes of information. That is, the same amount as about 600 floppy disks. A key difference between the two, however, is that a CD-ROM has faster access time allowing for the use of digital sound and video.

chatrooms a designation for private spaces used in Internet Chat Relay programs that allow for discussion on individual topics. Two or more participants wishing to discuss an issue may construct the virtual rooms at any time.

CMC Computer-mediated Communication refers to a situation in which computer-based discussion may take place but without necessarily involving learning.

CMI Computer-mediated Instruction refers to instruction that takes place through the use of a computer and may, for example, include learning that occurs when a learner communicates with a distant tutor through email or simply uses some form of computer hardware and software. The term *instruction* shows a teacher-centred approach.

cognitive overhead refers to the learning that needs to be done before using a software program.

cognitive overload refers to a computer software presentation which distracts the learner from the purpose.

Colossus the first British mainframe computer, used to assist in deciphering German Enigma cryptograms.

computer literacy vaguely refers to a set of skills and a base of knowledge required of learners. Because of continuous advances in technology, it is difficult to define such standards.

computer-adaptive testing is a program in which the learner is directed along easier or more difficult tasks or links depending on answers to questions at key points of the program. *See also* **CALT** above.

congruence Hoogeveen (1995) notes, 'The level of congruence is the degree to which different information types are used redundantly to express the same ideas' (p. 351). Inappropriate and unnecessary interruptions, such as flashing screens and senseless noises are *incongruent*.

cyberspace author William Gibson created the metaphor *cyberspace* in his 1984 science fiction novel *Neuromancer. Cyberspace* retains its original (although poetic) definition as 'a consensual hallucination' and 'a graphic representation of data' (Gibson, 1984: 51).

database a corpus of information which is accessible for selection and reorganization by predetermined criteria, as simple as alphanumeric ordering or by more complicated searches, such as by semantic field.

DDL Data Driven Learning, a term used in corpus linguistics to describe learner activities using a corpora.

DVD Digital Video Disks have approximately ten times the storage capacity of CD-ROMs. *See* **CD-ROM** above.

EAP English for academic purposes.

EFL English as a foreign language.

Eliza a program which simulates human intelligence by selecting portions of a learner's responses and fashioning them into further questions.

ENIAC Electronic Numerical Integrator and Calculator, an American computer intended for cryptography, but built too late to be of use in the Second World War (completed in 1945).

ERIC Educational Research International Clearinghouse.

ESL English as a second language.

EUROCALL European Association of Computer-assisted Language Learning.

FAQ Frequently Asked Questions.

fidelity refers to the degree of realism in a computer simulation.

FLEAT Foreign Language Education and Technology (conference organized by IALL and LLA).

GUI Graphical User Interface: icons used on the computer screen to automate some functions.

HCI Human Computer Interface, a term found in early publications in CALL, but now usually abbreviated to *interface*.

hotlink *see* **hyperlink**.

Hotsync refers to one device sharing data automatically with another, for example, a PDA with a desktop computer.

HTML Hyper Text Markup Language, text files that contain formatting instructions so that certain design and typographical conventions can be shared across computers.

HTTP Hyper Text Transfer Protocol, the method used to make hypertext documents available and readable on the World Wide Web.

HyperCard a software program developed by Apple Computer which creates a set of virtual index cards that can be extensively cross-referenced. On these cards, text, images, audio, animations and video can be added, along with questions and buttons to take users to other cards that might feature further questions, information and/or answers.

hyperlink refers to the hypertext link usually indicated by blue underline beneath text or a thin blue line around an image. Clicking on the hyperlink takes one to a new page or a pop-up page with further information.

IALL International Association for Learning Laboratories.

IATEFL International Association for Teachers of English as a Foreign Language.

ICALL Intelligent Computer-assisted Language Learning refers to a program or system that adapts to the learner and assesses his or her mistakes and provides tailored feedback recommending, for example, how typical errors might be remedied by going on to complete other tasks within the program. The computer may do so by asking questions of the learner about preferences and interests. A learner may also be asked simple knowledge questions which, if unanswered or answered incorrectly, lead the software into a subroutine to provide information on the topic and then present the questions or versions of the questions again.

ICQ I seek you, an Internet Relay Chat (IRC) program which allows users to be alerted to other designated users when they are both using the WWW.

incongruence *see* **congruence**.

IRC Internet Relay Chat, a form of WWW-based email that allows multiple computer users to engage in an online discussion.

IT Information Technology, a general term referring to computers as well as services such as the WWW.

ITS Intelligent Tutoring System, a term that once included non-computer learning applications (e.g. mechanical) that have now been largely replaced by computer-based applications.

KWIK Key Word In Context, a process used in concordancing.

LAN Local Area Network, a system of connecting a series of computers so as to allow them to share resources and communicate with each other.

LLA Language Laboratory Association of Japan.

LLT Language Learning and Technology.

locus of control refers to the continuum between the program's and the learner's responsibility for decisions about the outcomes, sequence of learning, learner interactions and even the content.

Memex a desk-sized (MEMory EXtension) system which would access and organize large amounts of information (Bush, 1945).

misaffordance *see* **affordances**.

MIT Massachusetts Institute of Technology that includes the *Media Lab*, site of many innovations in computing.

MT machine translation refers to the use of a computer to translate from one natural language to another.

multimedia offer two or more communication channels such as video and text. Early CALL programs primarily displayed text-only, either as teletype printouts or on video display screens. As the capabilities of the technology have increased, most programs increasingly offering multimedia, particularly pictures with text, but increasingly, sound and video as well.

netiquette rules about discussion on the WWW, including the avoidance of *flaming*, or abusive talk.

NLP Natural-language Processing.

PDA Personal Digital Assistant.

PLATO Programmed Logic/learning for Automated Teaching Operations, an early computer platform for teaching and learning.

Q&A Question and Answer papers typically bring those new to the field of CALL up to date on specific technologies and terminology.

scaffolding is the process by which one learner helps another grasp words and ideas by providing and building upon partial information.

schema theory 'A theory of language processing which suggests that discourse is interpreted with reference to the background knowledge of the reader or listener' (Nunan, 1993: 124).

SLA Second-language Acquisition.

synchronous refers to communication that takes place at the same time, such as through chatlines.

TEFL Teaching English as a Foreign Language.

TELL Technology Enhanced Language Learning usually includes CALL but also refers to any other technology that might be used in the classroom. For example, video, tape-recorders or even entire listening labs. These distinctions are becoming blurred as computers incorporate and become incorporated in other technologies. For example, modern CALL software often includes video and audio tape-recording facilities and language labs are increasingly computerized.

TESOL CALL-IS Teachers of English to Speakers of Other Languages CALL Interest Section.

UNIX UNiversal Interactive eXecutive or UNiversal Inter-eXchange *or* UNIversity eXchange; the etymology is so far only anecdotal.

virtual classroom Derycke, Smith and Hemery (1995) credit Roxanne Hiltz as coining the term and explain its qualities: the electronic classroom becomes virtual because it can relax the spatial constraints (users at different locations no matter how far apart) and the temporal constraints (users interacting over time via asynchronous communications). In fact the classroom is a virtual place where the learner can find not only pedagogical resources but also human (social) resources to support him/her in the distance learning process (p. 182).

VRML Virtual Reality Modelling Language.

WebCT Web Course Tools is a commercial educationally orientated web-authoring program developed at the University of British Columbia, Canada.

WELL Web-enhanced Language Learning.

wizard a program used to automate choices in creating a software program, particularly in authoring programs.

WWW World Wide Web (WWW) is a protocol that enables Internet users to share information with other Internet users.

ZPD Zone of Proximal Development, associated with Lev Vygotsky, refers to the idea that the potential for cognitive development is limited to a certain time span.

References

Ahmad, K., Corbett, G., Rogers, M. and Sussex, R. (1985) *Computers, Language Learning and Language Teaching*. Cambridge: Cambridge University Press.

Alessi, S. and Trollip, S. (2001) *Multimedia for Learning: Methods and Development*. Harlow: Allyn and Bacon/Longman.

Alexander, J.G. (1993) *Medieval Illuminators and their Method of Work*. Boston, MA: Yale University Press.

Allwright, D. (1988) *Observation in the Language Classroom*. London: Longman.

Anderson, T.G. (1988) Beyond Einstein. In Ambron, S. and Hooper, K. (eds), *Interactive Multimedia*. Redmond, WA: Microsoft Press.

Argyle, M. (1991) *Cooperation: The Basis of Sociability*. London: Routledge.

Arnold, D.J., Balkan, L.S., Meijer, S., Humphreys, R.L. and Sadler, L. (1994) *Machine Translation: an Introductory Guide*. London: Blackwells-NCC.

Atkins, M.J. (1993) Theories of learning and multimedia applications: an overview. *Research in Education*, 8(2), 251–71.

Bailey, K.D. (1991) Diary studies of classroom language learning: the doubting game and the believing game. In Sadtono, E. (ed.), *Language Acquisition and the Second/Foreign Language Classroom* (28: 60–102).

Bailin, A. (1995) AI and language learning: theory and evaluations. In Holland, V.M., Kaplan, J.D. and Sams, M.R. (eds), *Intelligent Language Tutors: Theory Shaping Technology*. Mahwah, NJ, Lawrence Erlbaum Associates: 327–43.

Barker, D. (1995) Seven new ways to learn. *Byte*: 54–5.

Barker, P. (1993) *Exploring Hypermedia*. London: Kogan Page.

Barker, P. (1994) Electronic libraries – visions of the future. *The Electronic Library* 12(4): 221–9.

Barnes, D. (1969) Language in the secondary classroom. In Barnes, D., Britton, J. and Rosen, H. (eds), *Language, the Learner and the School*. Harmondsworth: Penguin.

Basch, R. (1996) *Secrets of the Super Net Searchers*. Wilton, CT: Pemberton Press.

Beatty, K. (2001) Into the maze of learning: collaboration at the computer, *Department of Education*. Hong Kong: University of Hong Kong.

Beaumont, I. and Brusilovsky, P. (1995) Adaptive educational hypermedia: from ideas to real systems *ED-MEDIA* 95, Graz, Austria: AACE.

Belcher, T. and Young, B. (1974) Planning for change. In Briggs, Asa (ed.), *Essays in the History of Publishing*. Harlow: Longman: 389–419.

Benson, P. (2001) *Teaching and Researching Autonomy in Language Learning*. Harlow: Longman.

Benson, P. and Lor, W. (1998) *Making Sense of Autonomous Language Learning: Conceptions of Learning and Readiness for Autonomy*. Hong Kong: English Centre, University of Hong Kong.

Benson, P. and Voller, P. (eds) (1997) *Autonomy and Independence in Language Learning*. Harlow: Addison Wesley Longman.

Berger, S. (2000) *Education is the Underpinning of Technology*. *http://www.compukiss.com/ck/columns/article.cfm?id=33&year=2000*

Berleant, D. *et al.* (1997) LEARN: Software for foreign language vocabulary acquisition from English unrestricted text. *Computer Assisted Language Learning* 10(2): 107–20.

Berwick, R. (1994) Towards an educational framework for teacher-led tasks. In Crookes, G. and Gass, S. (eds), *Tasks in a Pedagogical Context: Integrating Theory and Practice*. Clevedon: Multilingual Matters: 97–124.

Biggs, J. (1988) The role of metacognition in enhancing learning. *Australian Journal of Education* 32(2): 127–38.

Biggs, J. and Collis, K. (1989) Towards a model of school-based curriculum development and assessment using the SOLO Taxonomy. *Australian Journal of Education* 33(2): 151–63.

Biggs, J. and Moore, P. (1993) *The Process of Learning* (3rd edn). New York: Prentice Hall.

Birkerts, S. (1995) *The Gutenberg Elegies: The Fate of Reading in an Electronic Age*. Winchester, MA: Faber.

Blease, D. (1986) *Evaluating Educational Software*. London: Croom Helm.

Bloom, H. (1956) *Taxonomy of Educational Objectives, the Classification of Educational Goals* – Handbook I: *Cognitive Domain*. New York: McKay.

Boag, Charles (1989) What makes a great teacher? *The Bulletin* (18 July).

Bolter, J.D. (1991) *Writing Space: the Computer, Hypertext, and the History of Writing*. Hillsdale, NJ: Lawrence Erlbaum Associates.

Boorstin, D.J. (1983) *The Discoverers*. New York: Random House.

Boswell, J. (1791) *Life of Samuel Johnson*, London.

Boswood, T. (ed.) (1997) *New Ways of Using Computers in Language Teaching*. Arlington, VA: TESOL.

Boyd, G.M. and Mitchell, D.P. (1992) How can intelligent CAL better adapt to learners? *Computers Education* 18(1–3): 23–8.

Bradbury, R. (1958) *The Martian Chronicles*. Garden City, NY: Doubleday.

Breen, M. (1998) Navigating the discourse: on what is learned in the language classroom. In Renandya, W.A. and Jacobs, G. (eds), *Learners and Language Learning* (39th edn, vol. 39). Singapore: SEAMEO Regional Language Centre, 115–44.

Brown, J.D. (1988) *Understanding Research in Second Language Learning*. New York: Cambridge University Press.

Brown, R. (1973) *A First Language: The Early Stages*. Cambridge, MA: Harvard University Press.

Brumfit, C.J. and Carter, R. (eds) (1986) *Literature and Language Teaching*. Oxford: Oxford University Press.

Bruner, J.S. (1961) The act of discovery. *Harvard Educational Review*, 31 (Winter), 21–32.

Bruner, J.S. (1966) *Toward a Theory of Instruction*. Cambridge, MA: The Belknap Press of Harvard University Press.

Bump, J. (1990) Radical changes in class discussion using networked computers. *Computers and the Humanities* 24: 49–65.

Burns, A. (1999) *Collaborative Action Research for English Language Teachers*. Cambridge: Cambridge University Press.

Burston, J. (1993) Exploiting available technology. *CALICO*, 11(1), 47–52.

Bush, M.D. and Crotty, J. (1991) Interactive videodisc in language teaching. In Smith, W.F. (ed.), *Modern Technology in Foreign Language Education: Applications and Projects*. Lincolnwood, IL: National Textbook Co: 75–96.

Bush, V. (1945) As we may think. *Atlantic Monthly*, 176(1), 101–8.

Cahill, D. and Catanzaro, D. (1997) Teaching first-year Spanish on-line. *Calico Journal* 14: 97–114.

Candlin, C.N. (1981) Form, function and strategy in communicative curriculum design. In Candlin, C.N. (ed.), *The Communicative Teaching of English: Principles and an Exercise Typology*. Harlow: Longman: 24–44

Carlson, P.A. and Larralde, V. (1995) Combining concept mapping and adaptive advice to teach reading comprehension. *ED-MEDIA 95*, Graz, Austria.

Cazden, C.B. (1988) *Classroom Discourse: the Language of Teaching and Learning*. Portsmouth, NH: Heinemann.

Chambliss, J.J. (ed.) (1996) *Philosophy of Education: an Encyclopedia*. New York: Garland.

Chan, M. (1997) No talking please, just chatting: collaborative writing with computers. *Teaching in the Community College Online Conference*. ERIC Document Reproduction Service no. ED 415 836.

Chandler, D. (1984) *Young Learners and the Microcomputer*. Milton Keynes: Open University Press.

Chanier, T., Pengelly, M., Twidale, M.B. and Self, J.A. (1991) Conceptual modelling in error analysis in computer assisted language learning. In Swartz, M. and Yazdani, M. (eds), *Intelligent Tutoring Systems for Second Language Learning: Bridge to International Communications*. Berlin: Springer-Verlag: 125–50.

Chapelle, C. (1997) CALL in the year 2000: still in search of research paradigms. *Language Learning and Technology* 1(1): 19–38.

Chapelle, C. and Jamieson, J. (1983) Language lessons on the PLATO IV System. *System* 11(1): 13–20.

Chapelle, C. and Jamieson, J. (1991) Internal and external validity issues in research on CALL effectiveness. *Computer-assisted Language Learning and Testing*. New York: Newbury House: 37–59.

Chapelle, C., Jamieson, J. and Park, Y. (1996) Second language classroom research traditions: how does CALL fit? In Pennington, M. (ed.), *The Power of CALL* Houston, TX: Athelstan: 33–53.

Chapelle, C.A. (1998) Multimedia call: lessons to be learned from research on instructed SLA. *Language Learning and Technology*, 2(1), 22–34.

Chaudron, C. (1988) *Second Language Classrooms: Research on Teaching and Learning*. Cambridge: Cambridge University Press.

Chen, D. and Zhao, Y. (1997) EWeb and HomePage Maker: making it easier to develop content on the WWW. *Computer Assisted Language Learning*; 10(5), (Nov) 427–41.

Chomsky, N. (1965) *Aspects of the Theory of Syntax*. Cambridge, MA: MIT Press.

Clark, R.E. (1985a) Confounding in educational computing research. *Journal of Education Computing Research*, 1(2), 137–48.

Clark, R.E. (1985b) Evidence for confounding in computer-based instruction studies: analysing the meta-analyses. *Educational Communications and Technology Journal*, 33(4), 249–62.

Coe, Marlana (1996) *Human Factors for Technical Communicators*. New York: Wiley.

Cohen, A. and Oxford, R. (in preparation) *Teaching and Researching Learning Strategies*. London: Longman.

Collentine, J. (1998) Cognitive principles and CALL grammar instruction: a mind-centered, input approach. *CALICO Journal*, 15(1–3), 1–18.

Collie, J. and Slater, S. (1987) *Literature in the Language Classroom*. Cambridge: Cambridge University Press.

Collins, A. (1991) The role of computer technology in restructuring schools. *Phi Delta Kappa* 73: 28–36.

Coniam, D. (1997) A preliminary inquiry into using corpus word frequency date in the automatic generation of English language cloze tests. *CALICO Journal*, 14(2–4), 15–33.

Conklin, J. (1987) Hypertext: an introduction and survey. *IEEE Computer* (September): 17–41.

Conner, P.W. (1991) The Beowulf workstation: one model of computer-assisted literary pedagogy. *Literary and Linguistic Computing* 5: 50–8.

Conrad, K.B. (1996) CALL-non-English L2 Instruction. *Annual Review of Applied Linguistics*, 16, 158–81.

Cook, G. (1989) *Discourse*. Oxford: Oxford University Press.

Cooper, J. (ed.) (1990) *Classroom Teaching Skills* (4th edn). Toronto: D.C. Heath.

Corbel, C. (2000) Beyond burn rate: Sustainability online. *Lens on Literacy*. Proceedings of the Australian Council for Adult Literacy Conference, 21–23 September. Perth, Western Australia: ACAL.

Cotton, B. and Oliver, R. (1993) *Understanding Hypermedia*. London: Phaidon Press.

Coulthard, M. (1985) *An Introduction to Discourse Analysis* (3rd edn). Harlow: Longman.

Crook, C. (1994) *Computers and the Collaborative Experience of Learning*. London: Routledge.

Cummins, J. and Sayers, D. (1995) *Brave New Schools: Challenging Cultural Illiteracy through Global Learning Networks*. New York: St Martin's Press.

Cunningham, D.J., Duffy, T.M. and Knuth, R.A. (1993) The textbook of the future. In McKnight, C., Dillon, A. and Richardson, J. (eds), *Hypertext, a Psychological Perspective*. New York: Ellis Horwood: 19–49.

Davies, G. (1986) Authoring CALL Courseware. In Leech, G. and Candlin, C.N. (eds), *Computers in English Language Teaching and Research: Selected Papers from the 1984 Lancaster Symposium: Computers in English Language Education and Research*. London: Longman.

Debreceny, R., Ellis, A. *et al.* (1995) The integration of networked learning delivery – from strategy to implementation. *ED-MEDIA 95*, Graz, Austria.

Deegan, M. and Sutherland, K. (1990) *Towards Computer Illiteracy: Hypertext, Computing, and Literary Studies*. Workshop on Computer Literacy, University of Durham, CTISS.

de Graaff, Rick (1997) The eXperanto experiment: effect of explicit instruction on second language acquisition. *Studies in Second Language Acquisition* 19(2): 249–76.

Derycke, A.C., Smith, C. *et al.* (1995) Metaphors and interactions in virtual environments for open and distant education. *ED-MEDIA 95*, Graz, Austria.

Detweiler, R.A. (1995) Leading the transition to information technology. *Educational Record* (Winter): 53–7.

Dias, J. (2000) Learner autonomy in Japan: transforming 'Help yourself' from threat to invitation. *Computer Assisted Language Learning.* 13(1): 49–64.

DiBella, I.A. (1997) German in Cyberspace: Tips and Strategies for Beginners. *Unterrichtspraxis/Teaching German*, 30(2), (Fall) 206–9.

Dillenbourg, P. (1992) *Interactive Learning Environment* 2(2): 111–37.

Dillenbourg, P. (1999) What do you mean by 'collaborative learning'? In Dillenbourg, P. (ed.) *Collaborative Learning: Cognitive and Computational Approaches.* Amsterdam: Pergamon.

Dillenbourgh, P., Baker, M., Blaye, A. and O'Malley, C. (1995) The evolution of research on collaborative learning. In Reimann, P. and Spada, H. (eds), *Learning in Humans and Machines. Towards an Interdisciplinary Learning Science.* London: Pergamon: 189–211.

Dillon, A., McKnight, C. *et al.* (1993) Space – the final chapter or why physical representations are not semantic intentions. In McKnight, C., Dillon, A. and Richardson, J. (eds), *Hypertext, a Psychological Perspective.* New York, Eillis Horwood: 169–92.

Dodigovic, M. (1998) Elements of research in CALL software development projects. *CALICO Journal*, 15(4), 25–38.

Dörnyei, Z. (2001) *Teaching and Researching Motivation.* Harlow: Longman.

Dörnyei, Z. and Csizér, K. (1998) Ten commandments for motivating language learners: Results of an empirical study. *Language Teaching Research*, 2, 203–29.

Druin, A. and Solomon, C. (1996) *Designing Multimedia Environments for Children.* New York: Wiley.

Dunkel, P. (1991) The effectiveness research on computer-assisted instruction and computer assisted language learning. In Dunkel, P. (ed.), *Computer-Assisted Language Learning and Testing: Research Issues and Practice.* New York: Newbury House.

Dunkin, M.J. and Biddle, B.J. (1974) *The Study of Teaching.* New York: Holt, Rinehart & Winston.

Duquette, L., Renie, D. *et al.* (1998) The evaluation of vocabulary acquisition when learning French as a second language in a multimedia environment. *Computers and the Humanities*, 31(4), 327–49.

Edwards, A.D.N., Holland, S. *et al.* (1994) *Multimedia Interface Design in Education.* Berlin/New York: Springer Verlag.

Egbert, J.L., Jessup, L.M. *et al.* (1991) Interactive CALL for groups: new technologies for ESL. *CAELL Journal* 2(1): 18–24.

Ellis, R. (1985) *Understanding Second Language Acquisition.* Oxford: Oxford University Press.

Ellis, R. (1994) *The Study of Second-language Acquisition.* Oxford: Oxford University Press.

Ellis, R. (1997) *SLA Research and Language Teaching.* Oxford: Oxford University Press.

Ellis, R. (1998) Discourse control and the acquisition-rich classroom. In Renandya, W.A. and Jacobs, G. (eds), *Learners and Language Learning*, 39: 145–71.

Emihovich, C. (1992) Computer discourse: classroom conversations with a machine. *Education and Urban Society* 24(4): 498–507.

Entwistle, N., Hanley, M. and Hounsell, D. (1979) Identifying distinctive approaches to studying. *Higher Education* 8: 365–80.

Faerch, C. (1986) Negotiating language in the foreign language classroom. *Confidence through Competence in Modern Language Learning*. CILT Reports and Papers 25.

Falvey, P. and Kennedy, P. (eds) (1997) *Learning Language through Literature: a Sourcebook for Teachers of English in Hong Kong*. Hong Kong: Hong Kong University Press.

Ferrara, K., Brunner, H. *et al.* (1991) Interactive written discourse as an emergent register. *Written Communication* 8(1): 8–34.

Firth, J.R. (1935) The Technique of Semantics. *Transactions of the Philological Society*: 36–72.

Ford, N. and Ford, R. (1994) Toward user models for intelligent computer-assisted learning; an empirical study. *Journal of Education for Library and Information Science* 35 (Summer): 187–200.

Fosnot, C.T. (1996) Constructivism: a psychological theory of learning. In Fosnot, T. (ed.), *Constructivism: Theory, Perspectives and Practice*. New York: Teachers College Press: 8–33.

Fox, J. (1991) Learning languages with computers: a history of computer assisted language learning from 1960 to 1990 in relation to education, linguistics and applied linguistics. Unpublished doctoral thesis, University of East Anglia.

Fox, M. (1997) Beyond the technocentric-developing and evaluating content-driven, Internet-based language acquisition courses. *Computer Assisted Language Learning* 10(5): 443–53.

Friedman, T. (1995) Making sense of software: computer games and interactive textuality. In Jones, S.G. (ed.), *CyberSociety: Computer-mediated Communication and Community*. London: Sage: 57–72.

Frizler, K. (1995) *The Internet as an Educational Tool in ESOL Writing Instruction*. *thecity.sfsu.edu/%7Efunweb/thesis.htm* (Dec. 1996.).

Frizler, K. (1997) Creating web sites – Students discover HTML: Teaching web page creation the inductive way. In Boswood, T. (ed.), *New Ways of Using Computers in Language Teaching*. Arlington, VA: TESOL.

Fucaloro, L. and Russikoff, K. (1998) Assessing a virtual course: Development of a Model. ERIC Document Reproduction Service no. FL025168.

Gaer, S. (1998) Using software in the adult ESL classroom. ERIC Document Reproduction Service no. FL801221.

Gale, L.E. (1989) Macario, Montevidisco, and Interactive Dígame: developing interactive video for language instruction. In Smith, W.F. (ed.), *Modern Technology in Foreign Language Education: Applications and Projects*. Lincolnwood, IL: National Textbook Co.

Ganderton, R. (1996) Télématique et didactique des language (Telematics and language learning and teaching). *On-CALL* 11(1), 27–32.

Gibson, W. (1984) *Neuromancer*. New York: Ace Science Fiction.

Gibson, W. (1986) *Count Zero*. New York: HarperCollins.

Gibson, W. (1988) *Mona Lisa Overdrive*. London: Gollancz.

Gould, J.S. (1996) A constructivist perspective on teaching and learning in the language arts. In Fosnot, C.T. (ed.), *Constructivism: Theory, Perspectives and Practice*. New York: Teachers College Press: 92–102.

Grace, C. (1998) Personality type, tolerance of ambiguity, and vocabulary retention in CALL. *CALICO Journal*, 15(1–3), 19–45.

Grice, H.-P. (1975) Logic and conversation. In Cole, P. and Morgan, J.L. (eds), *Syntax and semantics* Vol. 3. New York: Academic Press.

Grotjahn, R. (1987) On the methodological basis of introspective methods. In Faerch, C. and Kasper, G. (eds), *Introspection in Second Language Research*. Clevedon: Multilingual Matters.

Gunn, J. (1995) Dreams written out: libraries in science fiction. *Wilson Library Bulletin* (February): 26–9.

Hague, A.C. and Benest, I.D. (1995) Implementing CAL Technique for Deep Learning. *ED-MEDIA 95*, Graz, Austria.

Haining, P. (ed.) (1995) *The Frankenstein Omnibus*. London: Orion.

Hamm, M. (1992) *The Collaborative Dimensions of Learning: Cultural Diversity and Restructuring Schools with Cooperative Learning across the Curriculum*. Norwood, NJ, Ablex.

Hammond, N. (1993) Learning with hypertext: problems, principles and prospects. In McKnight, C., Dillon, A. and Richardson, J. (eds), *Hypertext, a Psychological Perspective*. New York: Ellis Horwood: 51–70.

Hannafin, M.J. (1984) Guidelines for using locus of instructional control in the design of computer-assisted instruction. *Journal of Instructional Development*, 7(3), 6–10.

Hanson-Smith, E. (n.d.) Technology in the Classroom: Practice and Promise in the 21st Century, TESOL Professional Papers no. 4. *http://www.tesol.org/pubs/catalog/downloadable/hanson-smith-1.html*

Hart, R.S. (1981) Language study and the PLATO system. *Studies in Language Learning* 3: 1–24.

Hatim, B. (2001) *Teaching and Researching Translation*. Harlow: Longman.

Higgins, J. and Johns, T. (1984) *Computers in Language Learning*. London: Collins ELT.

Holliday, A. (2002) *Doing and Writing Qualitative Research*. London: Sage.

Holliday, L. (1999) Theory and research: input, interaction and CALL. In Egbert, J. and Hanson-Smith, E. (eds), *CALL Environments: Research, Practice and Critical Issues*. Alexandria, VA: TESOL.

Hoogeveen, M. (1995) Towards a new multimedia paradigm: is multimedia assisted instruction really effective? *Ed-MEDIA 95*, Graz, Austria.

Howe, K. and Eisenhart, M. (1990) Standards for qualitative (and quantitative) research: a prolegomenon. *Educational Researcher* 19(4), 2–9.

Howlett, V. (1996) *Visual Interface Design for Windows*. New York: Wiley.

Hubbard, P. (1992) A methodological framework for CALL courseware development. In Pennington, M. and Stevens, V. (eds), *Computers in Applied Linguistics*. Clevedon: Multilingual Matters.

Hutchings, G.A., Hall, W. *et al.* (1992) Authoring and evaluation of hypermedia for education. *Computers Education* 18(1–3): 171–7.

Hwu, F. (1997) Providing an effective and affective learning environment for Spanish phonetics with a hypermedia application. *CALICO Journal* 14(2–4), 115–34.

Ingraham, B. and Emery, C. (1992) France interactive: a hypermedia approach to language training. *ETTI* 28(4), 321–33.

Jacobs, G. (1998) Co-operative learning or just grouping students: the difference makes a difference. In Renandya, W.A. and Jacobs, G. (eds), *Learners and Language Learning* 39: 172–93. Singapore: SEAMEO Regional Language Centre.

Jacobson, R.L. (1995) The virtual college. *The Chronicle of Higher Education* (27 January): 23–4.

James, C. (1998) *Errors in Language Learning and Use*. Harlow: Addison Wesley Longman.

Johnson, D. and Johnson, R. (1990) *Learning Together and Alone: Cooperation, Competition and Individualisation*. Englewood Cliffs, NJ: Prentice Hall.

Johnson, D.M. (1991) Second language and content learning with computers. *Computer-assisted Language Learning and Testing*. New York: Newbury House: 61–83.

Jones, R. (2001) Beyond the Screen: a participatory study of computer mediated communication among Hong Kong youth. A paper presented at the Annual Meeting of the American Anthropological Association 28 November–2 December 2001. *http://personal.cityu.edu.hk/~enrodney/Research/ICQPaper.doc*

Jones, S. (ed.) (1994) *The Mammoth Book of Frankenstein*. London: Robinson.

Jonnassen, D.H., Wilson, B.G., Wang, S. and Grabinger, R.S. (1993) Constructivist uses of experts systems to support learning. *Journal of Computer-based Instruction* 20(3): 86–94.

Kaye, A.R. (ed.) (1992) *Collaborative Learning Through Computer Conferencing*. Berlin: Springer Verlag.

Kenning, M.-M. and Kenning, M.J. (1990) *Computers and Language Learning: Current Theory and Practice*. New York: Ellis Horwood.

Keobke, K. (1994a) The patient but stupid teacher: Computers in the classroom. *CAELL Journal* 5(2): 2–9.

Keobke, K. (1994b) Approaching co-operation on the Internet: lessons for Asia. *Presentation to the Association of Southeast Asian Institutes of Higher Learning*. Chinese University of Hong Kong, December 1994.

Keobke, K. (1998a) Computers and collaboration: adapting CALL materials to different learning styles. In Reid, J.M. (ed.), *Understanding Learning Styles in the Second Language Classroom*. Upper Saddle River, NJ: Prentice Hall: 46–52.

Keobke, K. (1998b) What computers do best, what teachers do best. *Language Studies Working Papers* Vol. 2 (1997).

Keobke, K. (2000) *Better English with the WWW*. Hong Kong: Hong Kong Educational Publishing Co.

Kerr, S.T. (1986) Instructional text: the transition from page to screen. *Visible Language* XX(4): 368–92.

King, W.E., Tolzman, A. *et al.* (1998) Integrating technology tools into the language curriculum. *Journal of Instruction Delivery Systems* 12(2), 14–18.

Kinsella, K. and Sherak, K. (1998) Designing ESL classroom collaboration to accommodate diverse work styles. In Reid, J.M. (ed.), *Understanding Learning Styles in the Second Language Classroom*. Upper Saddle River, NJ: Prentice Hall: 85–99.

Kitao, K. (1997) World Wide Web Resources for EFL/ESL. *Doshisha Studies in English* March 68, 329–72.

Knowles, G. (1986) The role of the computer in the teaching of phonetics. In Leech, G. and Candlin, C.N. (eds), *Computers in English Language Teaching and Research: Selected Papers from the 1984 Lancaster Symposium Computers in English Language Education and Research*. London: Longman.

Kohonen, V. (1992) Experiential language learning: second-language learning as co-operative learner education. In Nunan, D. (ed.), *Collaborative Language Learning and Teaching*. Cambridge: Cambridge University Press: 14–39.

Kohonen, V., Jaatinen, R., Kaikkonen, P. and Lehtovaara, J. (2001) *Experiential Learning in Foreign Language Education*. Harlow: Longman.

Krashen, S. (1981) *Second Language Acquisition and Second Language Learning*. Oxford: Oxford University Press.

Kumpulainen, K. and Wray, D. (1999) *Analysing Interactions during Collaborative Writing with the Computer: an Innovative Methodology*. *http://www.warwick.ac.uk/staff/D.J.Wray/Articles/facct.html* (24 April 2001)

Lai, P. and Biggs, J. (1994) Who benefits from mastery learning? *Contemporary Educational Psychology* 19: 13–23.

Laidlaw, B. and McCall, J. (1997) Computer-assisted language learning. *Computer-Assisted Language Learning. Literacy Broadsheet*: 47 (December): 20–8.

Landow, G.P. (1989) Hypertext in literary education, criticism, and scholarship. *Computers and the Humanities* 23: 173–98.

Lanham, R.A. (1993) *The Electronic Word: Democracy, Technology and the Arts*. Chicago, IL: University of Chicago Press.

Leech, G. and Candlin, C.N. (1986) *Computers in English Language Teaching and Research: Selected Papers from the 1984 Lancaster Symposium Computers in English Language Education and Research*. London: Longman.

Leech, G., Myers, G. and Thomas, J. (eds) (1995) *Spoken English on Computer: Transcription, Mark-up and Application*. Harlow: Longman.

Legutke, M.K., Müller-Hartmann, A. and Ulrich, S. (1998) Neue Kommunikationsformen im fremdsprachlichen Unterricht. In Fritz, G. and Jucker, A. (eds), *Kommunikationsformen im Wandel der Zeit. Vom Heldenepos zum Hypertext*. Tübingen: Niemeyer.

Lenzo, K. (1992) Computers and Research Writing for Graduate Learners: A course Outline. *CAELL Journal* 4(1): 2–5.

Levy, M. (1997) *Computer-assisted Language Learning: Context and Conceptualization*. Oxford: Oxford University Press.

Lewis, D. (1997) Machine translation in a modern languages curriculum. *Computer Assisted Language Learning* 10(3), (June): 225–71.

Liou, H.C. (1997) Research of on-line help as learner strategies for multimedia CALL evaluation. *CALICO Journal* 14(2–4): 81–96.

Little, D. (1996) Freedom to learn and compulsion to interact: promoting learner autonomy through the use of information systems and information technologies. In Pemberton, R. *et al.* (eds), *Taking Control: Autonomy in Language Learning*. Hong Kong: Hong Kong University Press: 203–18.

Liu, M. (1992) Hypermedia-assisted instruction and second-language learning: a semantic-network based approach. Paper presented at the Annual Meeting of Eastern Educational Research Association, Hilton Head SC.

Logan, R.K. (1995) *The Fifth Language*. Toronto: Stoddart.

Lunde, K.R. (1990) Using electronic mail as a medium for foreign language study and instruction. *CALICO Journal* 7(3): 68–78.

Lyall, Sarah (1994) Are these books or what? CD-ROM and the literary industry. *New York Times Book Review* XCIX: 33.

McAleese, R. (1989) Navigation and browsing in hypertext. In McAleese, R. (ed.), *Hypertext: Theory into Practice*. Norwood: Ablex: 6–44.

McArthur, T. (1983) *A Foundation Course for Language Teachers*. Cambridge: Cambridge University Press.

McConnell, D. (1994) *Implementing Computer Supported Cooperative Learning*. London: Kogan Page.

McLean, James (1995) Improving education through action research: a guide for administrators and teachers. *The Practicing Administrator's Leadership Series: Roadmaps to Success*. Thousand Oaks, CA: Corwin Press.

McLuhan, M. (1962) *The Gutenberg Galaxy: The Making of Typographic Man*. Toronto: University of Toronto Press.

McMeniman, M. and Evans, R. (1998) CALL through the eyes of teachers and learners of Asian languages: Panacea or business as usual? *On-Call* 12(1), (January): 2–9.

McMurtie, D. (1937) *The Book: The Story of Printing and Bookmaking*. New York: Covici Friede.

Magid, L.J. (1998) *Child Safety on the Information Highway*. National Center for Missing and Exploited Children http://www.safekids.com/child_safety.htm

Marchionini, G. (1988) Hypermedia and learning: freedom and chaos. *Educational Technology* 28(11): 8–12.

Mardsjo (1996) Interfacing technology. *Computers and Composition* 13: 303–15.

Megarry, J. (1988) Hypertext and compact disks: the challenge of multi-media learning. *British Journal of Educational Technology* 19(3): 172–83.

Meich, E.J., Nave, B. and Mosteller, F. (1996) On CALL: a review of computer-assisted language learning in US colleges and universities. *ERIC* ED 394 525: 1–115.

Merrill, P.F., Hammons, K. *et al.* (1996) *Computers in Education*. Boston, MA: Allyn & Bacon.

Meunier, L.E. (1994) Computer adaptive language tests (CALT) offer a great potential for functional testing. Yet why don't they? *CALICO Journal* 11(4): 23–39.

Moeller, A.J. (1997) Moving from instruction to learning with technology: Where's the content? *CALICO Journal*, 14(2–4): 5–13.

Montali, J. and Lewandowski, L. (1996) Bimodal reading: benefits of a talking computer for average and less skilled readers. *Journal of Learning Disabilities*, 29(3): 271–9.

Moody, F. (1995) *I Sing the Body Electronic*. New York: Penguin.

Moore, Z., Morales, B. *et al.* (1998) Technology and teaching culture: results of a state survey of foreign language teachers. *CALICO Journal* 15(1–3): 109–28.

Morariu, J. (1988) Hypermedia in instruction and training: the power and the promise. *Educational Technology* (November): 17–20.

Murillo, D. (1991) Maximizing CALL effectiveness in the classroom. *CAELL* 2(2): 20–5.

Murray, J. (1991) *Knowledge Machines: Language and Information in a Technological Society*. Harlow: Longman.

Murray, J. (1995) Lessons learned from the Athena Language Learning Project: using natural-language processing, graphics, speech processing, and interactive video for communication-based language learning. In Holland, V.M., Kaplan, J.D. and Sams, M.R. (eds), *Intelligent Language Tutors: Theory Shaping Technology*. Mahwah NJ: Lawrence Erlbaum Associates: 243–56.

Murray, J., Morgenstern, D. *et al.* (1991) The Athena Language Learning Project: design issues for the next generation of computer based language-learning tools. In Smith, W.F. (ed.), *Modern Technology in Foreign Language Education: Applications and Projects*. Lincolnwood, IL: National Textbook Co: 97–118.

Nagata, N. (1997) The effectiveness of computer-assisted metalinguistic instruction: A case study in Japanese. *Foreign Language Annals* 30(2): 187–200.

Negroponte, N. (1996) *Being Digital*. New York: Vintage Books.

Neuwirth, C.M. and Kaufer, D.S. (1992) Computers and composition studies: articulating a pattern of discovery. *Re-imagining Computers and Composition*. Portsmouth: Boynton/Cook Heinemann.

Norman, D.A. (1993) *Things that Make us Smart*. Reading, MA: Addison-Wesley.

Nunan, D. (1987) Methodological issues in research. Applying second language acquisition research. Adelaide, National Curriculum Resource Centre: 143–71.

Nunan, D. (1989) *Designing Tasks for the Communicative Classroom*. Cambridge: Cambridge University Press.

Nunan, D. (1991) *Language Teaching Methodology: a Textbook for Teachers*. New York: Prentice Hall.

Nunan, D. (ed.) (1992a) *Collaborative Language Learning and Teaching*. Cambridge: Cambridge University Press.

Nunan, D. (1992b) *Research Methods in Language Learning*. Cambridge: Cambridge University Press.

Nunan, D. (1993) *Introducing Discourse Analysis*. London, Penguin.

Nunan, D. (1994) *The Learner Centred Curriculum*. Melbourne: Cambridge University Press.

Nunan, D. (1999) *Second Language Teaching and Learning*. Boston, MA: Heinle & Heinle.

Nunan, D. and Lamb, C. (1996) *The Self-directed Teacher: Managing the Learning Process*. Cambridge: Cambridge University Press.

O'Neil Jr, H.F. (1994) *Measurement of Teamwork Processes using Computer Simulation*. Los Angeles, CA: National Center for Research on Evaluation Standards and Student Testing.

Oxford, R. (1995) Linking theories of learning with intelligent computer-assisted language learning (ICALL). In Holland, V.M., Kaplan, J.D. and Sams, M.R. *Intelligent Language Tutors: Theory Shaping Technology*. Mahwah, NJ: Lawrence Erlbaum Associates: 359–69.

Papert, S. (1980) *Mindstorms: Children, Computers and Powerful Ideas*. New York: Basic Books.

Papert, S. (1984) *Microworlds: Transforming Education*. Cambridge, MA: MIT Press.

Papert, S. (1987) Computer criticism vs. technocentric thinking. *Educational Researcher* 16(1): 22–30.

Papert, S. (1992) *The Children's Machine: Rethinking School in the Age of the Computer*. New York: Basic Books.

Paris, S.G. and Oka, E.R. Strategies for comprehending text and coping with reading difficulties. *Learning Disability Quarterly* 12(1): 32–42.

Pask, G. and Scott, C.E. (1972) Learning strategies and individual competence. *Man-Machine Studies* 4: 217–53.

Pennington, M. (1996) The power of the computer in language education. In Pennington, M. (ed.), *The Power of CALL*. Houston, TX: Athelstan Publishers: 1–14.

Peyraube, A. (1996) Is Cantonese really Chinese? *China Perspectives* (5): 52–5.

Pica, T. (1994) Research on negotiation: What does it reveal about second-language learning conditions, processes and outcomes? *Language Learning* 44(3): 493–527.

Pica, T. (1998) Second language learning through interaction: multiple perspectives. In Regan, V. (ed.), *Contemporary Approaches to Second Language Acquisition in Social Context*. Dublin: University College Dublin Press: 9–31.

Postman, N. (1993) *Technopoly: the Surrender of Culture to Technology*. Toronto: Random House.

Preiss, B. (ed.) (1991) *The Ultimate Frankenstein*. New York: Dell.

Quentin-Baxter, M. and Dewherst, D. (1992) A method for evaluating the efficiency of presenting information in a hypermedia environment. *Computers and Education* 18(1–3): 179–82.

Rao, M. (1998) Multilingual publishing on the Asia-Pacific Internet. *On The Internet*. July–August *http://www.isoc.org/oti/articles/0798/rao.html*

Ravitch, D. (1987) Technology and the curriculum: promise and peril. *What Curriculum for the Information Age?* New York: Lawrence Erlbaum Associates.

Renzulli, J.S. and Smith, L.H. (1978) *Learning Styles Inventory: a Measure of Student Preference for Instructional Techniques.* Mansfield Center, CT: Creative Learning Press.

Richards, J.C. (1997) Preparing language teachers for tomorrow's language classrooms. In Jacobs, G.M. (ed.), *Language Classrooms of Tomorrow: Issues and Responses* 38: 195–208. Singapore: SEAMEO Regional Language Centre.

Richards, J.C. (ed.) (1998) *Teaching in Action: Case Studies from Second Language Classrooms.* Alexandria, VA: TESOL.

Richards, J.C. and Rodgers, T.S. (1994) *Approaches and Methods in Language Teaching.* Cambridge: Cambridge University Press.

Richards, J.C. and Schmitdt, R.W. (1983) Conversational analysis. In Richards, J.C. and Schmitdt, R.W. (eds), *Language and Communications.* Harlow: Longman.

Rivers, W.M. (1981) *Teaching Foreign-Language Skills* 2nd edn. Chicago, University of Chicago Press.

Rozycki, E.G. (1996) Behaviourism. In Chambliss, J.J. (ed.), *Philosophy of Education: an Encyclopedia.* New York: Garland: 52–4.

St John, E. (2001) A case for using a parallel corpus and concordancer for beginners of a foreign language. *Language Learning and Technology* 5(3): np. *http://llt.msu.edu/vol5num3/stjohn/default.html*

Schery, T. and O'Connor, L. (1997) Language intervention: computer training for young children with special needs. *British Journal of Educational Technology* 28(4) (October): 271–9.

Schmuck, R. and Schmuck, P. (1988) *Group Processes in the Classroom* 5th edn. Dubuque, IA: William C. Brown.

Seaton, W.J. (1993) Computer-mediated communication and students' self-directed learning. *Open Learning* 8(2): 49–54.

Segalowitz, N. and Gatbonton, E. (1995) Automaticity and lexical skills in second-language fluency: implications for computer assisted language learning. *Computer Assisted Language Learning* 8(2–3): 129–49.

Serim, F. and Koch, M. (1996) *NetLearning: Why Teachers use the Internet.* Sebastopol, CA: O'Reilly and Associates.

Sharan, S. and Shachar, H. (1988) *Language and Learning in the Co-operative Classroom.* New York: Springer Verlag.

Shilling, W.A. (1997) Young children using computers to make discoveries about written language. *Early Childhood Education Journal* 24: 253–9.

Shirley, Veenema and Gardner, Howard (1996) Multimedia and multiple intelligences. *The American Prospect* 7(29) 1 November–1 December.

Siekmann, S. (1998) To integrate your language web tools-CALL WebCT. CLEARINGHOUSE_NO: IR019097

Sinclair, J.M. and Coulthard, R.M. (1975) *Towards an Analysis of Discourse: the English used by Teachers and Pupils.* London: Oxford University Press.

Sinyor, Roberta (1997) An analysis of student behavior and error sources in an Italian CALL context. *CALICO Journal* 14(2–4): 51–64.

Skinner, B.F. (1950) Are theories of learning necessary? *Psychological Review* 57(4): 193–216.

Skinner, B.F. (1953) *Science and Human Behavior.* New York: Macmillan.

Skinner, B.F. (1954) The science of learning and the art of teaching. *Harvard Educational Review* 24(2): 86–97.

Skinner, B.F. (1957) *Verbal Learning*. New York: Appleton-Century-Crofts.

Skinner, B.F. (1958) Teaching Machines. *Science 128* (3330).

Skinner, B.F. (1968) *The Technology of Teaching*. New York: Appleton-Century-Crofts.

Sloane, S.J. (1990) A new model of discourse: reader, author, programmer, text (R-A-P-T) in Estes N., Heene, J. and LeClercq, D. (eds), *The Seventh Internation Conference on Technology and Education: New Pathways through Educational Technology*. Brussels: March 1990, vol. 1, 52–3.

Smith, G. (1991) *Computers and Human Language*. Oxford: Oxford University Press.

Spiro, R.J., Feltovitch, P.J., Jacobson, M.J. and Coulson, R.L. (1991) Cognitive flexibility, constructivism and hypertext. *Eduational Technology*, (May): 24–33.

Spolsky, B. (1987) *Conditions for Second Language Learning: Introduction to a General Theory*. Oxford: Oxford University Press.

Stephenson, N. (1995) *The Diamond Age, or A Young Lady's Illustrated Primer*. New York: Bantam.

Stephenson, N. (2000) *Snow Crash*. New York: Bantam.

Stevens, V. (1992) Humanism and CALL: a coming of age. *Computers in Applied Linguistics: an International Perspective*. In Pennington, M. and Stevens, V. Clevedon, Avon, Multilingula Matters: 11–38.

Stevens, V. (1995) Concordancing with language learners: Why? When? What? *CAELL Journal* (Summer) 6(2): 2–10.

Susman, E.B. (1998) Cooperative learning: a review of factors that increase the effectiveness of cooperative computer-based instruction. *Educational Computing Research* 18(4): 303–22.

Swaffar, J., Romano, S., Arens, K. and Markley, P. (eds) (1998) *Language Learning On-line? Theory and Practice in the ESL and L2 Computer Classroom*. Austin, TX: Labyrinth Publications.

Swain, M. (1983) *Understanding Input through Output*. Tenth University of Michigan Conference on Applied Linguistics.

Sweeters, W. (1994) Multimedia electronic tools for learning. *Educational Technology* (May–June).

Thompson, A.D., Simonson, M.R. and Hargrave, C.P. (1992) *Educational Technology: A Review of Research*. Washington DC: Association for Educational Communications and Technology.

Tillman, F. (1997) Hypermedia fiction: A medium of forking paths. *Computer Assisted Language Learning* 10(4), (September): 387–97.

Tripp, D. (1993) *The Moral Base for Teacher Professionalism*. London: Heinemann.

Tsui, A.B.M. (1987) An analysis of different types of interaction in ESL classroom discourse. *IRAL* 25(4): 336–53.

Tsui, A.B.M. (1991) Learner involvement and comprehensible input. *RELC Journal: A Journal of Language Teaching and Research in Southeast Asia* 22(2), (December): 44–60.

Tsui, A.B.M. (1994) *English Conversation*. Oxford: Oxford University Press.

Tsui, A.B.M. (1995) *Introducing Classroom Interaction*. London: Penguin.

Tsui, A.B.M. (1996) Reticence and second language learning anxiety. In Bailey, K. and Nunan, D. (eds), *Voices from the Language Classroom*. New York: Cambridge University Press: 145–67.

Turkle, S. (1995) *Life on the Screen: Identity in the Age of the Internet*. New York: Simon & Schuster.

Turner, J. (1998) A walk on ice. *On-Call* 12(3): 20–4.

Tuzi, F. (1997) Using Microsoft Word to generate computerized tests. *The Internet TESL Journal* III (11).

Van Handle, Donna, C. and Corl, K.A. (1998) Extending the dialogue: Using electronic mail and the Internet to promote conversation and writing in intermediate German language courses. *CALICO Journal* 15(1–3): 129–43.

van Lier, L. and Corson, D. (eds) (1997) *Knowledge about Language*. Boston, MA: Kluwer.

Vygotsky, L.S. (1962) *Thought and Language*. Cambridge, MA: MIT Press.

Vygotsky, L.S. (1978) *Mind in Society*. Cambridge, MA: Harvard University Press.

Warschauer, M. (1995a) *E-mail for English Teaching: Bringing the Internet and Computer Learning NetWorks into the Language Classroom*. Alexandria, VA: TESOL Publications.

Warschauer, M. (1995b) Heterotopias, panopticons, and Internet discourse. *University of Hawai'i Working Papers in ESL* 14(1): 91–121.

Warschauer, M. (ed.) (1995c) *Virtual Connections: Online Activities and Projects for Networking Language Learners*. Honolulu: University of Hawai'i Second Language Teaching and Curriculum Center.

Warschauer, M. (1996a) Comparing face-to-face and electronic discussion in the second language classroom. *CALICO Journal* 13(2/3): 7–26.

Warschauer, M. (1996b) *Computer-mediated Collaborative Learning: Theory and Practice* (Research Note no. 17). Honolulu: University of Hawai'i, Second Language Teaching and Curriculum Center.

Warschauer, M. (1996c) Motivational aspects of using computers for writing and communication. In Warschauer, M. (ed.), *Telecollaboration in Foreign Language Learning*. Honolulu: University of Hawai'i Second Langauge Teaching and Curriculum Center: 29–46.

Warschauer, M. (ed.) (1996d) *Telecollaboration in Foreign Language Learning*. Honolulu: University of Hawai'i Second Language Teaching and Curriculum Center.

Warschauer, M. (1997) Computer-mediated collaborative learning: theory and practice. *The Modern Language Journal*, 81(iv): 470–81.

Warschauer, M. (1999) *Electronic Literacies: Language, Culture and Power in Online Education*. Mahwah, NJ: Erlbaum.

Warschauer, M. and Healey, D. (1998) Computers and language learning: an overview. *Language Teaching* 31: 51–7.

Wegerif, R. (1996) Collaborative learning and directive software. *Journal of Computer Assisted Learning* 12: 22–32.

Wegerif, R. and Dawes, L. (1998) Encouraging exploratory talk around computers. In Monteith, M. (ed.), *IT for Learning Enhancement*. Exeter: Intellect.

Wegerif, R. and Scrimshaw, P. (eds) (1997) *Computers and Talk in the Primary Classroom*. Clevedon: Multilingual Matters.

Weizenbaum, J. (1976) *Computer Power and Human Reason: From Judgment to Calculation*. San Francisco, CA: W. H. Freeman.

Wesley Jr, M.T. and Franks, M.E. (1994) The virtual classroom and vertically integrated technology training for education: new paradigms for telecommunications technology training of school personnel. The Mid-South Educational Research Association Annual Conference, Nashville, TN: ERIC.

Weyer, S.A. (1982) The design of a dynamic book for information search. *International Journal Man-Machine Studies* 17: 87.

Weyer, S.A. (1988) As we may learn. In Ambron, S. and Hooper, K. (eds), *Interactive Multimedia: Visions of Multimedia for Developers, Educators and Information Providers*. Redmond, WA: Microsoft Press: 87–103.

White, M.A. (1984) Information and imagery education. In White, M.A. (ed.), *What Curriculum for the Information Age?* New York: Lawrence Erlbaum Associates: 41–65.

Wild, M. (1996) Mental models and computer modeling. *Journal of Computer Assisted Learning*, 12: 10–21.

Williams, N. (1998) Educational multimedia: where's the interaction. In Montreith, M. (ed.), *IT for Learning Enhancement*. Heereweg, Netherlands: Swets & Zeitlinger: 153–70.

Wright, D. (1997) The quest for spece-CD-ROM and capacity constraints. *On Call* 11(2), (May): 52–7.

Wu, Kamyin and Tsui, A.B.M. (1997) Teachers' grammar on the electronic highway: Design criteria for 'Telegram'. *System* 25(2): 169–83.

Wu, M.H. (1992) Towards a contextual lexico-grammar: an application of concordance analysis in EST teaching. *RELC Journal* 232, 18–34.

Yang, J.C. and Akahori, K. (1998) Error analysis in Japanese writing and its implementation in a computer assisted language learning system on the World Wide Web. *CALICO Journal* 5(3): 47–66.

Index